Ïyagaag̣miut

People Who Live Among the Rock Caches

Ïyagaagmiut

People Who Live Among the Rock Caches

by
Ch'igiioonta'
She Holds a Child

Iyaġaaġmiut: People Who Live Among the Rock Caches

An Arivahan Book

Copyright © 2025 Adeline Raboff — Ch'igiioonta' *She Holds a Child*

All rights reserved. No part of this book may be reproduced, stored in a retrieval system, or transmitted in any form or by any means, electronic, mechanical, photocopying, recording, or otherwise, without express written permission of the author.

Edited by: Carole Anderson
Design and layout by: McKenzie Long, Cardinal Innovative
Cover: *Fog and hills above Demarcation Bay, 2022. Photo by Claude Fiddler*
Frontispiece: *Stephen Peter Ch'igiioonta'. Photo by James Barker*
Final page: *Tundra Along Koluktuk Creek, 2004. Photo by Claude Fiddler*

ISBN: 978-0-9720980-0-7

Contents

Introduction 6

Chapter 1
Location, Location, Location 9

Chapter 2
Mastodons and Such: Late Prehistory.............31

Chapter 3
Kǫ'ehdan and Saityen/Nitsehduu 49

Chapter 4
Too Loghe and That Dits'iigiitł'uu!.................69

Chapter 5
The Last Eight Years 95

Glossary I
Regional Names..119

Glossary II
Placenames by Estate......................................123

Glossary III
Placenames 131

Glossary IV
Family and Personal Names 137

Glossary V
Indigenous Word Definitions.........................149

Glossary VI
Chronology..153

Acknowledgments..157

Introduction

This book, *Iyaġaaġmiut: People Who Live Among the Rock Caches* is and is not a follow-up on *Iñuksuk: Northern Koyukon, Gwich'in, and Lower Tanana 1800–1901*, 2001. It is a continuation of knowledge sharing because I am going to elucidate upon the history of the Northern Tl'eeyegge hut'aane groups and concentrate heavily upon the Nendaaghe hut'aane Denaa. I will not be using footnotes, nor the academic vocabulary of ethnographers and anthropologists, except in cases where it will just make sense and add more clarity to do so. However, I must forewarn readers that there will be Denaakk'e, Dinjii Zhuh K'yaa, Lower Tanana, Yupiit, and Iñupiaq vocabulary, which will be included in the glossaries. The reader will also be compelled to rely heavily on the use of maps provided. Place names of the 18th and 19th century will be used throughout this book, and a placenames glossary will be included. Multiple glossaries will provide information in the following categories: (I) Regional Names, (II) Estates, (III) Place Names: Rivers, Lakes, Creeks, and Mountains, (IV) Family and Personal Names, (V) Indigenous Word Definitions, and (VI) Time Chronology. Be prepared to leaf back and forth. There will be parentheses used for the following reasons; 1) for another dialect variation, or another word for the same thing, and 2) within quotation marks to indicate what is understood by the speaker and listener, but not explicitly verbalized, and back slash for two dialects (Khehkwaii/Khaihkwaii).

As with all my writing, this will not be your bedside reading.

Being a creature of habit, I must acknowledge all the people who have helped me get to this point in my work either through example, through academic papers, or through encouragement and recommendations.

None of my work would exist without the patience and stored knowledge of my father, Stephen Peter Tsee Gho' Tsyaa Tsal Ch'igiioonta, 1906–1997, and the life and work of my mother, Katherine Joseph Senaaneyo Peter Ch'igiioonta', 1918–2010, as well as the extraordinary dedication and faithfulness of my paternal grandmother, Soozun John Dahjalti' Peter Ch'igiioonta', a remarkable oral historian. She was a beloved matriarch. Furthermore, this work would NOT be possible without the larger Neets'aii community whom I grew up among.

As to the academic community, I want to thank the teachers at the University of Oklahoma, Norman, Oklahoma for recognizing the value of my then extensive family genealogies and oral traditions of the Dinjii Zhuh community for what they were. The Alaska Native Language Center and the Alaska Native Knowledge Network, and Ray Barnhard, to the life and work of Tatqaviñ Ruthie Ramoth-Sampson and Niayuq Rachel Craig. To the Iñupiat oral historians; Panniaq Simon Paneak, Isasan Justus Mekiana, Immałurauq Joe Sun, and many generous unnamed others. The encouragement of Adolf Gray, Mr. Wiggans, and Donna Van Wechel, Robin Renfroe, Jeff Rasic, and the life and work of Eliza Jones, Miranda Wright, Kenneth L. Pratt, and Katherine L. Arndt.

Thanks to Qalhaq Barbara Atoruk for Upper Kobuk genealogies and Kobuk dialect Iñupiaq language spellings, Lorraine Williams, and to the late Tiger Ernest S. Burch, Jr., whose loving patient dedication to his work was and is incomparable.

Many thanks to Nancy Alexander Joseph, Marcy Okado, Mildred Peter-Allen, Jeff Rasic, Kathleen Hildebrand, Virginia Ned, Jane Bird, Haley McCaig, Chris Cannon, Jimmy Fox, Bill Schneider, Bob Sattler, Kathy Walling, Thomas Lowenstein and Bill Simeone for reading through the various stages of this work.

Thank you to Carole Anderson for agreeing to edit this book.

In memory of Virginia Boys Osborne and Walter Hannum.

My immediate family and circle of friends who have been loving and encouraging mentors of another order, who know who they are.

Ch'igiioonta'
She Holds A Child
2025

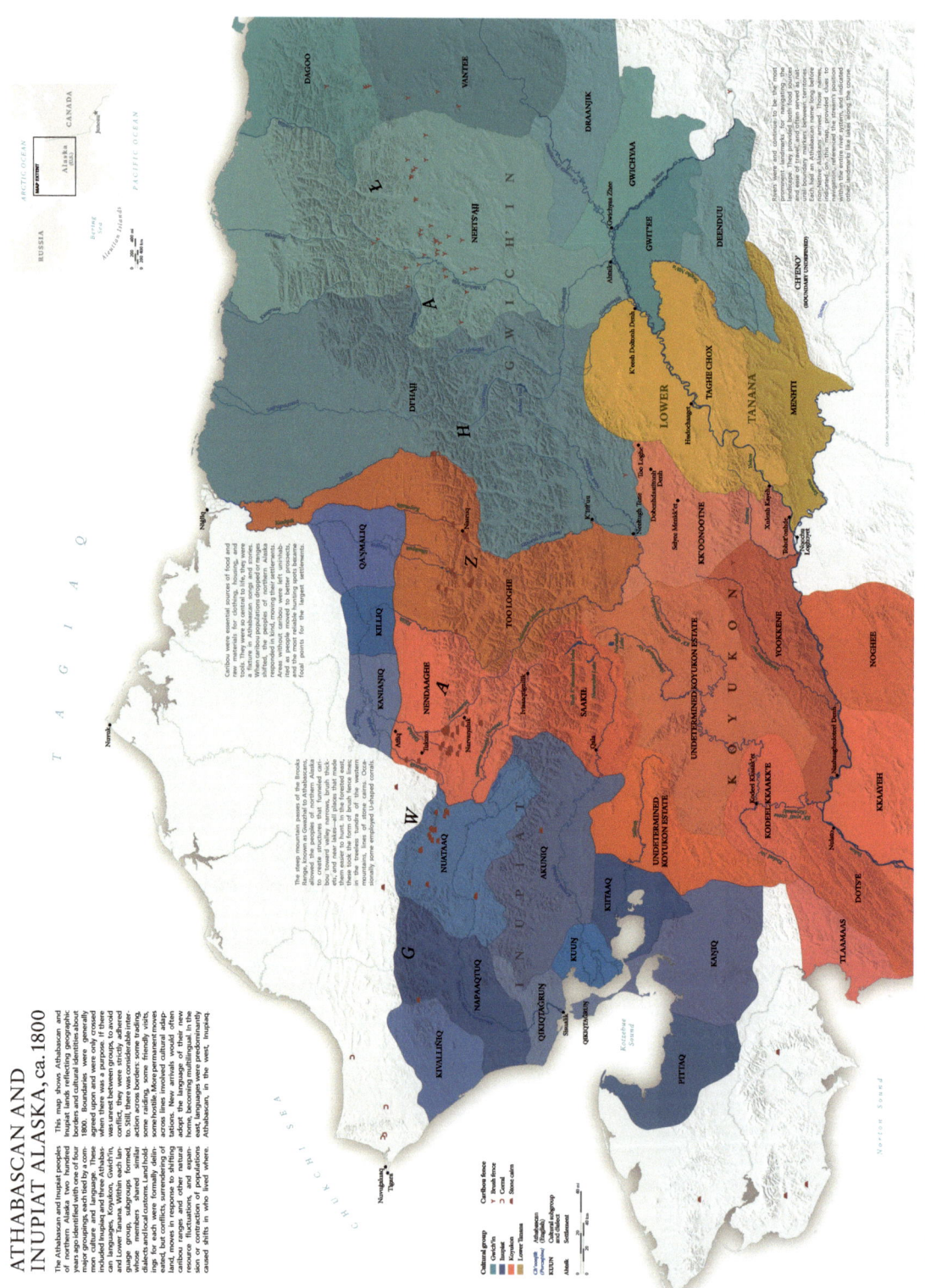

Fig. 1. Estimated Distribution of Alaska Tribal Peoples, circa 1800. Map publication by the Gates of the Arctic National Park and Preserve, and Jeffery T. Rasic.

Chapter 1

Location, Location, Location

This is a map (Fig. 1) of the estimated distribution of Indigenous groups in Northern Alaska in 1800. There are maps which cover more tribal groups, but this is an effort to narrow the focus of this book, and I might emphasize here, that this is a "Map in Progress." That is, as a work in progress it is bound to get more accurate as more information is gathered and more groups are added. I dream: one day there will be a map of all Indigenous groups in the present State of Alaska before the coming of the Russians, Spanish, English, and all Euro-American settlers.

It is important to note that after contact with Russians and Europeans, the subsequent movements of these peoples, and the process of acculturation that was imposed by various influences, and along with periods of environmental disruption, that the exact territories and boundaries of each group had to be re-elicited during the 20th century. There were still elders alive in these communities to pass on this information, and thanks to the forethought of the Iñupiat leadership of the time, for making the retention and recording of oral histories a top priority. These oral histories, in Iñupiaq text and in English translation represent a tremendous amount of work and a wealth of cultural knowledge.

It was thanks also to the work of ethnohistorian Tiger Ernest S. Burch, Jr., that much of the territories or estates of the Northwestern Iñupiat communities were delineated, and to the Gates of the Arctic National Park and Preserve and Jeffery T. Rasic that this map was compiled and published.

Exactly how these estates or territories were formed stems from the peoples' knowledge of the fauna, flora, land, and landscape, and the existence of trail systems. Natural boundaries occurred with encircling mountain ranges, rivers, and marked landscape features such as abrupt changes in elevation, swamps, and impassable mountain areas. Impassable mountain areas generally feature a cluster of mountains without passes through them, in this sense these features were often referred to by Dinjii Zhuh speakers as njuu or islands. Each of these estates had its own distinct environmental setting and ability to sustain a limited number of people. Populations in each region fluctuated by the amount and quality of resources, the season in which they occurred, and invariably by a period of food shortages which happened most often in the springtime.

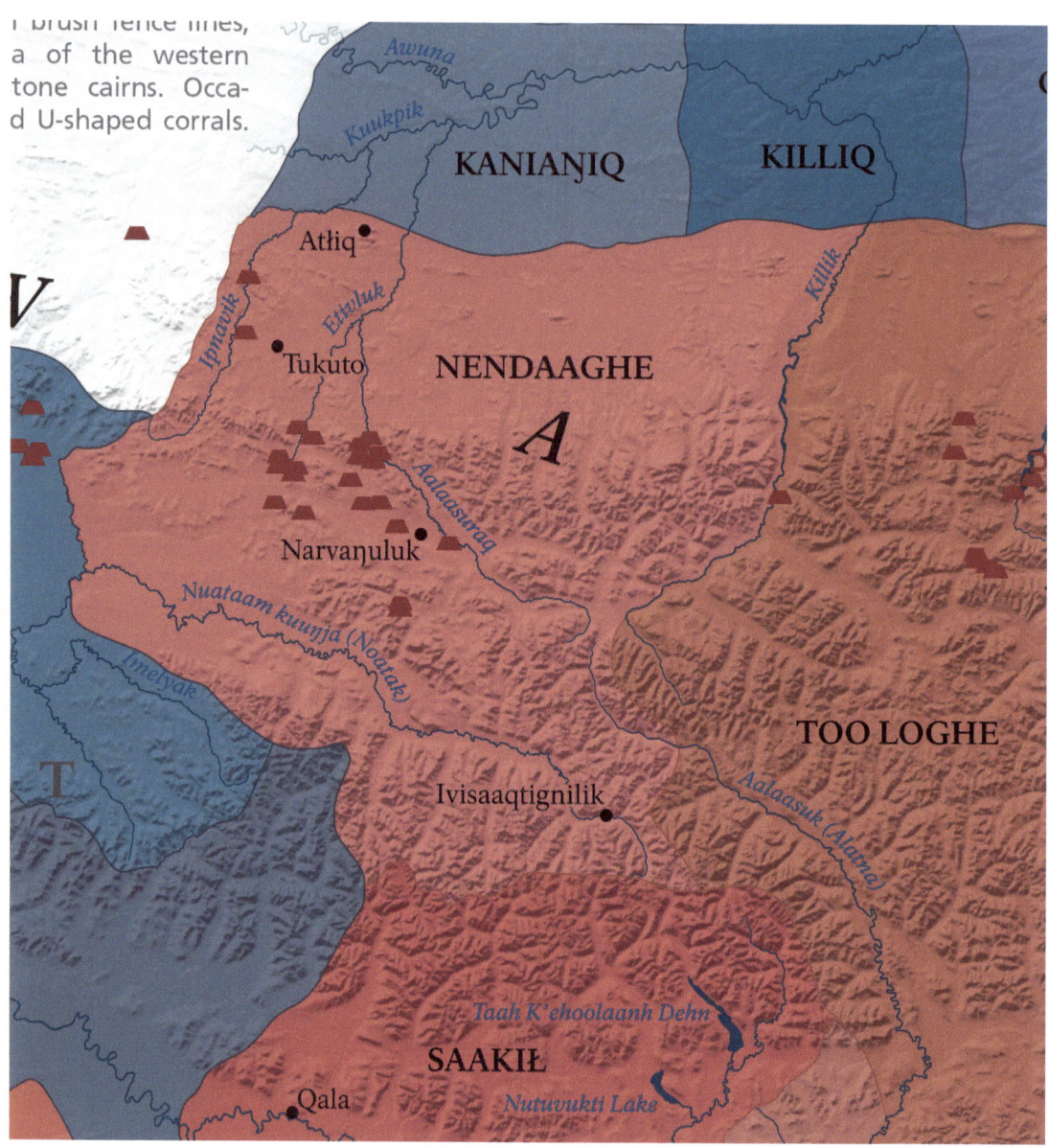

Fig. 2. Narrowing in on the Nendaaghe, Saaqił, Too Loghe Hut'aane and Dį'hąįį Estates. Raboff, GANPP, 2024

This map also shows the distribution of caribou rock fences, rock blinds (as in a rock fence of some size to seek refuge behind in case of strong winds or snowstorms), rows of rock cairns called *iñuksuk* used to direct the caribou towards the corrals, and brush fence locations. Some of these caribou rock fences date back 5000 to 6000 years. Note, the majority of rock fences are in northwestern Alaska, home to the Western Arctic Caribou Herd, or WACH as it is known by biologists. While the majority of brush fences are in the area of the Porcupine Caribou Herd (PCH) range, there is another smaller caribou herd called the Central Arctic Caribou Herd (CACH) between these two major herds. Whether they were corralled by rock or brush fences had to do with the materials that were/are readily available in the local area. All three of these herds wintered in the Gwazhał Cordillera, now commonly known as the Brooks Range.

Fig. 3. Itivlik (Pass), Nendaaghe Estate. Photo courtesy of Gates of the Arctic National Park and Preserve. GANPP

I will be concentrating on the Nendaaghe hut'aane Denaa people of the Upper *Nuataam kuuŋa* (Nuataaq River) and the headwaters of the *Ipnavik, Itivluk (Itivliim Kuuŋa), Aalaasuraq, Aalaasuk* and *Killiq* rivers. These people were known to their Iñupiat neighbors as **Iyaġaaġmiut** and **Uyaġaaġmiut**. These are dialect variations on the same word. People of the upper Kobuk say Iyaġaaġmiut and the people further north say Uyaġaaġmiut. The word stems from the word, *iyaġak* and *uyaġak* meaning rock and *iyaġaqtat*, which in the upper Kobuk dialect means a meat storage pit lined with grass or willow branches and covered with willows and rocks. The name can be translated as "People who live among the rocks," or as "People who live among the rock caches." From the Dene Athabascan perspective, the latter meaning would be most accurate, "People who live among the rock caches." This method of caching was a good way to store large quantities of meat in this treeless, high latitude setting. It was dug just to or below the level of the permafrost and made for excellent meat storage. It was said by the late elder *Immaturauq* Joe Sun, that meat stored in this way was a very good tasting meat and could be eaten raw.

Note however that **Iyaġaaġmiut** and **Uyaġaaġmiut** are not an estate specific ethnonym (ethnic name). Iñupiaq speakers of the recent past have not differentiated the Nendaaghe from the Saakił hut'aane Denaa people. The people of each estate have a specific ethnonym only for that estate. The Iñupiaq ethonym for the people of this specific estate has been lost. Although in "Maniiḷaq (Maniiḷauraq)" Compiled and translated from oral tapes by Ruth Ramoth-Sampson and Angeline Newlin [and Minnie Gray] 1981, it is written, "She (Maniiḷauraq's wife) was Siḷalliñgmiu[t]), "one who lived beyond the mountains to the North," around Noatak area." Pg. VII. There are several entries in this book about Maniiḷauraq's wife. Burch, in 1988 also has a **Silaliñirmiut** (Silaliñaġmiut) for the estate immediately to the north of Tikararmiut (Tikġaġmiut).

LOCATION, LOCATION, LOCATION **11**

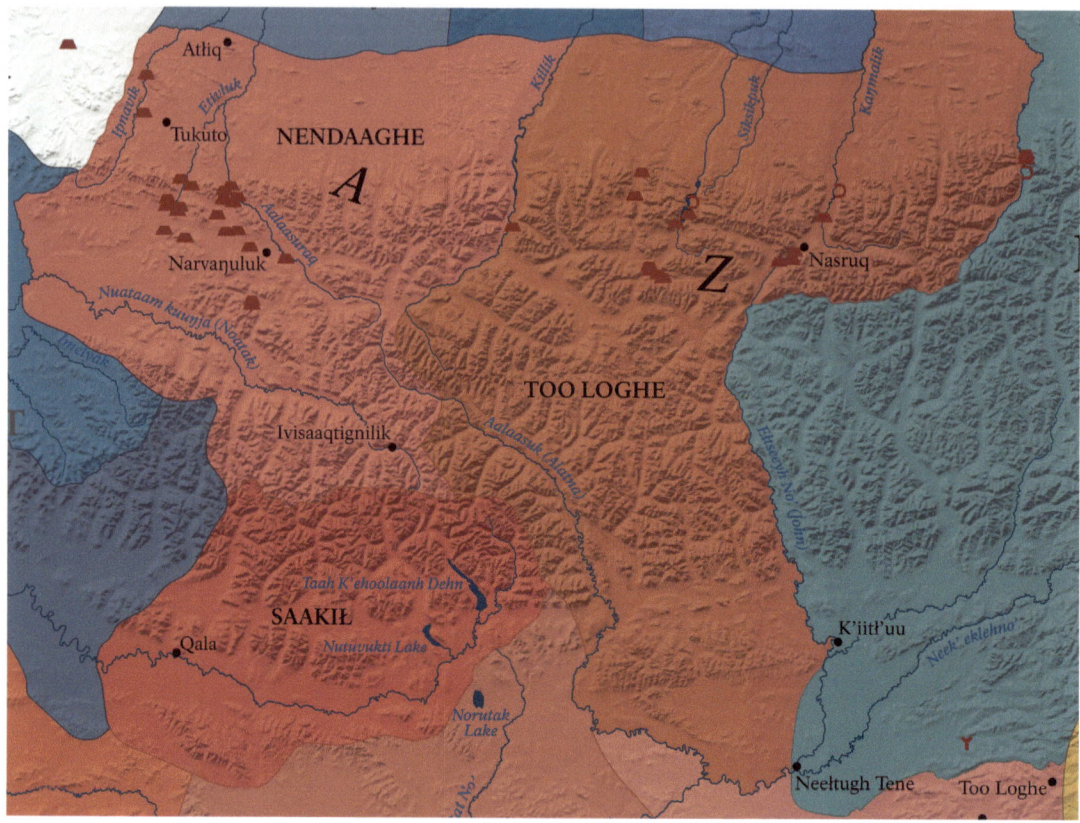

Fig. 4. Nendaaghe Estate, 1800. Raboff, GANPP, 2024.

Tatqaviñ Ruth Ramoth-Sampson was not an Upper Kobuk River speaker as evinced by her preference for Maniiḷaq over the Upper Kobuk dialect Maniiḷauraq. The familiarity of older speakers with Iñupiaq ethnonyms of earlier times was not necessarily understood by younger generations. Two questions loom, north of which mountains? The Baird Mountains or the De Long Mountains? If it was north of the Baird Mountains, then it definitely is the old Iñupiaq ethnonym for the people of the upper Noatak River, the Nendaaghe Estate. On the other hand, if it was north of the De Long Mountains, then are the **Siḷalliñġmiut** and **Silaliñaġmiut** the same people or is it a dialect variation and was the last statement, "around Noatak area," interjected as understood by the writers or spoken by the speaker?

In Iñupiatuun Uqaluit Taniktun Sivuniŋit on pages 360 we have two words, "A) **Siḷaliñauraq** outskirts, adjacent area around the main area, and B) **Siḷaliñiq** Arctic Slope (north of the Brooks Range.)." In entry, "A) outskirts, adjacent area around the main area," makes sense because they were adjacent to the long time dominate and prominent estate of Tikiġigak. In entry "B) Arctic Slope (north of the Brooks Range.)," this definition may be what the word has grown to mean in the North Slope dialect, not necessarily what it meant to the speakers along the Upper Kobuk. This does bear further research and discussion within the Iñupiaq speaking communities.

The Nendaaghe hut'aane called themselves **Tl'eeyegge hut'aane**, "inhabitants of the area." Tl'eeyegge meaning "coming down into the house," and hut'aane meaning referring to a residential area, as in "resident of." The Nendaaghe referred to themselves as **Denaa**, meaning "mankind" or "real human being" and referring specifically to a man, *denaa*. Nendaaghe hut'anne means "inhabitants of Nendaaghe (the area)." The Tl'eeyegge hut'aane language is known as **Denaakk'e**.

The ethnonym Nendaaghe hut'aane was a recent assignation by this author. The name of this group became lost over a hundred years ago, so a name had to be assigned to them to at least write about them and differentiate them from other Denaa groups. Although traditionally Dene people did not name their estates after rivers, it is for a matter of convenience that this name was chosen. The word *Nendaaghe* itself is the Denaakk'e name for the upper *Nuataaq* River (*Nuataam Kuuŋa*) in the central valley dialect of the Nuataaqmiut (also Nunataaġmiut) who live in the area, and called *Nunataaq* by the present and former upper Kobuk River community. In common usage, *Nunataaq* often refers to the whole of the former Nendaaghe hut'aane estate in the upper Kobuk dialect.

Generally, Dene Athabascan groups in Alaska did not name themselves after rivers, but rather in relation to other groups in the tribe, and with reference to mountain ranges and rivers in the region. For instance, *Di̧'ha̧i̧i̧ gwich'in*, are the most western Dinjii Zhuh group among all Gwich'in estates, and furthermore distinguished by their home behind a range of mountains. Therefore *Di̧'ha̧i̧i̧*, "ones who live at the furthest edge or border (of known Dinjii Zhuh peoples' occupation)," in other words people who lived at the edge of the Gwich'in Estates behind the mountains, out of sight.

Nendaaghe is the Denaakk'e word for the upper Nunataaq River. The Koyukon Athabaskan Dictionary says, "*meaning uncertain but probably from this verb theme.*" The noun theme is **nen**, meaning spinal ridge, backbone, and sloping, and **daa**, **daak** meaning in Group 5, "*the following themes express the movements of a mass of objects or of amorphous substances.*" And **tsaał** meaning darkness. Furthermore, **daaghe** means "*dead people, spirits, souls, ghosts of the dead.*" This is a difficult word to translate without the interpretation of an actual person from the area in the last century.

Keeping in mind that Dene Athabascan groups also named bands in relation to each other, we can look at the self-applied ethnonym for the former Tl'eeyegga hut'aane residents of the upper Kobuk River, *Saaqił hut'aane*. **Saaqił** is the way an upper Kobuk Iñupiaq speaker, Jenny Jackson, said the word. **Sookeł** is a word that might mean "sunny river bank," in the modern Denaakk'e language.

Putting all this information together, and including the movement of the sun and periods of darkness, geographic location of each community in relation to each other, the weather, and the predominate geography of the Nendaaghe Estate, we have a way to determine a meaning.

Part of the Nendaaghe Estate is on the north slope of the Gwazhał Cordillera (present day Brooks Range) where during the winter the sun does not come over the horizon for well over a month. This causes the Nendaaghe Estate to be incrementally darker during the winter months than the Saaqił Estate which is further south, making it comparatively sunnier than the darker Nendaaghe region. Continuing in this vein, we have spine and sloping, as part of the meaning. To get to the Nendaaghe Estate from the Saaqił region one must pass over mountain ridges, as there was no other way to reach the Nendaaghe Estate without the advantages of modern transportation. Then we have <u>daaghe</u> as part of the word. Here the idea of amorphous substances, and mass movement of objects is introduced. Souls, ghosts of the dead, spirits, yes, but blowing snow, rock particles, ice crystals, animal and plant remains, and dense fog are also amorphous substances and if a person or animal is walking towards a person, it takes a few moments for them to walk out of the dense fog or blowing snow, and hence the momentary appearance of an apparition. Shifting snowy particles and amorphous substances can appear as ghostly spirits. As a footnote, the whole area was totally abandoned except seasonally by the 1850s by the Nendaaghe hut'aane. Only the memory of long-gone people imbues the place.

All of this is precisely descriptive of the Nendaaghe Estate in the 1800s.

It is necessary to discuss the words; Nunataaq, Nuataaq, and Noataaq. These words are not translated by Iñupiaq speakers of the middle Nuataam Kuuŋa. Burch in his discussions of the word said, "*Just what the word Nuataaq means, however, is problematic: none of my sources has ever been able even to hint at a translation for it. It might be a contraction of nunataq, which, in the eastern Arctic, denotes an isolated mountain projecting up through an ice cap.*" This is a valid conclusion. In "Iñupiatun Uqaluit Taniktun Sivuniŋit" compiled by Ahgeak Edna MacLean, (2014) *nunataq-*, *nunatchi-*, and *nunataqaġvik* are all words associated with sod, and the storage of (caribou) meat underground in the North Slope dialect. The words for cache in Kaŋiqsisautit Uqayasraġnikun (1997) dialect of the Kobuk River basin is *saiyut*, *saiyuurat*, *siġluaq* and *siġluuraq*. Many of the former residents of the middle Noataaq River were forced during the crash of the Western Arctic Caribou Herd of the 1880s to migrate east, west, north, and south due to the real threat of starvation. When people moved from estate to estate, they normally adopted the language and dialects of the area they moved into. Most of the people interviewed by Burch were from the Northwest Arctic. In this context, a word can be lost or modified in one generation. Local multi-lingual speakers would have found the need to differentiate the <u>meat cache</u> from the name of <u>the river</u>. I think this is borne out by the fact the Kuuvaum Kaŋiaġmiut consistently refer to the Nuataaġmiut as Nunataaġmiut, and the Noataaq River, and the area of their summer caribou hunts as Nunataaq. Nunataaq then may have been the Iñupiaq name for the Nendaaghe Estate. It may also have been reshaped, but I am less certain about that.

To break this down further it appears that Nuataaġmiut and Nunataaġmiut in former times referred to the inhabitants of two distinct districts, separate nations, and language groups. The Nunataaġmiut would have been the Tl'eeyegge hut'aane above the Aniġaak River who spoke Denaakk'e, and the Nuataaġmiut would have referred to the Iñupiat Estate below the Aniġaak River along the middle Noatak River, who spoke/speak Iñupiaq. The terms *Iyaġaaġmiut* and *Uyaġaaġmiut* then are generic terms for a people long since gone from the region, but as names become obsolete or get repurposed, the ethnonym Nunataaġmiut has persisted. The Kuuvaum Kaŋiaġmiut of the upper Kobuk River valley being former Saaqił hut'aane in generations past carry on that name for the former Nendaaghe Estate, Nunataaq.

In conclusion I would like to suggest that *Iyaġaaġmiut* and *Uyaġaaġmiut* are general Iñupiaq terms for people who once occupied both the Nendaaghe and Saaqił former Denaa Estates, and it appears but far from settled, that the Upper Kobuk Iñupiat retained the old word for their Iñupiat ethnonym for the former Nedaaghe hut'aane Denaa as *Silalliñġmiut*. Furthermore, the former self-ethnonym of the Sookeł hut'aane Denaa as *Saaqił hut'aane* was gathered through Jenny Jackson. These two ethnonyms were gathered well into the twentieth century.

It is one thing to talk about the land and its inhabitants and to view photographs of the landscape, but now we need to think about it in terms of the terrain, that is, how easy or difficult was it to get from point A to point B, and in what season, and by what mode of transportation? Where was the best place to live and in what season? Then one must also regard

Fig. 5. Killiq River, A border river, GANPP.

the distribution of edible vegetation, and the vegetation that is useful for making tools and homes, even temporary homes. Special attention was demanded for the presence of resident and seasonal fauna. When and where was the best time to hunt ptarmigan, ducks, geese, rabbits, bears, sheep, wolves, moose, and caribou and to trap fish. This land and its resources had to be sought out to sustain the people who lived there. What was their predominate food source?

The Nendaaghe Estate is a vast area covering 4,307,002.9 acres or roughly 6,729 square miles. As a comparison, the states of Connecticut and Rhode Island combined are 7,029 square miles. Shikoku Island, the smallest major island of Japan, is 7,259 square miles.

The Nendaaghe Estate is firmly nestled in the mountain ranges and foothills of the Gwazhał Cordillera. The Northern border travels along the ridges of the De Long Mountains on the west end, and down the Ipnavik River to just below the Smith Lakes, crossing over to the confluence of the Itivluk and East Fork Itivluk River, then east through headwaters of a number of north flowing streams, to the confluence of the Killiq River and Kalukruatchiak Point. The western border consists of the Pupik Hills and the south flowing Anigaak River, across or down the Nuataam Kuuŋa (Noataaq) then south up the Imailim Kuuŋa (Imelyik) along the ridge of the Schwatka Mountains to Natmaqtuġiaq (Ambler Pass). All of this must of necessity follow Ernest S. Burch, Jr. in "The Iñupiaq Eskimo Nations of Northwestern Alaska," 1998 (TIENNA).

The southern border begins in the high ridges of the Schwatka Mountains beginning in the area of Natmaqtuġiaq Pass (Natmaktuġiaq, Nakmaktuak) and heads eastward towards Mount Papiġuq. The eastern border is long, starting at Quunġunaq and Gull Pass in the Endicott Mountains to the Aalaasuk River and upstream to where it ends in Killiq Pass and then portage to the Killiq River seven miles east as the crow flies. Down the Killiq River to

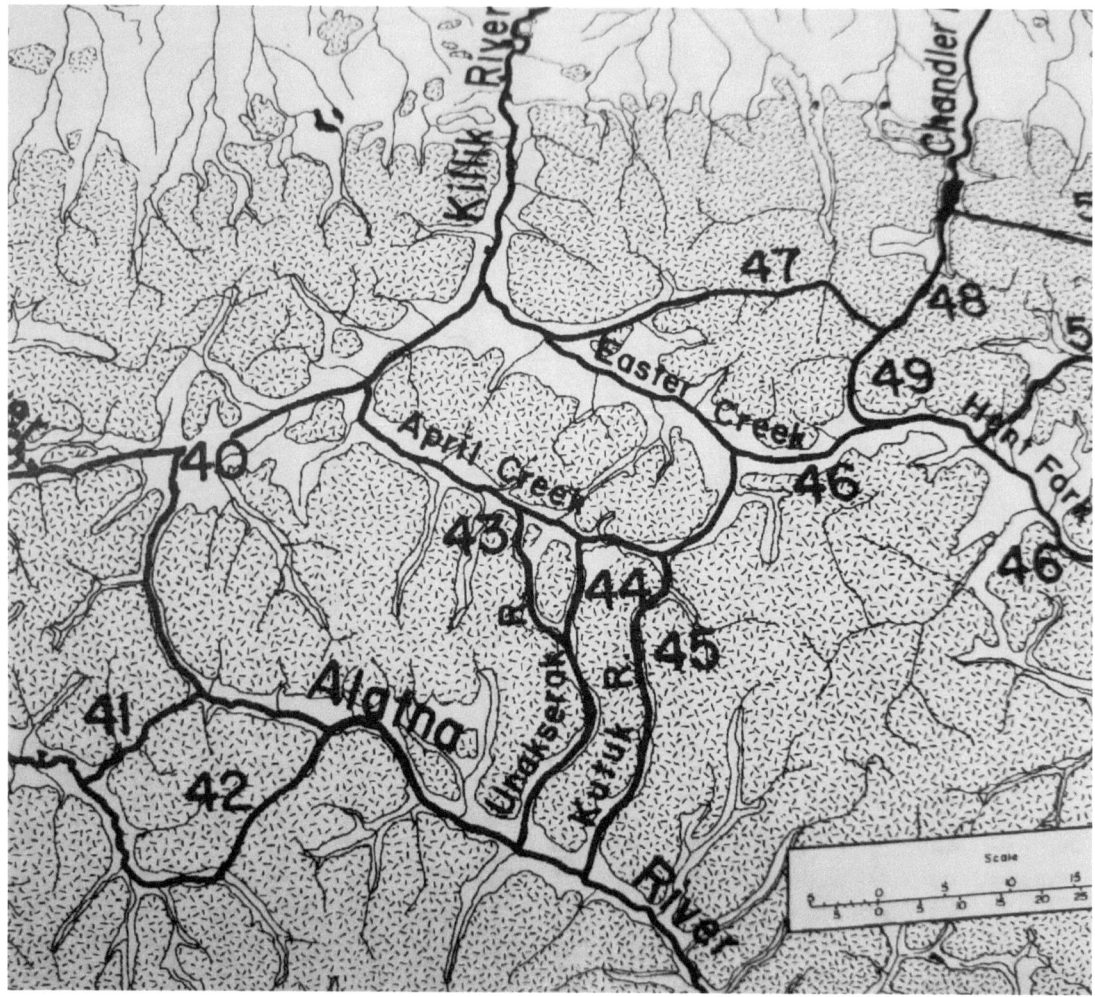

Fig. 6. Burch Trade Routes, "Alliance and Conflict," 2005

the confluence of the Okpikruak River.

However, taking Burch's trade route system through the Endicott Mountains in "The World System of The Iñupiaq Eskimos, Alliance and Conflict, 2005," (A&C) into account we have some options to consider.

First, we must keep in mind that borders must be clear, discrete, and accessible. A border through Killiq Pass, if such were the case, would qualify as such. The Nendaaghe and Too Loghe hut'aane were mountain people who hunted for caribou, their primary food and a big source of their trade items. Caribou choose routes to and from their winter and summer grounds by, among other factors, the forage available and snow conditions on mountain passes. Their routes changed from year to year. Therefore, although the Nendaaghe/ Too Loghe border might have been in the Killiq Pass, route 40, I'm of the opinion that there was flexibility between the Nendaaghe and Too Loghe border so that route 45 Kutuk River and down Easter Creek, route 46 and route 40 formed a wedge of land that was sometimes and seasonally shared (See Burch trade routes).

It is well known that elderly and physically challenged people were left behind in certain locales because the area was easier to walk around and there was enough small game, ground squirrels, ptarmigan, and fish available to sustain them and plants to gather while the main body of people went on their seasonal food gathering rounds. Other times elders as two or three individuals would leave the group to be on their own for the summer months and only later rejoin the group. This was done to reduce the number of people who had to be fed by the main provider, and when in search of food long distances had to be traversed in a timely way, so they would have posed a burden.

Other situations in which this wedge of land was shared was during the late June to August/early September hunts and the time of year when other people from the surrounding regions, such as the Saaqił hut'aane of the Hulghaatne River, and the Akuniġmiut Iñupiat, from lower down the river, came through the region or stayed. It is possible that an unknown and un-named group at and near the mouth of the Aalaasuk and *Koyitł'ots'ina* rivers might also have come through the area to hunt caribou, sheep, and bear during this season, however this is uncertain. Only some members of the latter group came, others were busy with salmon fishing during these times.

One aspect that must be explained about these groups concerns their biological relationship, therefore determining who stayed behind to hunt sheep, and those who went on further north to hunt caribou depended upon age and/or physical fitness. Their mutual relationships hinged on trading partners and co-sibling status. The old adage, "blood is thicker than water," was never taken lightly here, and it follows that the people who stayed behind to hunt sheep, and those who went out onto the tundra to hunt caribou, although of different estates were all inter-related over generations.

To conclude, the Nendaaghe/Too Loghe border was along route 40, but there was a sometime seasonally shared areas between, routes 40, 45, and 46.

In recreating the possible settlements of the time, we turn to Burch, the journeys of U.S. Naval Ensign William Lauriston Howard, (Pt. Barrow Expedition papers [microform], 1885–86, UAF), the accounts of George Morse Stoney, 1884–86, and archaeological records. The settlements and or camps are from North to South, 1. Atłiq, 2. Tukuto Lake, 3. Tooloouk, 4. Kinyiksukvik Lake, 5. Kikitliorak Lake, 6. Itivuk Lake and Narvaŋuluk, (it appears that Narvaŋuluk was the original name of Itivluk Lake), 7. Isheyak (in Howard), Issakuq (in Burch which probably jives with modern spellings). At the confluence of the Aalaasuraq and Itilyiurgiok Creek, 8. Qupyuq or Kipmik Lake, 9. Ugpigruaq, 10. Ninŋuq, 11. Tupilik, 12. Ivisaaqtiġnillik, 13. Quunġunaq, 14. Shotcoaluk, 15. Aneyuk, and 16. Koolooguak (reportedly at the Cutler and Imelyak confluence). At the very top along the Kuukpik is 17. Etivolipar. Recorded in 1885 by Howard, it appeared to be at that point a staging area before people proceeded down the river for trade. There was a camping site in the vicinity of Inyorurak Pass which Howard called 18. "Innugararuck's Village." Uncertain if this site was to the north or south of Inyorurak Pass. It then appears that there were at least sixteen or seventeen settlements of varying sizes occupied throughout the estate and utilized perhaps seasonally. If we assume that the first eight settlements were peopled with from ten to thirty residents, then we have from 80 to 240 people in the region. That would represent at least seven or eight large extended families. This population swelled during the summer and fall hunts with Tl'eeyegga hut'aane and Akuniġmiut Iñupiat relatives from other areas to the south and west.

Although this is a story about the Nendaaghe hut'aane people, there are other neighboring estates that have a larger part in this story, they are the Too Loghe Estate and Saaqił Estate, and the Di' haii Estate. Still other groups will be introduced later.

As the Nendaaghe and Too Loghe hut'aane

Fig. 7. Historic Nendaaghe Settlements after Burch, Howard and Raboff, 2024. Map by H. McCaig and Adam K. Freeburg.

were the farthest north Denaa groups in the 1800s, I will continue with the Too Loghe people and their estate.

The Too Loghe Estate abuts the Nendaaghe on the west/east border. They shared a section of east/west border, from the Okpikruak and Killiq River confluence south to Killiq Pass. As I commented earlier, they shared a small wedge of land on a seasonal basis. This area of the Gwazhał Cordillera, is currently regarded as the Central Brooks Range and forms a large portion of the Gates of the Arctic National Park and Preserve.

Here we run into two thorny issues regarding what records or oral traditions are available for the north, south, and eastern borders of the Too Loghe Estate. Since we are talking about events that took place over two hundred years ago, this reconstruction must be necessarily construed, extrapolated, and followed through in terms of what is known about land use and available resources including archaeological evidence if available or reliable for the not-too-distant past.

The first problem area is what Burch (1998) calls, "the headwaters district of the upper Noatak River." The Nendaaghe Estate is backed up by oral and written traditions on the Iñupiat side. However, it was not called the **Nendaaghe Estate**, and in Burch and Craig W. Mishler, 1995, they claim that these people were the Di'haii Gwich'in. I can understand this since the main study area of Burch was always the Northwestern Arctic Iñupiat communities. It is tremendously difficult to acquire information, then to organize it, and finally see a bigger picture, then to reorganize it, return for more inquiries, reorganize again, and finally to write about things that happened years ago. It requires time to understand that each community has a shared body of knowledge that others don't necessarily catch on to at the onset. Furthermore, to acculturate oneself to relations with the study group community all takes years. Finally, to present all this information with the latest and tested theories within a specific field, as in anthropology, requires collaboration of academic colleagues who are able to help and contribute. Burch was therefore relying on Mishler for the Di'haii gwich'in side of the story.

The corpus of knowledge about the mystery people assumed to be the Di'haii gwich'in were told by Elijah Kakinya, Maptiåaq Billy Morry, Isasan Justus Mekiana, and Panniaq Simon Paneak in oral histories, and sometimes through the interpretation and writings of Helge Ingstad, Edwin S. Hall, Jr., Nicholas J. Gubser, Knut Bergsland and John M. Campbell. These men were repeating stories told by an older generation of the events that took place during the lives of their grandfathers and great grandfathers. What they imparted is invaluable information.

The result is that Ingtad, Hall, Gubser, Bergsland, Campbell, Burch, and Mishler all have repeated the assumption that the Di'haii gwich'in were in the upper Nuataam Kuuŋa (Noataaq), and also the Indians who were displaced in the Anuktuvuk Pass area. Collectively, these are most of the anthropologists who have written about the area in question.

The second issue is; What constitutes evidence of events that took place two hundred years ago? Everyone here, including myself, has used oral tradition and written records by early observers.

Then the question becomes; Why does this author claim that these people were Northern **Tl'eeyegge hut'aane** Denaa? The principal reason is the added extensive genealogy of the Tl'eeyegge hut'aane and Dinjii Zhuh people that goes back five to seven generations. It is the transition of these communities of people through a number of stages from one estate to another, and one language area to another which has posed the major obstacle to understanding or seeing this picture. The other reasons being that informants of Di'haii gwich'in origin primarily all died by the 1940s, and that the anthropologists that worked with the Neets'aii gwich'in community were not aware as to the extent of the community's movement just in the last three generations, since 1800. As a result, no one asked, or pursued the question. Perhaps due to time constraints and lack of deeper knowledge and good interpreters.

There are two people in the last forty-five years upon whom we can rely: Johnny Frank Drit of Venetie, Alaska, and Stephen Peter Ch'igiioonta' of Arctic Village, Alaska.

Johnny Frank Drit was raised around his paternal grandmother, Dik Sarah Aldzak Ch'igiioonta' Drit (later known as Sarah Shaaghan Dik) who was a remarkable storyteller. She imparted the mythology cycle and cosmology of the Nendaaghe hut'aane and Di'haii gwich'in communities and shared stories about her early life. The problem with relating her life stories is that she had no way to pinpoint the location of any places beyond the general area of the Kobuk, K'iit'it, and the Ch'ataanjik, which the younger generation of her time could associate or connect with. She might have imparted place names, but no one subsequently made any effort to repeat them. Therefore, they only knew that she was raised far to the west of the Dį'hąįį and Neets'ąįį gwich'in estates. In person, her voice came through Johnny Frank Drit very clearly, he was a great storyteller in his own right, and had an abiding sense of humor. Once when my father and I were visiting him he decided to speak in the Dį'hąįį dialect, my father had to translate into Neets'ąįį dialect, after sometime he laughed and resumed in Neets'ąįį gwich'in dialect. Johnny Frank Drit had the added good fortune to be raised during a time when the men in the Neets'ąįį gwich'in estate were raised according to strictly structured traditions. His upbringing served him well throughout his life. Johnny Frank Drit was a second generation Neets'ąįį gwich'in person.

The other person is Stephen Peter Ch'igiioonta' whose mother Soozun John Dahjalti' Peter Ch'igiioonta' was a family historian and genealogist. Soozun was raised on the Draanjik Estate, and her mother, Shaanaavee Vahan Drit Dahjalti' was Dį'hąįį gwich'in and Saaqił hut'aane Denaa. Her father was Shoh tsal John Dahjalti' a Neets'ąįį gwich'in. She grew up speaking both dialects of Dinjii Zhuh K'yaa, and eventually added the Neets'ąįį dialect. Later after her marriage to Shajol Peter John Ch'igiioonta' she moved to the vicinity of Teeląįį Tthal caribou corral and residence near her maternal Uncle Juuzii Tr'ootsyaa John Drit owner of *Teeląįį Tthal* corral on the south shores of Van K'eedii/K'ehdii. As a young girl Soozun lived with her maternal grandmother, Ilikuq Lucy Saityen Shijuu Tr'oonii Drit Shiigyaa Tr'oonii Khyahtthoo and her last husband Vindeegwaazhii Thomas (spelled Dhindeegwaazhii by Herbert Halvir Ginkhii Albert Tritt Drit) Khyahtthoo. Soozuns' residence in early life allowed her to see the Denaa Tl'eeyegga hut'aane coming into the region and where they settled subsequently, and if she didn't know details, her grandmother Ilikuq Lucy was there to inform her. Soozun's son Stephen was raised exclusively on the Neets'ąįį Estate. Stephen was a third generation Neets'ąįį gwich'in person.

As a young man Stephen was given two alternatives, he could become a *dinjii dazhan* (shaman) or he could study the bible. Stephen chose the latter. As a very young man Stephen Tsee Gho' became a prayer healer. In this capacity he traveled extensively among the Western Gwich'in Estates and as far as Old Crow and Dawson, Yukon Territory, Canada. His work required him to live for extended periods of time with sick and or dying people. Among the Dinjii Zhuh this meant helping the household with fishing, hunting, and behaving as a nurse-orderly for men. During these times the patient and/or his family would relate the stories of their lives, their genealogies and stories of the people and places in the local area. Coming from a family of genealogists; he had acquired an extensive knowledge of Dinjii Zhuh genealogy and history, and he had years in which to cross check those genealogies.

However, neither Johnny Frank Drit or Stephen Peter Ch'igiioonta' ever described the exact routes their families traveled to end up on the Neets'ąįį gwich'in estate nor the exact location of known confrontations, except for the last battle at K'iitł'it and the altercation at the mouth of Ch'ataanjik. Johnny Frank Drit does tell a story about dinjii dazhan (shaman) on the Kobuk River. This indicates that Sarah Shaaghan Dik may have journeyed through or lived temporarily in the Upper Kobuk to gain this tale, but that is a small aspect of the whole story.

Genealogy has been used as evidence of a peoples' movement across time and space, certainly in mass movements of human geography over the centuries, yes. However, in these remote sparsely populated areas of Northern Alaska, the genealogical information was not raw materials for clothing, housing, and tools. They were so central to life, they were a fixture in Athabascan songs and stories. When caribou populations dropped or ranges shifted, the peoples of northern Alaska responded in kind, moving their settlements. Areas without caribou were left uninhabited as people moved to better prospects, and the most reliable hunting spots became focal points for the largest settlements.

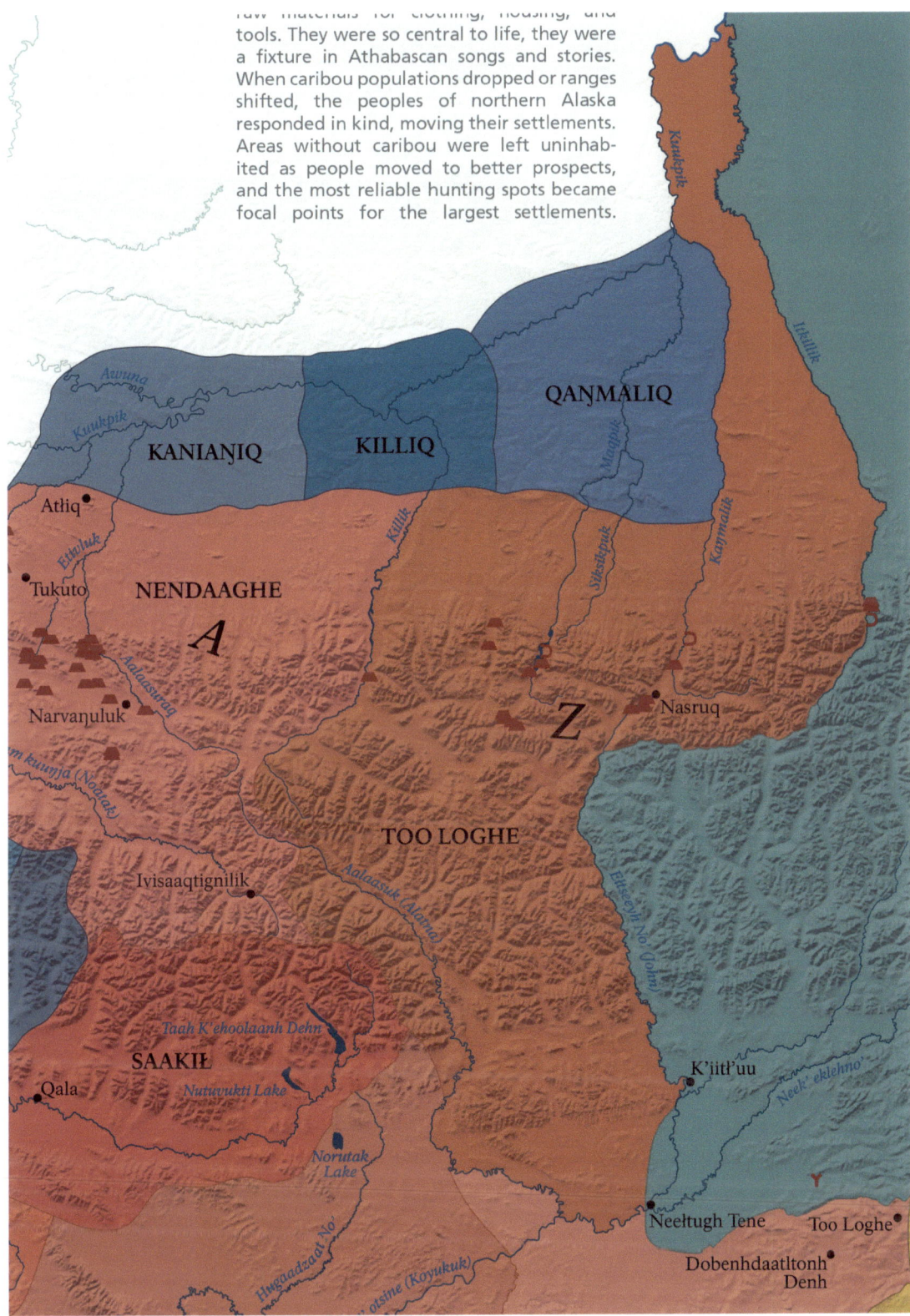

Fig. 8. Too Loghe Estate, 1800. Raboff and GANPP, 2024.

Fig. 9. Agiak Lake, looking north, Too Loghe Estate. Raboff and GANPP, 2024.

written. It is what I, through the teaching of my father, Stephen, bring to this study, and I will demonstrate this through various family histories.

In this context broad outlines of possible estate borders for the Too Loghe hut'aane and the Dị'haii gwich'in estates can be drawn.

The Too Loghe Estate is approximately 6,093,577 acres (9521 square miles in size). The estate is so large, full of higher elevation mountains, narrow valleys, and high elevation alpine tundra plateaus.

We resume then with the Too Loghe Estate. The western borders follow the same lines as the eastern border of the Nendaaghe Estate for most of its length. We resume at Killiq Pass. It follows the Aalaashuk River from its headwaters down beyond the foothills of the Endicott Mountains, but to the north of the Alatna Hills. There is a trough that runs from east to west to the Eł tseeyh no' (Kiitł'uu Dzk, Eł tseeyh no', Dn, Kiiñaqvak, I).

Once upon the Eł tseeyh no', this is followed north to its headwaters which end at the south end of K'iitł'it (Pass) (Dzk)/Naqsraq (Pass) (I), henceforth K'iitł'it/Naqsraq Pass. Before the Eł tseeyh no' ends the Inukpasugruk (I) enters from the east going up a deep mountain gorge which is included. The eastern border continues along the mountains that rim the whole Qaŋmaliq (Kaŋmalik) River drainage.

I must stop here to ponder upon the name of the Anaqtuuvak River. How long has it been known by this name? Burch through Surgeon John Simpson calls this river the Kaŋmalik from oral accounts, and segregated the Kuukpiġmiut into the Kaniaŋiq, Killiq, and Qaŋmaliq Iñupiat estates. The

Fig. 10. Agiak Lake, inuksuk driveline, Too Loghe Estate, 2005. Photographer Jeff Rasic, GANPP

Kanianigmiut were at the headwaters of the Kuukpik. The Killiġmiut and Qaŋmaliġmiut got their names from the rivers that they lived along, the Killiq and Qaŋmalik. According to Gubser (1965), the present residents of Anaktuvuk Pass are a people composed of five families of Tuluġmiut and eight families of Killiġmiut. Continuing with Gubser, the Tuluġmiut were members of and or descendants of the former Qaŋmaliġmiut. For a people to change names after a whole river drainage to one lake, Tulugag, represents suffering, hardship, and immense loss of a degree few people can fathom. I wonder at what point the name of this river was changed, since changing the names of rivers is a rare occurrence, except when there is a takeover or abandonment, and even then it is very difficult to wipe out the name completely as demonstrated by the Noataaq (Nunataaq).

However, Elijah Kakinya, stated that, *"Now Tulugaq has been named Anaktuvik... Qaŋmaliq, like that; it is said it is Qaŋmaliq, that up there, our land, Qaŋmaliq was its name since that time long ago. Qaŋmaliq...And then the white people changed it to Anaktuvik. What used to be Qaŋmaliq...Although they have as their roots "people of Qaŋmaliq and then they renamed it Anaktuvik, the cause of this being the white people." Puiguitkaat (1981).* Here is plainly stated that the designation of the Qaŋmaliq River to Anaqtuuvak River, and Tulugaq to Anaktuvik happened sometime during the 1950s and maybe as late as the early 1960s. Tulugaq was a former place of residence near Tulugaq Lake.

Naqsraq- is the name for a pass in the Iñupiaq language. *"Naqsraq- a ridge that divides watersheds of rivers; a pass, a valley or passage in the mountains;*

Fig. 11. Chandler Lake, Too Loghe Estate, Anderson Photos 2005, GANPP.

low point of a hill; (i) to travel via the lowest point; (t) to travel via its lowest point," Iñupiatun Uqaluit Taniktun Sivuniŋit (2014). The name for Anaaqtuvak Pass, the community, in Iñupiaq is Naqsraq (in Dn possibly Sehno'). The summit is nearby, called, **Naqsraġlugiaq**.

Continuing down the Qaŋmaliq River to its confluence with the Kuukpik and Uluskuk Bluff then we enter the summer range, proceeding down the Kuukpik from the mouth of the Qaŋmaliq River to the mouth of the Itqiliq. Then north up the Itqiliq to the area of Mt. Itigaknit and west skirting the foothills of the Gwazhał Cordillera back to the Qaŋmaliq River.

One glaring difference between the Nendaaghe and Too Loghe estates is the number of caribou rock cairns and corrals. Nendaaghe is in the region of the Western Arctic Caribou Herd (WACH), Too Loghe is in the region of the Central Arctic Caribou Herd (CACH). The WACH was and is a much larger herd covering a much larger area. The CACH was as stated earlier a smaller herd compared to the Porcupine caribou herd (PCH) and WACH. Naming the herd is important for current studies, but during some years the CACH intermixed with both the WACH and PCH. Each herd continues to winter in the Gwazhał Cordillera and to regions south across the whole range. During our study period there were other small herds in the region, but we are concerned here about the movement of the Northern Tl'eeyegge hut'aane.

Looking at where the caribou corrals and brush fences are on the Too Loghe Estate is a sure sign of where the people congregated if not during the winter months then on a seasonal basis. In this case 1. the Okokmilaga

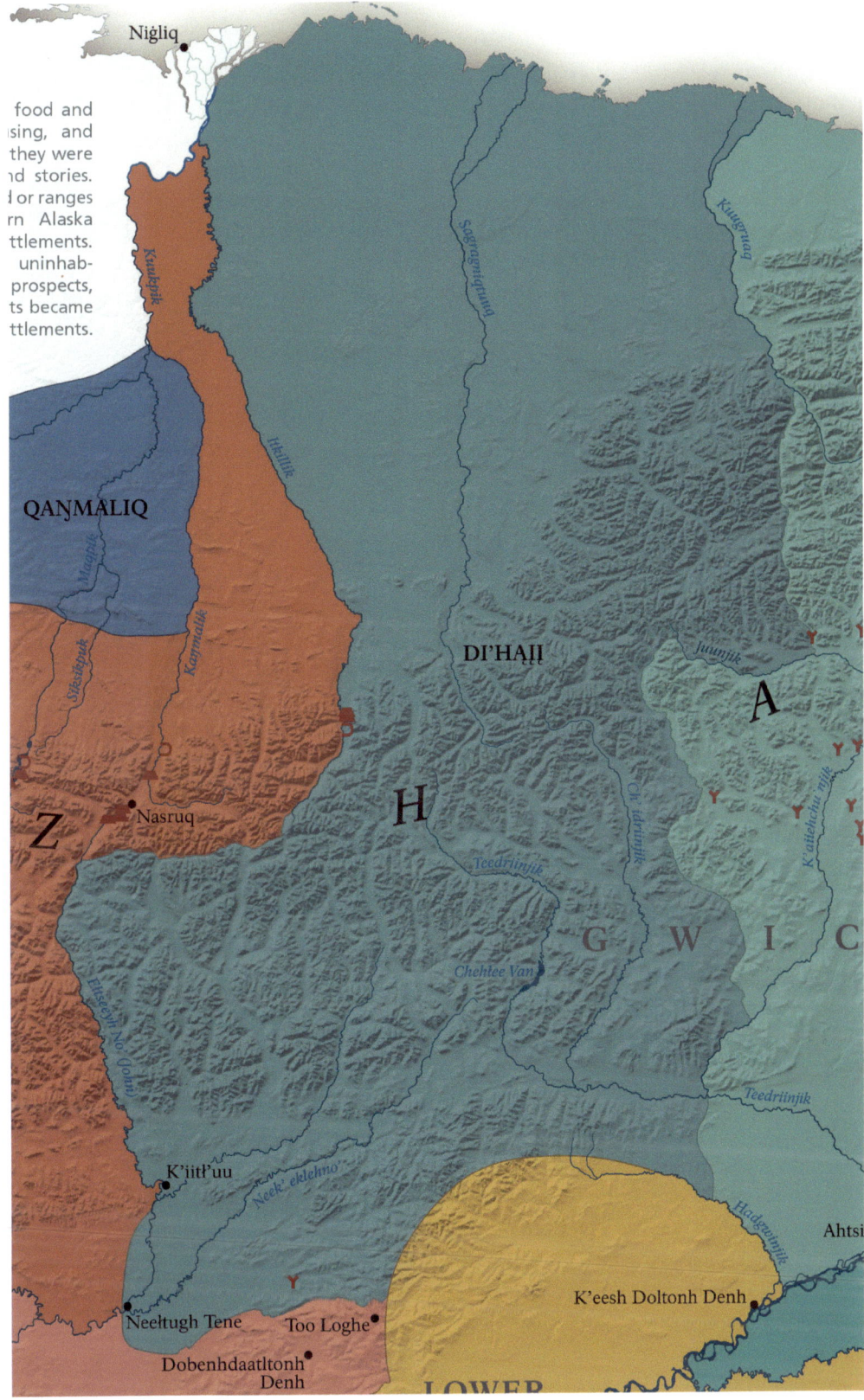

Fig. 12. Dį'hąįį Estate, 1800. Raboff and GANPP, 2024.

River headwaters, a tributary of the Killik, 2. the Maqpik drainage, and the Chandler Lakes, 3. the areas of Agiak and Amiloyak Lake, 4. the area of Easter Creek headwaters, Agiak Creek, and Hunt River, and 5. the area of north/south drainages of Qaŋmaliq (Kaŋmalik)/Eł tseeyh no', and K'iitł'it/Naqsraq Pass. Once again assuming from 10 to 30 residents for each possible community/ies you have a minimum of 50 to 180 people for the whole estate. Although we have no way of knowing with certainty, perhaps there were two or three other settlements along the Aalaasuk, Qaŋmaliq, or Eł tseeyh no'. That would be from five to seven large extended families.

In 1867 when Robert McDonald (Robert McDonald Journal 1862–1912) met three "Kitlit Gwich'in" while in the Neets'ąįį region, they said their population numbers were 40 men, 40 women, and 100 children. However, by this time they were entirely in the Koyitł'ots'ina river valley, removed from Too Loghe Estate completely for almost 20 years. Given the terrain and the yearly availability of food sources its doubtful that Too Loghe Estate could have supported more people than that.

Our next region of concern is the Di'hąįį Estate which is immediately to the east of the Too Loghe Estate. It is the largest estate so far. The open tundra represents the summer range all the way to the Chuu Choo Vee/Taġiuq/Tagiag between the Kuukpik to the Saġvagniqtuuq, and the south of the range represents the wintering grounds. The area to the southwest is dominated by the Koyitł'ots'ina River and its tributaries.

The whole central part is in the heart of the Gwazhał Cordillera and covered with high alpine tundra and narrow valleys. There are a series of craggy mountain passes known as **Nihteeindrat**, beginning with Oolah Pass and going eastward along the divide all the way to the Nagwichoonjik. This area in particular excluding the Ahtr'aiinjik/Ivaasak pass and those further east are known by this name. The passes **Nihteeindrat** are 1. Itqiliq /Kuyuktuvuk Creek (Oolah Pass), 2. Dietrich/Tlaakk'oł Neekk'e (on maps as Atigun River), 3. Tlaakk'oł Neekk'e/Teedriinjik, 4. Teedriinjik/Tlaakk'oł Neekk'e/ Saġvagniqtuuq, 5. Ch'idriinjik/ Saġvagniqtuuq, and 6. Kiitsal Tit.

However, the more traveled route appears to be the Itqiliq/Kuyuktuvuk Creek (Oolah Pass) where there are caribou drives, cairns, and subterranean caches, and tent rings. Then down the Itqiliq to its confluence with the Kuukpik and out to the ocean. From the mouth of the Kuukpik, the Chuu Choo Vee/Taġiuq/Tagiag shore was followed east to the Saġvagniqtuuq River from which they would proceed up to its headwaters and intersect with the Ch'idriinjik (Dzk) and the Teedriinjik (Dzk) or proceed to their eastern Vyàh K'it/Kuugruaq border to Ahtr'aiinjik. The area between the Ahtr'aiinjik and the Łuhtan Deetak Gwinjik was a quasi-shared spring/early fall (right of passage) area between the Łuhtan Deetak Gwinjik and Thoochyaa Tsalnjik.

I might note here that Hudson's Bay Company was aware of the extent of the "Loucheax" Indian occupation as far as the northern sea. The Dinjii Zhuh recognize the 1. Di'hąįį from the Kuukpik to the Vyàh K'it/Kuugruaq, 2. the Neets'ąįį from the Vyàh K'it/Kuugruaq to the Kaŋigqut, and 3. the Dagoo from Kaŋigqat to the area just to the west of Nanjuughat (Qikiqpagruk) along the Firth River. Furthermore, we have stories of Dahjalti' Khehkwaii going from the Łihteeraadal (Łeeridiidal, Qaaktuġvik) all the way to the Kuukpik to chase away and wipe out the Iñupiat attempting to spend the winter and spring in the region. Dahjalti' Khehkwaii would never have done this if the region was not already understood to be Dinjii Zhuh hunting lands.

The western border and Neełtugh Tene (after 1847, a Denaakk'e placename) at the confluence of the Koyitł'ots'ina and the Neek'eklehno' and following the Koyitł'ots'ina to the confluence of

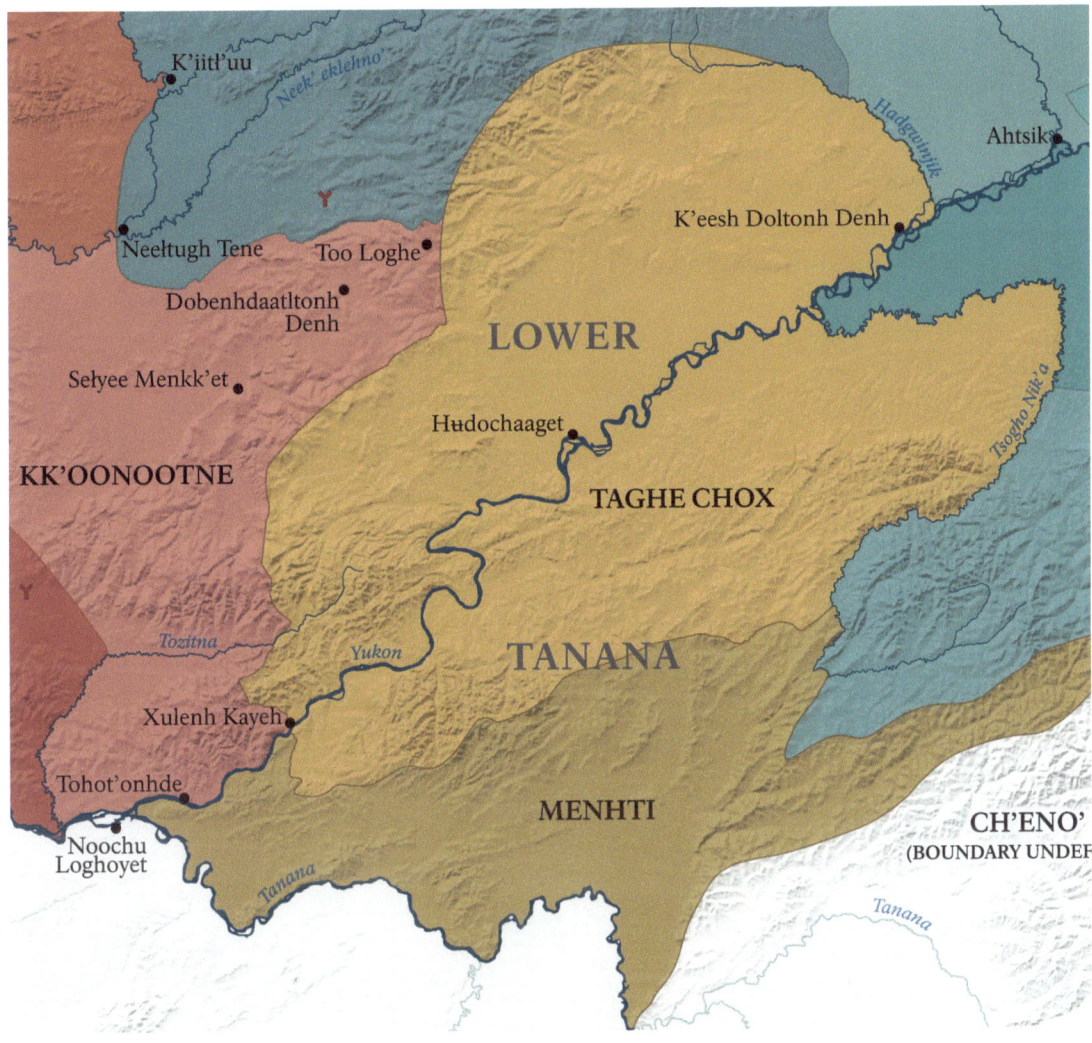

Fig. 13. Taghachʉx xwt'ana Lower Tanana Estate, 1800. Raboff and GANPP, 2024.

the Kiiñaqvak/K'iitł'uu/Eł tseeyh no' and the settlement of K'iitł'uu (Dzk birch bark shavings), then down the Qaŋmaliq which joins the Kuukpik above the Itqiliq. At this point we reach an area that might have been shared from time to time depending on the relationship of the members of each group. People who were co-sibling or trading partners might have met up in these places before spending the spring on the open tundra and trading at Niġliq near Taġiuq (Tagiaq) /Chuu Choo Vee, the great salt ocean shore.

Coming back from the shore they might choose to return by way of any of the other passes if they traded further to the east toward the mouth of the Nagwichoonjik. The eastern border then was along the Vyàh K'it/Kuugruaq to the Ch'idriinjik, down the Ch'idriinik to its confluence with the Łuhtan Deetak Gwinjik. Down the Łuhtan Deetak Gwinjik to the confluence of K'aiieh'chuu'njik to the Teedriinjik. Or as noted above down the Ahtr'aiinjik to the confluence of Teedriinjik with K'aiieh'chu'njik and then almost directly south to the headwaters of the Hadwinjik and along the mountain ridges to the south all the way to the area where the Hudochaaget portages to the Kk'oonootne, then north again to

LOCATION, LOCATION, LOCATION **27**

Fish Creek, a tributary of the Neek'eklehno', and to its confluence with the Koyitł'ots'ina.

The area is enormous, covering many square miles.

Finally, the last estate under review is the Taghachwx xwt'ana Lower Tanana estate along the Lower Yukon River ramparts and the lower part of the Yukon Flats.

This is the most mysterious of all these estates because by 1865 it was already abandoned by its original occupants.

Essentially the western border was along the mountain ridges to the southwest of Too Loghe settlement on the Kk'oonootne Estate that circled back west along the Tseet'o Dlele' downriver ridge from the mouth of Tseet'o Huno'. The northern and western borders continue east from Too Loghe to the end of the Kk'oonootne where it joins the Hudochaaget headwaters and following the northern ridgeline joining the border with the Dį'hąįį Estate to the north to the headwaters of the Hadwinjik to its mouth which ends at the Yukon River. The southern border then is the Yukon River all the way back to the Tseet'o Huno' or also the Ch'ataanjik. It is likely that the Yukon River as its southern border was a little more fluid in that they must have had some access to its near banks and bluffs. This then was the Taghachwx Estate before 1851.

I will get back to the Hadwinjik River in Chapter 5.

The estimated area of this estate then is unknown at present.

As we follow the displacement of the Nendaaghe, Saaqił, and Dį'hąįį in their eastern and southern movements we will revisit each of these estates.

In Memory of Niayuq Rachel Craig:

Kaŋiqsiñiaġataqtugiḷi Iñupianiñ uvagut piugut. Imma naluaġmiut iñugiaksiplugu aglaanikkaluaġaat iŋmiŋḷi kaŋiqsimmatimiktigun. Uvagulliasiiñ uvva Iñupianiñḷi kaŋiqsiñiaġataqtugu sivulliipta qanuq iñuuniatḷat iḷisimmataat uvva kipiġniuqtugut.

—Niayuq Rachel Craig, *In Puiguitkaat*, 1981

We do this because we are trying to understand fully what our own Iñupiat have to tell us. The white people have written a lot all right, but in their own understanding. And we, on the other hand are trying to fully understand from the Iñupiat themselves how our ancestors lived, their wisdom, and we are focusing all our attention our intent on acquiring this.

—Niayuq Rachel Craig, *In Puiguitkaat*, 1981

Sunset on Noatak River, 2008. A Claude Fiddler Photograph.

Chapter 2

Mastodons and Such: Late Prehistory

Now that we are somewhat familiar with the lay of the land, there are some other areas to explore before we can proceed.

The first of these is the seismic activity which encircles the North Pacific Rim. We all know that natural events have always been a part of the human experience, and its effects have been present in the course of human history. Alaska is not only in an area of active seismic activity, but also in the path of the long-range effects from major volcanic eruptions in the Pacific Rim. Coupled with that Alaska is also near the magnetic North Pole which attracts all sorts of atmospheric fall out, be it volcanic gases and debris, the nuclear fallout from detonated bombs, or pollutant gases which are currently amassing.

How volcanic activity in the Pacific Rim affects the late Prehistory of Alaska is rather profound. Unfortunately, very few academics have taken it into account to associate volcanic activity aftermath with what was happening on the ground with Indigenous Alaskan Late Prehistory.

Take for example the stories of William A. Oquilluk in "People of Kauwerak," (1973, 1981), and in Burch the story of Qayiayaqtualuk and his sister Maŋuyuk, in the Kivalliñiq Estate (Kivalina district). Both stories concern the survival of a few people after a catastrophic famine.

After a severe famine, Qayiayaqtualuk and his sister Maŋuyuk were the sole survivors of a couple who came from up the Wullik River in the Kivalina district. According to Ernest Burch's composite account no one knew who their parents or where they were specifically from (TIENNA 1998). Qayiayaqtualuk married a Napaaqtuġmiut (lower Noataaq) woman and his sister married a Tikiġaġmiut (Point Hope) man. Others joined them from inland and other areas in the region and formed the historic Kivalliñiġmiut population. Burch then proceeds to follow Qayiayaqtualuk's genealogy to Sivviq Chester Sevek born 1890, his 3rd great grandson. That is six generations. Through a few calculations, it is estimated that the historic Kivalina residents began minimally in 1780.

William A. Oquilluk's account is very clear, in his section on "The Third Disaster: The Time

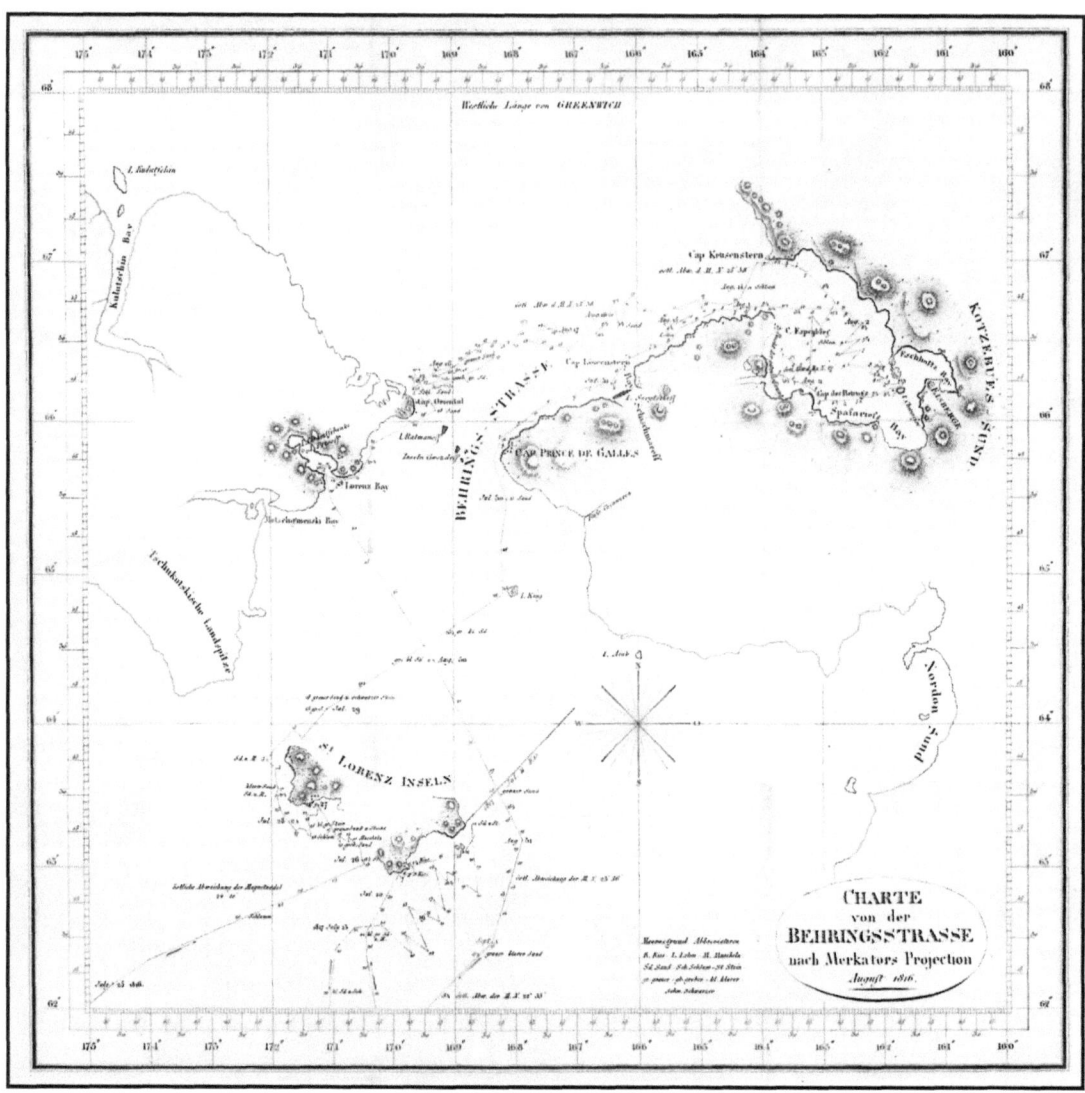

Fig. 14. Kotzebue Atlas (C0020), Archives, University of Alaska Fairbanks.

Summertime Did Not Come," he describes a normal spring, then at the end of June, winter arrived and stayed until the following spring. The stores of food needed for a whole winter had not yet been built up. During the ensuing famine, everyone died except for four people in the region. According to my estimation Mr. Oquilluk could be the 6th or 8th generation from these forefathers. Mr. Oquilluk was born 1896. I approximated the 6th generation as my estimate.

Gauging a time frame for six generations back for Chester Sevek and William Oquilluk can be done with the help of an existing genealogy of my father who was born in 1906. Putting all of them in the same generation. Taking my father back to the 6th generation that would take him to Tł'eevihti', a Nendaaghe hut'aane Denaa man, whom I guess to have been born circa 1760. Burch set 1780 as a minimal estimate for repopulation, which is the same estimate for Stephen Peter Ch'igiioonta'. Even if a middle figure of 1770 is assumed for William Oquilluk we end up with a period between 1770 and 1780 for all three families for the beginning of repopulation in these communities.

This, of course, does not answer the question of what precipitated the famine or famines. My hypothesis is a volcanic eruption. For this time period we have two possibilities; Laki, an Icelandic volcano which erupted in 1783, and Tambora which erupted between April 1815 to April 1816 in Indonesia. Both of these eruptions were big enough to cause worldwide weather cooling. Thirty-three years separate the eruption of these two volcanos. We have scant evidence for the effects of either eruption in Alaska, but there are a few leads.

For Alaska, there is tree ring evidence taken from the upper and middle Kobuk River region by James L. Giddings. Jr. in the 1940s. After studies, Roseanne D'Arrigo (1995) concludes that the tree rings are almost nonexistent for the year of the Laki eruption, 1783.

However, evidence for the effects of a Tambora eruption are present in the ship logs and maps of Baron Otto von Kotzebue. He writes that on July 11, 1817, a full 14 to 26 months after the eruption of Tambora he came upon solid ice off the coast of St. Lawrence Island and on July 14, 1817 he had to abandon any hopes of visiting Kotzebue Sound. St. Lawrence Island is at 63.3261 degrees North Latitude. By comparison, Unalakleet is at 63.8731 degrees North Latitude, and going north along Norton Sound, Shaktoolik is at 64.3339 degrees North Latitude. Nome is at 64.5 degrees North Latitude, and Port Clarence (the area of Kauwerak) is at 65.2622 degrees North Latitude.

Consequently, even taking into account the "warmer" waters on the Alaska side of the Bering Strait, there had to have been solid ice in all those places. In other words, all of Norton Sound and the Seward Peninsula were frozen in. There were no open leads for seals, walrus, or whales, which were prime food sources during that time of year. Evidently that included the Kivalina district which is to the north of Kotzebue Sound and Cape Krusenstern.

Then, taking into account the studies of Owen K. Mason and friends who have come to the conclusion that when the weather is colder, the coastal people struggle and find it harder to subsist because there are fewer or nonexistent leads in the ice, while interior people fared better. Conversely when the weather is warmer, the situation is reversed. That would have meant that the people in the interior would have fared better during the catastrophic years of 1816–18.

Now, was the eruption of Tambora the cause of the Kauwerak peoples' famine, and the Kivalina famine? Or was it Laki? It could only have been one of these events. William Oquilluk mentions only one such event. Only one famine caused the depopulation of the old Kivalliñigmiut community. Even with the paucity of written records and the few oral accounts in the Northwest region Tambora emerges as the most likely candidate. But the jury is still out as oral accounts from Native communities to the east and south have yet to be corroborated as regards volcanic effects of either event.

This means that on Kotzebue's first trip there were people who traded with each other over great distances and Siberia for hundreds of years. They were inter-related through generations, rich in the ancient Inuit/Yupiit cultures and languages. They knew which languages to use in each trade setting, including Siberian Yupik south of Wales. The whole of Burch's Pittaġmiut community was out in force in 1816. When the Russian Expedition of 1819 and 1821 Mikhail Vasiliev and Gleb Shishmarev came into the region in 1819 and 1820 they were dealing with a much reduced and devastated coastal population, and encountered many more interior people whose survival rate had been better who were moving in and intermarrying. As demonstrated by the story of Qayiayaqtualuk and Maŋuyuk coastal communities were repopulated by a few survivors within the region, and predominately by Athabascan speaking peoples from interior regions and later by Iñupiaq speakers in Norton Sound.

When Frederick W. Beechey came along in 1826 the Pittaġmiut were much reduced in population not having regained their former numbers. This speaks to why when Alexander Kashaverov came into the neighboring Kaŋiġmiut region in 1838, the people there told him that they were Kotsokhotana

1. Sixteen Eruptions before and during the Nendaaghe and Too Loghe displacement:
1812	Awu	Indonesia
1812	Usu	Japan
1813/14	Suwanosejima	Japan
1814	Mayon	Phillipines
1815/16	Tambora	Indonesia
1819	Mt. Wrangell	Alaska
1826	Avachinsky	Kamchatka Peninsula, Russia
1826	Kelud	Indonesia
1826	Ognedyshushchava Gora	Unalaska Island
1829	Klyuchevskaya	Kamchatka Peninsula, Russia
1831	Zavaritsky	Kamchatka Peninsula, Russia
1842	Shish-aldin	Unimak Island
1843	Mt. Agung	Indonesia
1845	Helka	Iceland
1846	Fonualei	Tonga
1846	Sinarka	Kuril Islands, Russia

2. Five Eruptions during caribou scarcity of the 1840s:
1842	Shish-aldin	Unimak Island
1843	Mt. Agung	Indonesia
1845	Helka	Iceland
1846	Fonualei	Tonga
1846	Sinarka	Kuril Islands, Russia

3. Eleven Eruptions during the Western Arctic Caribou Herd crash:
1872	Smarka	Kuril Islands, Russia
1872	Merapi	Java
1872/78	Sinarka	Kuril Island, Russia
1873	Grimovota	Iceland
1875	Askja	Iceland
1877/85/89	Suwanosejima	Japan
1883	Augustine	Alaska
1883	Krakatoa	Indonesia

4. Two Eruptions during the 1898 area wide Famine:
1892	Awu	Indonesia
1897	Mayon	Phillipines

(Kkotsox hut'aane) a Denaakk'e speaking community from the upper reaches of the Kaŋiq and Koyuk rivers. These people were moving in and intermarrying. Burch mentions people of Pittagmiut affiliation on the rosters of places like Deering, Kotzebue, and the upper Kobuk River in the 1910 US census. All of which leads to the genealogies of Qalhaq Barbara Atoruk, who mentions the intermarriage of three Buckland girls into the upper Kobuk families before and during that census. Furthermore, through DNA evidence these very families are related in the 4th to 6th generation to the descendants of the former Saaqił and Nendaaghe hut'aane Denaa people. We need to bear in mind that we are speaking about communities of people in the hundreds, not in the thousands, and that the fluidity of the gene pool was while limited, dynamic.

One can see then that centuries of regional development was interrupted by the 1816–18 famine, and this represented not only a major population shift, but regional language shifts which have persisted into the 21st century.

View a list of volcanoes which erupted globally and compare to events which took place in Alaska during the Later Prehistoric period.

All of these eruptions left their mark on the landscape, flora, fauna, and the people who were living at and during these events. As examples, two 21st century eruptions are: 1. When Mt. Pinatubo erupted in the Philippines in 1991, there was an unseasonably early and heavy snowfall. Because all the leaves were still on the trees and the snowfall was heavy, caused the branches and whole birch and alder trees to be permanently bowed over. There are full grown birch and alder trees which bear these features today. 2. When Nova Rupta erupted in June 1912. The snowfall was so heavy up the Ch'atoonjik that the caribou could not pass, and the females calved on the snowfields, causing a 100% mortality for that group. Subsequently, the Porcupine Caribou Herd crashed also the Central Arctic Caribou Herd, and it took almost thirty years for the herds to regain their previous herd size. Meanwhile people all along the Gwazhał Cordillera starved and moved out of the region for a span of time or never returned.

In looking at the aftermath of volcanic eruptions in the written records both past and present, there are a set of common occurrences. In this case we are referring to volcanos which erupted sometimes hundreds and thousands of miles away, but still some of these impacts may have been experienced in Northern Alaska in the Late Prehistoric period which we are concerned about here. First, 1. The weather gets colder and stays that way for up to 3 years, often bringing increased precipitation. 2. Florine poisoning or ash causes wildlife and domestic herds to die. 3. Volcanic ash falls and almost all the crops fail, simultaneously all the natural flora dies. 4. People die from the impact blast, and/or noxious fumes, and later from starvation. Furthermore, if the eruption is big enough to push debris into the higher atmosphere, the weather cools worldwide due to the obstruction of the sun by cloud cover.

In the Late Prehistoric period of Alaska, we have the graphic details of William A. Oquilluk's account of what happened, which we can take as evidence for what was happening all along the coast north of Unalakleet, Alaska. During a two-year period only two months (May and June of 1817) of warmer weather occurred. This was not enough time to gather all the stores of food needed for the coming winter. None of the medicinal herbs, and wild berries were harvested that year, a big source of vitamin C which is sorely needed during the winter months. Perhaps there were stores of dried fish put up, but nowhere near enough for an especially long winter. Not enough whales, ugruk and seal meat and skins, or caribou hides for clothing were gathered or could be traded.

In the upper Nendaaghe and Hulghaatne the women were forced to cut their fishing season short. They were also caught without warm clothing and in summer dwellings not meant for an abrupt winter. That means they had to hustle to put up a warm dwelling and gather firewood. Luckily any fish they caught would be frozen and available for consumption later. The men's annual caribou hunt to the north might have yielded a bumper meat haul because of the caribou's untimely return from the open tundra calving grounds. The herd did not have enough time to put on the weight and fat they needed for the coming winter. The calves might not have put on enough weight for the long trip to wintering grounds thereby increasing mortality rates. Regardless, as soon as the men began to realize the severity of the situation, they would have cached their store of meat as fast as they could and headed back to their wives and children with as many skins as possible for clothing, bedding, and other purposes, and as much meat with fat as they could acquire.

At some point during the aftermath of Tambora, the snow storms came and dumped a great deal of snow. From Iñupiaq and Dinjii Zhuh storytellers we come upon stories of heavy snows being associated with famine. Heavy snows mean the caribou herds suffered a very high mortality rate that winter. At the onset of sudden winter in July, caribou were not able to build up the fat resources to take them through the winter due to a shortened summer on the tundra, and then they were confronted with heavy snows which made it hard to move and forage enough. Heavy snow also makes it difficult to get small game, as in rabbits, muskrats, beaver, porcupine, and ptarmigan. Yes, people died everywhere, in both coastal and interior regions.

The winter of 1816–18 would have been extremely difficult, all regional groups would have been affected and were struggling to stay alive. As noted, the coastal regions were devastated. The summer of 1818 would have found survivors searching for other survivors and making efforts to put together family and community. Since work was divided between men and women, they could not survive without each other, and people had to find helpmates. Relationship meant survival. This is where one begins to appreciate the usefulness and the necessity of trade fairs, inter regional messenger feasts, and especially trading partnerships for establishing and forming lifelong friendships. They were a lifeline. Marriages were arranged for young people who survived because people had long term relationships across estates and regions.

By the summer of 1818 the picture of their positions was clearer, and the communities in every region started to get back to usual subsistence rounds and to continue interactions with neighboring groups. At these times they were able to access the strengths and weakness of the groups present, but especially their numbers. Inter marriage and group reorganization and hierarchies were being established anew.

This, then were the communities that Mikhail Vasiliev and Gleb Shishmarev, and William Pigot on the ship Pedler were dealing with in Kotzebue Sound in the summer of 1819.

This is also when the Iñupiat communities began to feel the shortage of women, and to see the trade route bottleneck that was created by Nendaaghe hut'aane occupation of the upper Nendaaghe. Right in the midst of Iñupiat occupation the Nendaaghe interrupted direct trade from north, west, and east and perhaps profited in all directions. Meanwhile the trade scene was changing, more and more ships began to appear in Kotzebue Sound and often traded with the coastal communities. Considering that it was only a two day portage between the headwaters of the Nunataaq and the headwaters of the Kuukpik (Rochfort Maguire, Bockstoce, 1988), the situation gradually began to be more than the Iñupiat were able or willing to tolerate. Looking at who would gain most by the eviction of the Nendaaaghe hut'aane, a group of Umialik began to make a strategic plan for that purpose. Once the decision was reached, they decided to make the preparations and initiate action the following year, which would have been 1819 or it is possible that this process started sooner.

The lingering effects of the eruption of Tambora and other volcanos throughout the Late Prehistoric period in Alaska had direct consequences for Indigenous Alaskan communities all over the state, and as played out in the Northwestern Alaska arctic. It meant, without a shadow of doubt, the catastrophic devastation of whole regions, group movement, displacement, and regional language shifts. Coupled with persistently colder weather all year around for a period of years, heavier precipitation, a dip or crash in availability of caribou, food scarcity, and higher mortality rates from volcanic aftermath led to major changes. This then is the mastodon in the Late Prehistoric history of Indigenous Alaskans.

* * *

Genealogy is at the heart of what my family did for many generations. Any genealogist will tell you that it is time consuming work, requiring hours of research, following every lead, and extensive talking to family members. In literate communities where records have been kept genealogies can span centuries. In Alaska we have oral tradition, which in our case goes back from four generations to ten generations for the current Dinjii Zhuh community.

I heard genealogies all through my childhood. Many stories that I heard were prefaced with abbreviated family histories where I was able to follow the main character to a living person, that I knew or knew of. When I first began to write out Gwich'in Estates family genealogies all those years of hearing about family relationships served me well.

When my father and I set about writing out these genealogies in earnest it was in the early days of computers. My father wanted this information to be passed on through writings. I lost or lost access three separate times to older material. The last time I lost access to my records was because I did not have a computer that had ports for three inch discs or floppy discs. It was through the kindness and ability of a dear cousin on my mother's side that some of the information was retrieved.

There were problems with computerized genealogy programs. First, there were no appropriate language fonts, secondly, the names did not fit into the allocated character space, and thirdly, programs could not handle multiple wives or multiple names. In the end I went with word processor files. That is the technical part.

Dinjii Zhuh culture is both patriarchal and matriarchal. It is patriarchy because the men made most of the decisions, it is matriarchal because the three phratries of the Dinjii Zhuh were determined along female lines. Ideally the three phratries were exogamous, that is they made every effort to marry a person outside of their own phratry.

This phratry system was shared with other Dena people in Alaska that is the phratries translated across language boundaries. There are the three basic phratries which are named differently in each region but have an equivalent in the next language region. If a woman marries into another language group her phratry has already been translated, and she is known by that phratry. An example; my mother Katherine Joseph Senaaneeyo was known in a Denaakk'e speaking region as Noltsene, however in Dinjii Zhuh K'yaa among the Dinjii Zhuh she is of the *Naatsąii* phratry. The two groups are mutually equivalent. This is a nutshell version of a very lengthy subject which will not be covered here.

There are some problems in working with Gwich'in Estate genealogies. Children are enumerated in order of birth, *kit* being the first born, and among the Neets'aii

Dahjalti' Khehkwaii Vizhee K'aa

A close relative or sister with another wife: Eliza Shaaghan Zhriah Ch'iji'oonta

2nd wife name lost: Dahjal m., Daanitysaa f., Ellen Treenahtsyaa Dahjalti' Shiteegwiłtthat, Shohtsal John Dahjalti'

Raised and adopted at different times:

Vuntut Gwich'in: Ch'eewhałti', Goghwaii and brother

Nendaaghe hut'aane: Di'ch'i' David Dzeegwaajyaa, Ndik Dzeegwaajyaa, Joseph Dzeegwaajyaa, Andrew Saityen, John Saityen, Khagooheenjikti', Deets'i'

Too Loghe: Shit'iigwiłtthat Taghachwx xut'aane: Ch'idził, and Tanacross: Saveah, Shahnyaati', Ch'adzahti

Fig. 15. Dahjalti' Khehkwaii Vizhee K'aa. Raboff, 2024.

khąįits'a/khaints'a' being the last born. My father enumerated every family in this way. For Instance, older and younger sister, older and younger brother are also applied to first biological brothers and sisters, and first cousins, and to adopted brothers and sisters. If a man had a number of wives then the last one alive was known as the mother of all the children. Furthermore, the adopted children also called each other brother and sister. The situation is further complicated in the household of a khehkwaii (khaihkwaii) where young orphan boys rotate through the household as a work force over the length of their active productive lives. This leads to a number of built-in pitfalls. As a prime example we can view the household of Dahjalti' Khehkwaii.

If all these people are calling each other in familial terms, one begins to see how this can cause confusion. If one is orphaned, the information will be lost or convoluted very easily. For example, fictitious Ellen, a biological daughter of Dahjalti' has a daughter who was abducted as a small child. The abducted child is later asked in another region about her phratry or her relatives, she would not know unless she was aware enough to know. But if by chance she heard her mother call Ch'eewhałti' brother, she would claim him as her uncle. As it turned out Ch'eewhałti' became a famous Vuntut gwich'in khehhwaii. If someone found out or knew his phratry, then she would be assigned that phratry and get a whole new relative roster. If she knew nothing of her phratry or who her relatives were then she would be assigned the Teenjaarahtsyaa phratry, the "ones we bring into the fold." In one generation biological descent and phratry can be lost and/or muddled throwing off all future generations.

Dahjalti' Khehkwaii himself has a long story which will not be fully disclosed here, but you see where he took in young boys from among the Vuntut gwich'in, Nendaaghe hut'aane Denaa, Taghachwx xut'aane, and Tanacross areas. All these young men were orphaned or given or taken in service to him. He was an enormously influential khehkwaii during his lifetime.

The naming system represents another problem area. At least among the Dinjii Zhuh, an infant was called infant, until some trait or predisposition came along and then someone would give him/her a 'childhood' or endearment name. Dahjalti' for instance was known as Shininduu as a child. He was a sickly child and spent many days just laying down, the willow ashes from the firepit fell upon his face. Therefore, he was known as Shininduu, "ashes and soot upon my face." Family members continued to call him Shininduu throughout his life as a term of affection and endearment. When he became a strong young man and a warrior he was known as K'eezhiizhal. His contemporaries called him K'eezhiizhal. When he became a father, he became Dahjalti', "the father of Dahjal." Dahjal being his firstborn son. Dahjalti' Khehkwaii was a well-known community leader throughout the Dinjii Zhuh world. Outside of the Neets'aįį Estate area few people know his other names, and even there mostly among direct line descendants.

Three personal names is a conservative number of names for a Dinjii Zhuh person to have. Some people had five different names. If they crossed estate borders they had a few translated versions of their names, or they were given altogether new names in the new estate. Names are often cryptic and difficult to translate, and they are often contractions of a longer phrase. Take the name for Europeans, Vanan goodlit, "for him/her there became more land than he/she was previously aware of." The word became Oonjit and Vanodlit in two different dialects. Personal names can even tell a snippet of what happened in that person's life or where they originated from. The upshot is that people were often known by different names in other estates, and if they happened to move from one estate to another, and across language regions, it was very difficult to follow. The other issue stemming from multiple names is that written accounts often use only one of those names and to identify people in those records often takes time or they may not be able to be identified at all.

In working with the genealogy of the Dinjii Zhuh I have learned to be very careful.

Robert McDonald the Anglican missionary who came to the Gwichyaa Estate in 1862 made a point to learn the language of the Dinjii Zhuh. He wrote all the personal names of people throughout the Gwich'in Estates region, Western Gwich'in Estates in Alaska, and the Eastern Gwich'in Estates in Canada. Although McDonald began his career in Alaska, after Alaska's purchase by the US government he moved first to Old and New Rampart on the Ch'oonjik and later to Teetł'it Zhee along the Teetł'it near the confluence of Nagwichoonjik. McDonald kept a journal which begins in 1862 and ends in 1912. The journal holds the largest repository of Gwich'in Estate personal names extant. Many of these personal names can be followed down to living descendants, and the person can be identified. Others cannot be placed. It has been a treasure trove in terms of who was where, and when. It has enabled me to follow Nendaaghe, Saaqił, and Too Loghe hut'aane families for generations and allowed me to pinpoint the Gwich'in Estate upon which they settled.

The last issue with the genealogies has to do with the English surnames in the Gwich'in Estates region and how they were assigned. Beginning with McDonald, he initially assigned English names to people as he baptized them. Shahnyaati' became John Hardisty, Ch'idził became Archibald Garret, and so forth. The women became Emma, Caroline, Julia, Salina, Christine, Matilda, and Biblical names. The men became Herbert, Alexander, William, Edward, and Biblical names. McDonald also named people after Anglican Church officials in England. Later in his career he successfully kept Native surnames. When McDonald relocated to Fort McPherson, Northwest Territories of Canada he intentionally used the Native personal names as surnames in the area. Therefore, the Dinjii Zhuh of that region have surnames like Kwatlatyi, Netro, Josie (an attempt at Juuzii), Kakavihchik, Kendi and others.

After McDonald left the American occupied regions of the Alaska Territory in 1867, the Episcopal Church as the sister church of the Anglican Church took over the Alaska ministry. With the coming of the American Episcopal Church missionaries and preachers, there was no effort to learn Dinjii Zhuh K'yaa or to perpetuate Dinjii Zhuh surnames in the region nor was literacy in Takudh (Dagoo Dialect) particularly encouraged. However, as McDonald had made it a habit to teach literacy. It was continued by the Indigenous lay-readers, clergy, and community members as a way to communicate with one another, and as a way to worship. Everyone with an Old or New Testament used these books as primers and as a way to learn English. The bibles were also used as a means to record births and deaths within the families who owned them.

Among the Neets'aii gwich'in, they deliberately converted to Christianity so that their young men could be taught, not only about the religion, but how to read and write in their own language and understand each other. McDonald was impressed with the eagerness of this community to learn.

A quote from McDonald in 1866, words of Shit'iigwiłtthat Simon Laryil Ralyil translated by McDonald:

We are just like deer in a forest, and you are come to seek for us, and catch us in snares. We are very thankful for being taught the knowledge of God. It is different with us now from formerly. We do not grieve for our relations, who have died of scarlet fever. But we are thankful that they had heard of the way of life; and we hope that they are now in heaven.

—Shit'iigwiłtthat Simon L'original Ralyil

Just as a footnote, Laryil or Ralyil is not a Dzk word, it was the only way Dzk speakers could say, L'original, the name given him probably by Antoine Hoole the French Canadian interpreter of the Hudson's Bay Company.

This was after the scarlet fever epidemic of 1865 which raged throughout the Hudson's Bay Company trade route in western, northwestern, and northern Canada to the Yukon Flats, and ended at the Lower Yukon River Ramparts. More on this in another writing.

The baptismal name was considered a Christian name, whereas the Dinjii Zhuh personal name was not considered a Christian name. As time went on, having a "baptismal name" became synonymous with being a Christian. This made a difference to HBC employees in that the Christian Indigenous Alaskans got preferential treatment because they wanted to Christianize the community. This was a way to encourage this process. Having a Christian name became a bragging point in the Indigenous community. By the turn of the 20th century it became an affront, an insult to call out to a Native person in their Dinjii Zhuh personal name to their face. It was alright to refer to him/her with the Indigenous name in conversation with others, but considered disrespectful to say to their face. However, in this regard it is more an affront to people in the Yukon Flats than it was/is to people on the Venetie Reservation. People who grew up together on the Reservation were more likely to refer to each other and face to face by their Dinjii Zhuh personal names. So much so that my father often had to think of peoples' English name, and in some cases simply could not remember or didn't know it.

For the usage of names it is worthwhile to allow Eliza Jones in "The Stories That Chief Henry Told," Chief Henry 1979, explain Denaa customary name usage, "Normally personal names are not used very much. In this story Uncle identifies himself by name mostly for the benefit of the tape recorder,… Throughout the story he does not call people by name but refers to them as friend, older sister, uncle, and so on; he uses their kinship term first. Children are not supposed to call adults by name, but only by kinship term—'mom', 'dad', and so on. It is also acceptable to call people by their English names. It is less disrespectful to address people by their English names than by their native names. In Central Koyukon [Denaakk'e], one may address someone by kinship term and make the distinction that he is not a member of the group by adding k'aala after the kinship term." This similarity in name usage for abutting language communities in this region seems quite natural.

American missionaries, traders, and frontiersmen only used English personal names in addressing Native people. Therefore, the last name of a person became a problem. It became a habit then to refer to people as the son or daughter of the persons English name. In Dinjii Zhuh K'yaa it goes like this "Stephen Peter vidinji' or vigii." That is "Stephen the man-child or child of Peter." When people outside of the community heard this, they heard Stephen Peter. That is what was written in records and when the US census came along, Peter became my father's surname. All of his brothers then got the Peter surname. This happened in many Indigenous communities in Alaska. Therefore, the last names, of Sam, Jimmy, William, Peter, Paul, Alexander, Ambrose and so forth. This did not only happen in one generation, this happened to multiple generations. This made following family lines very difficult, especially for people outside the community.

For instance: if you go to a community and assume that all the Peters', Williams', Roberts' and Adams' are close family, you would be mistaken.

It is for this reason that in the genealogies that my father and I have been able to piece together, all the heads of the families have an original Dinjii Zhuh personal name, and every descendant of his/her has that name attached to the "legal name" in government records, and other written records. It simply has not been possible to follow family lines without this "aide."

One last thing about names is the way that names were so easily recycled in the western Gwazhał Cordillera, but not the eastern part. In modern times this has changed. In the late prehistoric period the names in the west were recycled and there were juniors, sons and daughters with the same names as their fathers and mothers. Not so in the east.

The Dinjii Zhuh of the Gwich'in Estates believed strongly in reincarnation. This is not to say that the Iñupiat and Tl'eeyegge did not, far from it. I am focusing on the people of the eastern mountain regions here. The belief in reincarnation also said that the name of that person deceased could evoke the spirit/soul of that person, furthermore, the repetition of the person's name could in effect hold down, or hold back this person's spirit/soul to this earthly plain of existence thereby hindering him/her from continuing on their spiritual journey. This, in particular, was frowned upon. There were verbal admonitions against "holding on to that person's name." There was the added fear that if this spirit/soul did not leave this earthly plain, then it could harass the living and bring evil ominous portents. The person thus encountered could also die, be taken away by the spirit/soul of the deceased.

Among the Dinjii Zhuh only the western most community of the Dih'aii Estates recycled names and had juniors. Ditsiigiitł'uu Drit Khehkwaii was a junior as his name Ditsiigiitł'uu (in this case meaning, "I am named after my grand-father" [also father]) indicates. There are two Shiizin's among the Nendaaghe, and repeated usage of Anaaraq, Juuzii, and Ella (Aallaa). Once in Dinjii Zhuh country, the name Aldzak was not repeated for four generations. Whereas one of my father's personal names is Tsee Gho', in looking for another Tsee Gho', I found one in McDonald in 1863, then as translated surnames in 1891 and 1893. My father was born in 1906, over forty-six years after the last Tsee Gho'. No one, to my knowledge, has ever been called Dahjal or Dahjalti' in over one hundred and seventy years.

It was this fear of being taken away or harmed by the deceased spirit/soul that brought people who killed others intentionally or accidentally to observe a three- or four-day ceremony to pray for the soul of that persons' safe and speedy journey to the afterlife and rebirth.

Working with these genealogies has been a daunting endeavor, but it has been my life's work.

* * *

Another area to be considered here is the terms of usage. In order they are: Neets'aii, Neets'it, Neetsit, Neets'egwich'in and, Neets'uu, Neets'uuch'in. These are all dialect variants. Neets'uu is Di'haii dialect, Neetsit /Neeets'it is a dialect variant, and Neets'aii is a Yukon River Gwichyaa dialect and in Modern Dzk usage. Of the three Neets'uu and Neetsit are either no longer in usage or are rarely used by present day speakers. In literature Cornelius Osgood used Netsit Kutchin (1932), which was evidently the term used by John Fredson, his chief informant and translator. Johnny Frank Drit was the last person that I personally heard use the word Neets'uu or Neets'uuch'in. Paul Solomon Dzeegwaajyaa was the last person who said Neets'egwich'in. I heard other people say both the word and phrase as a small child. I will use Neets'aii throughout this text.

Another grossly misunderstood area is the matter of who the Dinjii Zhuh people are and what did they called themselves. The original people referred to themselves always as Dinjii Zhuh. "Dinjii Zhuh ihłii or tr'inlii," (I am, or we are Dinjii Zhuh) was a very common phrase I heard repeatedly as a child. The name for ourselves is Dinjii Zhuh, loosely translated as "the children of mankind." Gwich'in means "1) dwellers of, of (a specific region or estate), and 2) looks like." For a Dinjii Zhuh K'yaa (meaning language of the Dinjii Zhuh) speaker, the idea that we are the gwich'in people is highly questionable. We are the Dinjii Zhuh people, how did it come about then that we are known as the Gwich'in people?

The transition from Dinjii Zhuh people to Gwich'in people has everything to do with acculturation. When William Lucas Hardisty drew a map for the Hudson's Bay Company in 1854, he wrote out regional names for a wide area. The map includes the Denaa of the Tl'eeyegge region, Han, and the Lower Tanana areas. All of these outer regions are labelled in Dinjii Zhuh K'yaa, the language of the Dinjii Zhuh, not as the residents of these estates would call themselves. This was entirely appropriate from the Dinjii Zhuh perspective. It was only later that people began to sort out who belonged to which language group and estate. This nomenclature confused explorers, missionaries, early pioneers into the region, as well as scholars, and the Indigenous community of the area. At the time no one asked the Dinjii Zhuh people what they called themselves.

The label of Kutchin/Gwich'in was attached to the Dinjii Zhuh community with the Hardisty map. It was further reinforced by missionaries, fur traders, and early explorers. By the turn of the century this label was firmly attached by all non-Dinjii Zhuh people. The Dinjii Zhuh had no way to change this because although there was literacy among them, they were literate in the Dagoo dialect, most knew very little English, and it is not as if the early pioneers of the time cared what the Dinjii Zhuh called themselves. As far as they were concerned, the Dinjii Zhuh had a name, Kutchin/Gwich'in.

This label introduced other ideas and confusion within the Dinjii Zhuh community along the Yukon River. Since the Euro-American community called them Kutchin and later

Gwich'in, "Dinjii Zhuh!" became a derisive phrase. It was the habit then of more acculturated Indigenous people, those who had more interaction with Euro-Americans and lived along the Yukon River to use the word derisively for backwater Dinjii Zhuh people who were not familiar with the habits and expectations of the Euro-American community. "Dinjii Zhuh!" came to mean "you stupid ignorant native person" or "what an ignorant naïve Indian." This phrase was still in usage during the early 1960s.

In 1900 the Episcopal Church had a mission and orphanage in Fort Yukon. This first generation of mission educated orphans learned English and were raised in the Christian religion. Many of the old customs and beliefs were stripped away or replaced often with the wrong analogies. Boys learned how to garden and did all the wood gathering, water hauling, hunting, carpentry, and maintenance work of running a mission sometimes to the exclusion of learning English or learning to read and write. The girls learned how to housekeep, garden, jar preserves, knit, embroider, were encouraged to do beadwork, and taught to cook food the way it was eaten at the mission house. All these skills helped to maintain these facilities.

When Osgood came along he recognized what "Kutchin" meant, and proclaimed it the "Kutchin nation," however he failed to illicit their name for themselves unless they are in his notes, but not in his final paper. Apparently, the subject was not broached with John Fredson, his main interpreter. Emile Petitot was closest to the name with, Dèné-dindjié The Loucheax Indians. The long-term consequence of this confusion brought linguist Michael Krauss in 1997 to say, "The Gwich'in lack an all encompassing term for themselves."

The Dinjii Zhuh then are the people who occupy the Gwich'in Estates. Dinjii Zhuh K'yaa, translated as, "the essence or spirit of the Dinjii Zhuh," is the language of the Dinjii Zhuh. This is enormously profound and I find

Fig. 16. Joseph #6, Mable, and Ezias Joseph Khagooheenjikti', Nancy Joseph Collection.

it very difficult to forsake the vocalization of our ethnonym and our language.

Academia has foisted "The Gwich'in Language," as it is called, upon the Dinjii Zhuh people. Dinjii Zhuh K'yaa is the language of the Dinjii Zhuh who live on the Gwich'in Estates.

* * *

Another area of concern here is how the Indigenous people moved from estate to estate, and what happened during those transitions.

Ordinarily people moved from estate to estate through intermarriage and adoption. When a Khehkwaii gave one of his sisters in marriage to the Di'haii gwich'in, that was a deliberate way to strengthen ties and alliances. When Drit married his younger sister to Deets'i' Khagooheenjikti' and insisted on a matrilocal marriage, it was a way for him to recruit more men into the dwindling Di'haii community.

Adoption was common, when a couple could not have children, they adopted relative's children. Orphan children were often given to elder persons as live-in helpers. They gathered the wood and brought water and got small game. Stories abound with poor orphan children living with their grandmothers. When a mother died with young children all those children were taken in by community members. A man could not support a family alone. The

Fig. 17. Viłiiyił'yo, aka Beaver Creek William, Skidadlostal aka Stephen, Old Steven, Gochonayeeya, aka Charlie, Old Charlie. Circa 1910/12, Rivenberg Collection, Archives, University of Alaska, Fairbanks.

division of labor between men and women made that impossible. When young boys were orphaned they were more likely adopted by the community khehkwaii. They became a part of a food gathering work force, and as they got older became a ready-made raiding force.

Abduction of women and children was not uncommon. The women were commonly kept as female labor and the children were essentially slaves, they could be kept or sold and bartered away. As an example when Drit Khehkwaii took a group of small boys in 1850, he kept them for a few years and then handed them off to Ch'idził Khaihkwaii and Shahnyaati' Khaihkwaii.

Blood revenge was a common practice. If a person accidentally or deliberately killed another, then that person's family would take it upon themselves to avenge that killing. My maternal great grandmothers' first husband died of some illness, the family suspected her of maliciously intending him to die by using shan Dzk, or k'e'eenee' Dn (casting spiritual energy or magic). Therefore, after her husbands' death, they planned to pierce her legs with knives to debilitate her and thereby cause sure death. However, her younger cousin Ch'igwihch'in Lucy Gehikti' Drit warned her during the night, and she escaped with the clothes on her back, a knife, snares, and a fragment of McDonalds' written Dagoo text. She ended up along the Yukon River as the Dinyeet hut'aane Denaa were on their way up to trade in Fort Yukon. She hailed the person in the last canoe who happened to have traded in her community, William Viłiiyił'yo'. She got into Viłiiyił'yo's canoe, and in that moment Nich'it Gwilaii Agnes Hishinlai' Khagooheenjikti' became his wife, and she and all her children became Dinyeet hut'aane of Stevens Village, Alaska.

Men also removed themselves in this way. Sometimes taking along younger siblings and young families. Some of these events are recorded by missionaries, fur traders, and school teachers. This is not to say that they knew the exact nature of these occurrences, just some aspect of the events. After the steamships came along in 1868 travel to more distant places became easier.

Men were also more likely to hire themselves out as mercenaries. How this was carried out and what they were offered in return is an area that bears study. There are intimations of this practice here and there, however only what I assume to be within common language group estates. It might merit further study.

* * *

I have stated in the past that the coming of the Russian American Company, the Hudson's Bay Company, and later the American whalers and fur traders brought changes to the Alaskan Indigenous communities many years before any of the participants ever met each other. The main reason being the control of the trade, and trade routes.

I think this is another area which has not been adequately covered in the Late Prehistory of Alaska Indigenous communities because it represents major shifts within each community and in regional trade networks. This regional jostling for control of the trade routes by the major leadership in each area led to internecine warfare. Often these events took place ten to twenty years before actual contact with Europeans. It is a subject that is researchable because traders made comments about reported regional shifts within the communities that they traded in.

Since I am not as familiar with how this process presented in Northwestern Alaska this will not be thoroughly covered, except as it will be demonstrated in the story of the Iyaġaaġmiut. This shows the end result of this process, not the internal mechanisms of how it came about. This subject will be covered more thoroughly in another volume about the Alaska Western Gwich'in Estates proper, should it come to fruition.

When viewed as trillions, of trillions of electro-chemical transactions per nanosecond you begin to see the dynamics of life on the tundra on a different scale, as a land imbued with **Inua**.

—Sigiññaachiaq, 2022

"*Si l'on considère qu'il s'agit de trillions, de trillions de transactions électrochimiques par nanoseconde, on commence à concevoir la vie dans la toundra à une échelle différente, comme un territoire imprégné d'***Inua**".

—French Translation by Constance Thirouard

Leaving the Third Range, 2018. A Claude Fiddler Photograph.

Chapter 3
Kǫ'ehdan and Saityen/Nitsehduu

Kǫ'ehdan and Saityen are two of the most well-known Nendaaghe and Iyaġaaġmiut men of the 19th century. Together they tell the story of the Nendaaghe hut'aane people's gradual eviction from the Nendaaghe Estate. The story of Kǫ'ehdan is told throughout the Dinjii Zhuh region and the story of Saityen is told throughout the Kuuvaum Kaŋiaġmiut Northwest Arctic region. The older of the two stories is the Kǫ'ehdan story, I will begin with his story.

The Kǫ'ehdan story represents one of the first attacks and onset of hostilities in the western area of the Nendaaghe region beginning in the 1820s. In trying to pinpoint the location of this attack, there are three requirements. First, the location must include a bluff high enough so that it would be a waste of time to shoot arrows although it was often the case that one member of the community was left alive. Secondly, Kǫ'ehdan's settlement must be within minimally eight to twelve spring days walk from the next settlement. Thirdly, the attack occurred along the Nendaaghe, where there are fall chum runs. We will continue this discussion after the story. Here then is Kǫ'ehdan.

* * *

Kǫ'ehdan
As told by
T'ąąval Henry William Saityen and Stephen Peter Ch'igiioonta'

"It was springtime and Kǫ'ehdan (Without fire embers) and his brother were having a feast for the men in the men's house. It was hot, so they took off their outer garments. When the Iñupiat came upon them, Kǫ'ehdan and his brother skipped into their snowshoes and made a run for it. An Iñupiaq warrior hooked his brothers' snowshoes with something like a manaqtuq, a floating seal retrieval hook, but it was not designed to float. Evidently it was a hook designed specifically to hook snowshoes or things on land. His brother was killed and so were all the men in the men's house. Kǫ'ehdan escaped to safety on a steep rock face cliff. One Iñupiaq named "Khii Choo," (Big Silver/fall salmon Dzk) and in Iñupiaq that would be Iqaluġruaqpak (p.c., Lorraine Williams) was killing Kǫ'ehdan's brother with a ch'ankhwarh, an antler club with a sharp stone/s imbedded on the striking end. In Iñupiaq known as an anaullaun. As he was doing so he said, "Kǫ'ehdan, is that really you, is this your younger brother that I am doing this to?" Kǫ'ehdan looked down upon the scene. He was helpless. He had no clothes and no weapon.

The Iñupiat warriors finally marched off. Among them was his wife Łihteerąhdyaa "One whom we take back and forth." He asked her to mark her trail; she did this. She had a small bag of tsaih, red ochre on the inside of her coat which she took out when they stopped and rubbed a small quantity on the soles of her boots and then rubbed her boots on a stone leaving a mark. She also cut shavings and put them into rock crevices at camp sites. Finally, the last man was his trading partner. The man pleaded with him, "Kǫ'ehdan come down to me." But Kǫ'ehdan refused to come down to him, so his trading partner left him a pair of warm mittens, long beaver skin mittens.

He went back to the village and to his surprise saw smoke coming out of one kon, a permanent winter home. He found his younger brother's wife curled up by the fire badly wounded. When the fighting began she had crawled under a snow drift. The Iñupiat warriors had walked over the area with their barbed snowshoes. They tied sharp stone barbs to the bottom of their snowshoes to kill or wound anyone hiding under the snow. This was known among the Dinjii Zhuh as ch'ivihtr'ii. They had thus severed her tendons. She was unable to stand or walk. They cried together.

They snared rabbits. They ate them and made a rabbit skin wrap for Kǫ'ehdan. She asked him to leave her since she was badly wounded. She had four dogs and they stayed with her. He took some embers with him to light his fires and set out to find people. The embers went out and for some time he suffered greatly from the cold. That is why he is called Kǫ'ehdan, "Without fire embers." After a few days his sister-in-law's four dogs came after him, then he knew she had died.

He walked for many days and nights. He began to suffer greatly from hypothermia. He finally stumbled upon an old trail and followed that until he came to a new trail. He followed the new trail until he came upon a settlement.

He sneaked into the settlement and stumbled into the home of an elderly woman. He told her all that had happened and asked her not to reveal him right away. She fed him for a number of days, but a small boy who came to give her food inadvertently saw her put the food aside (as if for someone else). The little boy immediately told all that he saw. Then the community was in a state of alert, they were ready for a fight, all the men gathered. The elderly lady ran out and cried, "My grandson Kǫ'ehdan sneaked into camp, but I did not tell about him."

Kǫ'ehdan revealed himself and immediately began to put together a group of warriors to take his revenge. He spent the summer recuperating and the community made preparations for the coming battle.

Then they started off in late August or early September during the fall chum salmon run. They went back to Kǫ'ehdan's former settlement and followed the trail of the aggressors. It was the better part of a month that they followed their trail, and finally ended up along the shores of a big lake along the ocean shore.

His wife and the other women saw them and secretly brought them food. Then under cover of the fog they cut up all the umiaks. They killed the Iñupiat there and took back their women. Kǫ'ehdan's wife slit the throat of her Iñupiaq abductor. Meanwhile Kǫ'ehdan had warned his trading partner, and he was relieved to find that his trading partner was not among the dead men. He saw his trading partner at a distance then and asked him to come with them, but his trading partner replied, "You were the one whom I could not convince to come down to me, so now I must refuse you." Kǫ'ehdan left some food and those things that his trading partner would need to survive. They sang the "Divee ch'ilig, (sheep song)" and did a victory dance, then departed. That is how Kǫ'ehdan got his revenge."

* * *

In narrowing down the possible location of Kǫ'ehdan's community it was along the upper Nendaaghe, which has fall salmon runs possibly near a side stream. Although it has fall salmon runs, the Aalaasuk/Aalaashuk is too deep into the Nendaaghe Estate for perpetrators to come and go safely at that time. There are bluffs all along the middle and upper Nendaaghe which plays an important role in the story. It had to be an outskirt community, one closer to the western border, which would be below Ayayaak River and above or near the Imailim Kuuŋa. Wherever the settlement was located on the western edge of the Nendaaghe Estate, Kǫ'ehdan was not lost when he set out, he knew where he needed to go for assistance. Under ordinary circumstances, with all his gear and well prepared, he knew about how many days' journey that would take. He set out to get there, wherever 'there' was, alive.

At the time the Nendaaghe were strong enough to rely upon themselves. There were evidently enough men and women alive for it to be a viable community. They were still a few years from moving onto the Saaqił hut'aane estate.

Burch estimated 1820 as a likely date for this concerted effort to evict the Nendaaghe from the headwaters of both the Nendaaghe and Kuukpik rivers. I totally concur, it correlates with my previous estimates. The Nendaaghe had too many men and women for any one Iñupiat region to mount a successful campaign to evict them from their estate. As stated earlier it was a concerted effort by a group of Umialik in adjoining estates.

Even in the best of circumstances springtime is a difficult time to be traveling in Arctic Alaska. During the day the sun is reflecting off the snow potentially causing snow blindness, the snow is melting, water is flowing, and overflowing icy rivers, and at night everything freezes over. Spring snowstorms are not uncommon. However, Kǫ'ehdan is not adequately clothed, he has no change of footwear if his feet get wet, and because of the conditions during the day he must travel at night when temperatures drop below freezing and darkness descends. He must walk with a stout staff, otherwise he may fall over from breaking through the snow crusts or breaking through the ice. He has his snowshoes, a knife, snares for rabbits and ptarmigan, but he has no bow and arrow, no blankets or caribou skin mats, and no way to prepare warm food. Kǫ'ehdan is burning through the calories and barely eating. He was in desperate straits, grieving for all those he lost, and he suffered from the cold, which can cause disorientation and lapses of good judgment. Kǫ'ehdan slept during the day whenever possible and walked during the night.

He snared rabbits and ptarmigan and ate the internal organs and gave the meat to his dogs. When the rabbits jumped under the snow Kǫ'ehdan also trampled them with his snowshoes, (Neerihiinjik, 1995 Johnny Sarah Hàa Googwandak, edited by C. Mishler). He skinned the rabbits and turned them inside out and rubbed the skins from time to get them soft. When they were dried and soft Kǫ'ehdan then cut them into strips and wove them into his coat to stay warm. According to my father, while he was still with his sister-in-law, she helped him process rabbit skins and made him the rabbit skin coat.

Kǫ'ehdan's name is in Dinjii Zhuh K'yaa, the language of the Dinjii Zhuh people. His original Denaakk'e name has been totally lost but was probably known by direct line family until the turn of the last century at least. This Gwich'in Estate personal name added to the assumption that it was the Di'haii gwich'in who were all the way up the Noataaq River, not the Nendaaghe hut'aane Denaa people.

Once Kǫ'ehdan arrived at this settlement, people there knew exactly who he was, and in a heartbeat were ready to help him retaliate. The threat to the community was very clear.

There were already clues for Kǫ'ehdan and the community as to who these perpetrators were. First it was the composition of the raiding party, Kǫ'ehdan knew where his trading partner came from, Nuvuġaluaq, a settlement about seven miles to the north of Tigara on the Tigara Peninsula on the Tikiġaġmiut Estate. His trading partner may have been conscripted to join the raid. Secondly Iqaluġruaqpak knew him by name. They were not strangers he knew the community of Iqaluġruaqpak. It is likely that he at least recognized other members of the raiding party. The main objective after retaliation was to get the women back. The problem was locating them, they could have been taken to anyone of the communities of the members of the raiding party.

When they did leave in the fall of 1820, they walked for the better part of a month, which would be minimally three weeks or 21 days. If we assume, for instance, that they were at the Kipnik Lake settlement, the first 60 miles could have been traversed in three or four days. From there they would have been tracking, taking much longer, and covering less ground. They could also have been delayed by early winter storms. If they averaged ten miles per day on the low side they would have traveled 210 miles. That would be approximately the distance to Nuvuġaluaq. According to Burch (A&C, 2005) Nuvuġaluaq was a community of "between 50 and 60 people."

A clue about the dearth of women is the name of Kǫ'ehdan's wife, Łihteerąhdyaa (One whom we take back and forth). Her family name was Geh'ikti', "the father of Rabbit Coat." She came from a Nendaaghe Tl'eeyegge hut'aane family. If she had been the firstborn child, her name would have been Geh'ik "Rabbit Coat", and her mother would have been Geh'ik vinh. Geh'ik would not have been an unlikely name for a small child since they were often dressed in rabbit skin robes. The name Łihteerąhdyaa reflects the experiences of this segment of her life. This name could be a translation from the Denaakk'e original. Only the female members of this family survived their ouster from the Nendaaghe Estate. Her younger brother Shiizin Geh'ik did not survive the transition. We will follow her family into the Di'haii and Neets'aii Estates, and the Dinyeet/Dinyee hut'aane lands near Stevens Village. Her name will also appear in the Geh'ik, Dzeegwaajyaa and Drit family lines.

This retaliation party of Kǫ'ehdan led them to Nuvuġaluaq. Łihteerąhdyaa did her job of marking her trail well. The raid took place after the expedition of Mikhail Vasiliev and Gleb Shishmarev in 1819/1820, so that Nuvuġaluaq was a viable community of an estimated forty men at that point. From reconstruction the very fall after the visit of the explorers sponsored by the Russian Navy and the Russian American Company, Nuvuġaluaq was razed. When Beechey came along in 1826, there were only ruins.

In continuation of the Nuvuġaluaq story in Burch (A&C 2005) we find the revenge of Navaġiaq during the following fall, 1820, where he killed a group of fifteen or so Indians at Auksaakiaq (presently a camping area). First, that would have required 15 clean shots with a bow and arrow where the victims were rendered incapable of raising an alarm. Assuming these men were Nendaaghe hut'aane, this would have been a big blow to a community already reduced in numbers by inclement weather and food scarcity. However, for the

Dzeegwaajyaati' Vizhee K'aa

1st wife not named:
    1. Dzeegwaajyaa,
    2. Kǫ'ehdan and wife, Łihteerąhdyaa Geh'ik
    3. younger brother and wife who died

2nd wife:
    4. Dinjiitil David Dzeegwaajyaati',
        a. Solomon Nideech'i' Dzeegwaajyaati'
        1st wife Belle: 1. Ginnis and 3. Sophie?
        2nd wife Elizabeth Ch'itchy'aa zhuu, Tanacross
            2. Peter, 4. Myra, 5. Paul, and 6. Maggie
        b. Simon Dinjiitil Dzeegwaajyaati'
        1st wife Name unknown: 1. William, 2. Eliza
        2nd wife Jennie Shit'iigwiłtthat
    5. Ndik Tinjiitil Dinjiinindal Dzeegwaajyaa w. Joseph Vahan Drit
        a. Joseph Tsal Dzeegwaajyaati' w.Katherine John Saityen
            1.Peter, 2. Abraham, 3. Caroline, 4. Sarah
    6. Joseph Dzeegwaazyaati'w. Mary Ch'idii Khyahtthoo
        a. Laura Dzeegwaajyaati' Drit, 2. Albert, 3. Charlie.

Fig. 18. Dzeegwaajyaati' Vizhee K'aa. Raboff, 2024.

Nendaaghe to return in the following year to a community that they totally razed the previous year poses some questions. Why would they do that? Was it a raiding war party? Or did they have another purpose for heading into the vicinity? The intention and destination of this party of men is not clear.

This was also a story that Panniaq told in passing.

If, however, a party of fifteen Nendaaghe hut'aane men had been killed somewhere in 1820 this would have represented a real setback for the rest of the community. To lose so many men in one spot. This would have opened the flood gates for more immediate attacks. It would have led directly to the Kuukpiġmiut attack at Atłiq in the following years, or possibly concurrently. Some of these men might have been mercenaries, but this is a vague area for that to be proven.

By 1822 two Nendaaghe communities were abandoned, Atłiq and Tukuto, the western most settlements on the Nendaaghe Estate. The community started to contract, abandoning Tukuto Lake, and the lower Itivluk to defensible positions in Itivluk Pass, the Aalaasuraq, Aalaasuk, and Killik river valleys.

There is a footnote to this story. Since the Nendaaghe hut'aane men came into the Nagwichoonjik (Han Gwachoo) area, Teetł'it Gwich'in Estate as early as 1865, a variation of the Kǫ'ehdan story was told as far south as Fort Good Hope on the Mackenzie River (Petitot 1870). This caused Richard Slobodin (1971) to look for the possible location where these events could have taken place since the local terrain did not fit neatly into the story.

Now to tell more of Kǫ'ehdan's extended family after the death of Kǫ'ehdan, circa 1822/26. Kǫ'ehdan was an older half-brother (same father different mother) or a first cousin to Dinjiitil Di'chi' Choo David Dzeegwaajyaati'. After the death of Kǫ'ehdan Dinjiitil and his younger brothers, Ndik Dinjiinindal and Joseph, were orphaned. It is unclear how it happened that they became a part of Dahjalti' Khehkwaii's household. This represents the first eastward movement of Nendaaghe hut'aane across three estates and a language region. Here then is Kǫ'ehdan's family line.

All the names in bold represent families of Nendaaghe Tl'eeyegge hut'aane origin. Even after the transition onto the Neets'ąįį Estate people of Nendaaghe hut'aane heritage continued to marry each other. This family as represented here are only the family members who survived into the 20th century. The ones who survived the transition from the Nendaaghe Estate and the ones who survived to and after the 1898 famine. The mortality rate during the initial transition was very high. Kǫ'ehdan and Dinjiitil probably had many more family members.

In examining how Dahjalti' Khehkwaii came to take in the orphan family members of Kǫ'ehdan there are a few scenarios. Kǫ'ehdan was a contemporary of Dahjalti' Khehkwaii. Perhaps it was that he made arrangements for his brothers to be taken by Dahjalti' Khehkwaii if he did not survive, or as a khehkwaii Dahjalti' just decided to take the children as they were orphaned. Other possibilities are that they were trading partners and he knew the family situation or that he was intermarried in some way. It was not uncommon for the mountain Indians to intermarry since they made a living in the same type of environmental settings. Whatever the circumstances, Dahjalti' Khehkwaii raised these boys in his household on the upper western Neets'ąįį Estate.

The Khyahtthoo family member not in bold type is Mary Ch'idii. The Khyahtthoo family is Tl'eeyegge hut'aane in origin, but it is unclear to me which estate they originated. Teetsii Tsik John Khyahtthoo and his younger brother (name lost) were the original Denaa members of this family to move into the eastern Neets'ąįį region. Because of the subsequent marriage patterns of this family, my guess lays strongly with the Too Loghe hut'aane, but this is just my best guess. My father did state emphatically that the family was Teetsii gwich'in (Denaa) in origin. They came into the region, however as full-grown men with families, which means they were sponsored by Dahjalti' Khehkwaii. The composition of the Khyahtthoo family is real brothers and sisters, and several close male cousins. As "new-comers," Shahnyaati' Khaihkwaii treated them as subservients, as they did not have status in the larger Gwich'in Estates communities. According to Robert McDonald Teetsii Tsik John Khyahtthoo's younger brother died during the scarlet fever epidemic of 1865. I will return to this family in another section.

Now for the family of Łihteerąhdyaa Gehik Dzeegwaajyaati' Drit. I will combine the Gehik family with the Khagooheenjikti' family. Geh'ik Vihn and Khagooheenjik Vihn are sisters. The names of their parents have been lost. The vihn at the end of their names is an indication that their firstborn child was a girl. Vihn means the first born child is a girl, vahan if the firstborn child is a boy. Geh'ik is the older of the two sisters. They were both Nendaaghe hut'aane women in origin. Geh'ik's youngest sister Ch'igwihch'in Lucy was born on the Dį'hąįį Estate. Once again please note, all their names have been translated into Dinjii Zhuh K'yaa from their Denaakk'e originals.

The three families in bold print are not Nendaaghe hut'aane in origin, **Drit** is Dį'hąįį, **Viłiiyił'yo'** is Too Loghe Denaa, and **Ch'idził** is Taghachwx xwt'ana.

The Geh'ikti' and Khagooheenjikti' families are a good snapshot of the Nendaaghe hut'aane, Too Loghe hut'aane, and Dį'hąįį in transition, from circa 1823 right to the turn of the 20th century. As with the Dzeegwaajyaa

Sisters: Geh'ik Vihn and Khagooheenjik Vihn

	Geh'ikti'	Geh'ik Vihn
1.	Geh'ik	
2.	Łihteerąhdyaa Geh'ik Dzeegwaajyaa Drit	
	a. 1st husband Kǫ'ehdan Dzeegwaajyaa	
	2nd husband Ditsiigiitł'uu Drit Khehkwaii	
	No children	
3.	Shiizin Geh'ikti': a son	
4.	Toh Vał'i' Geh'ik	h. Vindeegwiizhii John Ko'nii'ak
	a. Phillip, Eliza, Lucy	
5.	Ch'igwihch'in Lucy Geh'ik Drit	h. Drizhuu Fraum Frank **Drit**
	a. Maggie, Annie, Julia, Jennie, Mary, Johnny, Francis, Elijah, Alice, David, Stephen, Harry, Nihshuk, Elisha, Jimmy	

	Khagooheenjikti'	Khagooheenjik Vihn
1.	Khagooheenjik Agnes Hashinlai'	h. William **Viłiiyił'yo'**
	a. Kenneth, Edmond, Ann, William, Belle, Ellen	
2.	Joseph Khagooheenjikti'	w. Khaihkwaiigii Emma **Ch'idził**
	a. Ezias, Rachel, Sarah, Sampson, James, Gladys	
3.	Brother Deets'i's son: Adopted John Leviti' Khagooheenjikti'	
	a. W. Jennie **Ch'idził**	
	b. Levi, Robert, Sophie, Collin, Caroline, Elijah, o, o, Myra, Laura, Sarah, Silas, Jimmy	

Fig. 19. Sisters: Geh'ik Vihn and Khagooheenjik Vihn. Raboff, 2024.

family this represents only family members who survived the transition to the Dį'haįį Estate, and because they were nearer the Yukon River and the subsequent unfamiliar diseases.

Geh'ik Vihn's three older children were born on the Nendaaghe Estate. Toh Vał'i' was married to a fellow Nendaaghe hut'aane man, Vindeegwiizhii John Ko'nii'ak. Lucy Ch'igwihch'in Geh'ikti' Drit was born on the Dį'haįį Estate circa 1854 and married someone also born there and a first generation Dį'haįį gwich'in Dinjii Zhuh. She and her husband Fraum Frank Drit were fluent Dį'haįį speakers.

Khagooheenjikti' was a generation younger then Dinjiitil David Dzeegwaajyaa and no doubt came into the household of Dahjalti' after 1838 with his younger brother Deets'i'. They were young boys. Now in the 1840s he was old enough to be looking for a wife. He married Khagooheenjik vihn, but because he was a young warrior and conflicts were still ongoing they had a patrilocal marriage. Some years later marriage arrangements were made for his younger brother, Deets'i', to marry the younger sister of Ditsiigiitł'uu Drit Khehkwaii. That marriage was matrilocal. By the time of this marriage Drit Khehkwaii died circa 1855 and the Dį'haįį abandoned the upper Koyitł'ots'ina and were along the upper Teedriinjik and at Chehłee Van.

Note as of 1850s Dzeegwaajyaati', Khagooheenjikti', Geh'ikti', and Ko'nii'ak families were all considered Neets'ąįį and Dį'haįį gwich'in men and women.

Saityen
As told by Immałurauq Joe Sun

Saityen had many Iñupiaq dialect variations for his Nendaaghe Tl'eeyegge name. Among them are: *Sayyen, Saiyyen, Sai'ya, Saityet, Satnik,* and *Sannik*. Saityen means meat cache in the upper Kobuk dialect of the Iñupiaq language. This is predominately the Immałurauq Joe Sun version of this story. It was originally a Nendaaghe hut'aane Denaa personal name. His name in modern Denaakke might mean something associated with the word "knife," *tsaaye* and "blade," *sai'ye*. Since this dialect of Denaakk'e has not been spoken in over two hundred years, it's unlikely that we can re-illicit it. There is a similar name in a list of families of the upper Koyitł'ots'ina, **Senaaneeyo** which means, "He followed me," (p.c. E. Jones) and possibly "He followed me (across)," (p.c. J. Kari). Jetté might have the same name spelled differently, **Tsenani'o**, however he offered no translation, but might be "he brought something out." (p.c. J. Kari)

As a young boy Saityen was displaced from the Nendaaghe Estate sometime after 1822. Or his parents were displaced and he was born shortly after on the Saaqił Estate. In either case his parents fled the Nendaaghe Estate. His father would have joined others on retaliatory raids, and at some point, most likely lost his life in the effort. His mother died, and as an orphan, Saityen was raised by a Saaqił hut'aane family along the upper Hulghaatne. This family may have been related or his stepfather had been a trading partner of his father. According to Iñupiat story tellers there were a number of young men who were raised in this way on the Saaqił Estate.

From upper Kobuk oral renditions it seems that a larger group of Nendaaghe hut'aane stayed at the extreme headwaters of the Nendaaghe and Hulghaatne rivers and the Taah K'ehoolaanh area of the country. Plus, according to Isasan Justus Mekiana it was during his grandfather Maptiåaq's time that these events took place and also during the time of Panniaq's great grandfather, Suvlu (Sowlu). Together they placed the Nendaaghe hut'aane in the upper Aalaasuraq, Itivluk, Killik, and Aalaasuk river valleys.

From the upper Hulghaatne, and the much-reduced Nendaaghe Estate post 1823 the Nendaaghe began a war of attrition. In Burch (A&C) the perpetrators in the raids are often referred to as Kobuk people, in Iñupiat renditions, which then caused Burch to ask; "the Kobuk Koyukon or Kobuk Iñupiat people?" All of the stories in (A&C) are told strictly from the Iñupiat perspective.

When the refugee Nendaaghe hut'aane first arrived among their midst, the Saaqił hut'aane, were at first eager to help their Nendaaghe neighbors, and relatives regain their Nendaaghe estate. They probably helped through the gathering of food, clothing, and materials for weapon making, with planning stages, talking about the best routes and what time of year to carry out these raids, and in Saityen's case taking in orphans. Young men joined as mercenaries. These things were no small matter.

At first there was cooperation, but later as the years went on having so many extra people in the region stressed resources. Their relationship with their Iñupiat relatives, and trading partners to the north, south, and west began to deteriorate. Many of their young men who joined in these raids as mercenaries died. For a small community of people (est. populations 300/650) to lose a few young men meant hardship and vulnerability. As the years passed, dealing with the Nendaaghe in their midst became an increasing burden.

No one knows how Saityen was orphaned, perhaps he was a toddler. It is known that Saityen was taken to safety, he was raised by an Upper Hulghaatne Saaqił hut'aane family. Evidently this family had some status, because Saityen was never described as a "poor

Fig. 20. Saaqił Estate, 1800. Raboff and GANPP, 2024.

orphan." Saityen was raised with his adopted brother Qatïya'aana. They were as brothers.

Growing up among the Saaqił hut'aane would have meant that Saityen knew all or most of his adopted parents' relations, and all the children his own age and those younger and older, and that he shared a life and identity with them. If growing up there was anything like among the Dinjii Zhuh, it would have meant he was kicked out of the house long before the first morning light appeared in the sky. Saityen and Qatïya'aana would have been out there with all the other little boys playing around and learning about the cosmology of the Denaa, and the stars and navigation long before breakfast.

Saityen also shared in the subsistence round of activities. As a child he would have helped his step-mother collect the right willow branches to make fish nets, and later when the fish surged up the river, he would be among all the other little naked boys pulling and pushing in the loaded nets and processing the fish for winter. He would help pick edible plants and roots, and in the fall be picking berries, and all the time learning what was and was not hutlaane, rules of behavior and relation to the greater spirit of the universe. With Qatïya'aana and all the boys in their age group, Saityen would have been laughing and giggling long into the summer nights, practicing with their bow and arrows, and wrestling.

Throughout these early years he learned all the place names in the region, and listened when the men came back from their caribou hunts up north and enumerated place names of the regions in which they hunted during those hunts.

Also during these formative years he would have heard again and again the stories of his people, the creation myths, hunting stories, stories of tribal conflicts, the cosmology of their world, and the stories of the deyenh, (commonly known as shaman or medicine men). All of which were moral tales of how to live ones' life. As he got older the star lore and navigation by the stars became more important for him to remember and use.

When Saityen became old enough to go hunting for caribou and sheep with the men in the upper Itivluk, Aalaasuraq, Killik, and Aalaasuk river headwaters, and sometimes out onto the open arctic plains. He saw in person those many place names of the region he heard as a young boy. Saityen began to join in the life of the men on an expanded level and scale. They added to his ever-deepening knowledge of proper conduct, and the concepts of the energy of life. The men would have known Saityen and joked around with him. He would have met men and women from different regions and learned their dialects and languages. He heard Denaakk'e, Iñupiaq, and Dinjii Zhuh K'yaa.

Later when he became a denaa, a real human being, he moved back to what was left of the Nendaaghe estate where he was reported by Immałurauq Joe Sun to have relatives. Here it's important to interject that by this time it was dangerous for Nendaaghe hut'aane men and even Saaqił hut'aane men to be hunting on the middle upper Nendaaghe or to go through the area to hunting grounds further north. It was an area that was no longer in "possession" of the Nendaaghe hut'aane Denaa. There were remnants of the community who stayed in the area between the headwaters of the Itivluk, Aalaasuraq, Killik, and Aalaasuk river headwaters. Evidently by this time they had been removed from the Itivluk Pass region. There was a small community there known later by Iñupiat speakers as Narvaŋuluk. They maintained relationships with the upper Kuukpik river Iñupiat, of the Kaniaŋiq, Killiq, and Qaŋmaliq estates, and with the Too Loghe Tl'eeyegge hut'aane further east at the headwaters of the Eł Tseeyh no' (Dn), Kiiñaqvak (I), K'iitł'it (Dzk).

Saityen would have been at trade gatherings and acquired sighok'elaayh, trading partners among other Denaa groups to the east, west, and south, Iñupiat to the north, and Di'haii and Neets'aii Estates to the east. It was because of this trade network that Saityen was a young man who became well known in the region.

Saityen was then married to Nach'aatsan (probably a Dzk translation of her Denaakk'e name) the daughter of Aldzak, a Kkohkkee with a caribou corral of his own, and responsible for the lives of extended family. At the time, most marriages were arranged along three exogamous maternal lines. Nach'aatsan was from the Noltseene/Naats'aii marriage lineage. This was a major alliance and social connection for Saityen. It bound him to the Nendaaghe hut'aane Denaa. Because his father-in-law was a Kkohkkee his marriage was matrilocal.

Saityen became a Kkohkkee in his own right. He was recognized as a Kkohkkee among later Iñupiat story tellers. This recognition meant status and respect. Saityen became a successful hunter and leader, and sought another wife.

Saityen's second wife came from the Hulghaatne area where he had spent a large part of his formative years. He probably grew up knowing his second wife and her family, and whose Denaa name has been lost, but according to Panniaq (in Bergsland) her Iñupiat name was Ilikuk or Ilikuq. Later she became known on the Di'haii Estate as Shijuu Tr'oonii "I don't have any more younger sisters," and years later after her third marriage, Shigyaa Tr'oonii "I ran out of snares [to catch men]." Because of Saityen's status, this marriage was patrilocal.

This caused Panniaq Simon Paneak and Isasan Justus Mekiana to say that Saityen had an Indian wife and an Eskimo wife. Two wives. These events happened in Panniaq's great grandfathers Suvlu, Ququuq, Ilikuk, and Uqriñŋunalġaa's time, which means that at least one or all of them would have known Saityen by sight.

Now, to look more closely at the timing of the events of Saityen's life. Saityen was described by Iñupiat sources as a young man with two young wives. Looking at young Dinjii Zhuh men, as a comparison, looking for a second wife, we can safely assume that they would be in their very late teens or early 20s, the first marriage being in the 17 year + range. Young women were often married between 14 and 17 years of age. At the time of this story Saityen would have been between 20 and 23 years of age. Yes, a young man. And looking closer, if Saityen was married at 17 years, and his first marriage was matrilocal, then he was living on the Nendaaghe Estate for minimally a good five years during the final events of this story.

Meanwhile life in the upper Hulghaatne area and the headwaters region became more adversarial. The deyenh of both communities began to compete, and increasingly there was bad blood. Disease and death were often looked upon as the "work" of deyenh from other communities and regions. This growing animosity set the stage for what happened next.

Smallpox. In May of 1838 smallpox arrived at St. Michael's Redoubt on Norton Sound just before and with the actual arrival of a Russian American Company transport. The company made every effort to inoculate native communities, but given the transport of the times, it was too late for the Lower Yukon.

The Yupiit, Iñupiat, and Denaa communities of the region were preparing for the spring trade gatherings and were amassing. The conflagration raged throughout the summer and into early 1839 in more distant regions. From company estimates nearly half the Indigenous population of the immediate region was taken away by the disease by late fall.

Given the prevailing attitude that diseases and death could be sent to distant locations by deyenh, not only did the Russians suffer repercussions, the scene also played out between adjoining groups and communities even in more remote regions.

Pock marks were noted on people of the Upper Kobuk in 1889. One could call that evidence of the disease having travelled there, or maybe those persons were recent arrivals in the vicinity. We may never know for sure.

However, just looking at the proximity to the smallpox disease, and the trade routes of both communities, Saaqił hut'aane in the Hulghaatne traded to the south and west. They traded as far south as Unalakleet, right in the center of the epidemic. Towards the epidemic. Nendaaghe hut'aane would have been more likely, even then, to trade at Niġliq near the mouth of the Kuukpik River. Away from the smallpox. The majority of Nendaaghe were in more remote locations, not necessarily in a congregated group. The Too Loghe hut'aane who also traded at Niġliq, Noolaaghe Doh, and Noochu Loghoyet were further east along the Gwazhał Cordillera.

Be that as it may, the fear, anxiety, and even the rumor of disease caused an already volatile situation to erupt into an all-out confrontation. The timing of this event would have depended upon when smallpox was contacted, the length of time to recovery, and the preparation time for a confrontation of this sort. Or perhaps smallpox did not reach them, in which case the very threat of it would have triggered aggression.

My guess would be in the early spring or late fall of 1838, the early spring of 1839 is a possibility, but unlikely due to issues of food shortages. If the disease was contracted in the Hulghaatne then it could have been no later than fall 1839.

Given these developments Saityen did not have a choice as to which side he would be on. He was a Nendaaghe hut'aane Denaa.

The weakened state of the Saaqił hut'aane became apparent and they immediately sent for help from their downriver Akuniqmiut Iñupiat neighbors. As it turned out, that was only a temporary stop gap. The Nendaaghe were ejected from the upper Hulghaatne for good.

Surviving Nendaaghe went north and east. Once again, a small group went across the open tundra to join family, trading partners, and to become household slaves, and mercenaries. If you note, this is the second small group of Nendaaghe hut'aane to travel east and join the Neets'aii, the first being circa 1820/22. Others joined relatives among the Too Loghe hut'aane. The main body of Nendaaghe stayed along the mountain headwaters, as before.

The altercation of 1838/39 along the Hulghaatne was a tragedy. It amounted to a large violent family feud where fathers, uncles, brothers, sons, mothers, daughters, and sisters were torn apart. They all knew each other; some never saw each other again. There were many tears.

Every community in the region became more vigilant in watching who came and went upon their estates. Each community was diametrically opposed to the other.

The Saaqił hut'aane meanwhile began to see that they had invited the wolf to a fight. The Akuniqmiut Iñupiat began to see the weakened state of the Saaqił hut'aane community and realized without a doubt that the upper Kobuk was theirs for the taking. Accordingly, they made an ultimatum, "you either leave the upper Kobuk or become Iñupiat in language, speech, and custom, and stay."

The larger body of Saaqił hut'aane choose to leave the Hulghaatne region. They went south to the mouth of the Koyitł'ots'ina and along the north bank of the Yukon River. Their adventures in this region will not be covered here.

The people who stayed became Iñupiaq in every sense of the word, and they never looked back. The Saaqił hut'aane Denaa who stayed became the Kuuvaum Kaŋiaġmuit Iñupiat community and the Denaa Hulghaatne became the Kobuk River for its whole length. They were also known for many years by others in the region as Itqiliaġruitch, the Indians.

The word is no longer in usage.

Now it so happened that the Saaqił hut'aane were accustomed to hunting in the Nendaaghe Estate in June after their summer trading, but before the fish runs, much as the present day Kuuvaum Kaŋiaġmiut Iñupiat of the upper Kobuk did in the recent past and still do. They followed familiar routes through the passes.

So it was that Qatïya'aana, Saityen's adopted brother, did not take into account the changed nature of the relationship between the now newly Kuuvaum Kaŋiaġmiut Iñupiat people of the upper Kobuk, and the Nendaaghe hut'aane Denaa people along the Aalaasuk. He followed his usual route through what was now enemy territory. He unwittingly risked his own life and that of his companion Kataksiñaq.

Meanwhile it fell upon Saityen as a young Kkohkkee to defend the area of Ivisaaqtignillik. His small community group was across the divide in the Aalaasuk Valley. It was from there that he maintained his guard. He was accompanied by his nephew Qïvlïuraq. Together they killed anyone other than Nendaaghe hut'aane people who came up the Ivisaaqtignillik by way of ambush.

It was in such circumstances that Qatïya'aana, along with his hunting partner, Kataksiñaq, took his usual route through Ivisaaqtignillik intending to go up the Aalaasuk from there. Saityen and Qïvlïuraq ambushed them in the early hours of the morning. Unbeknownst to him, Saityen shot his brother, Qatïya'aana outright, but his hunting partner, Kataksiñaq ran off without proper clothing and died of exposure later down the Manïilaq River. It was later reported by Saityen's nephew, Qïvlïuraq and his two wives, that when he discovered what he had done, Saityen truly wept.

Some story tellers do not say but given the nature of relationship between Saityen and Qatïya'aana, I believe that Saityen buried his brother in the ways of their father.

It was the practice of the day that when a person took another person's life, they must fast for three to five days and stay away from the community. This ceremony was called Nachuksut (natchiksaq?) along the Kobuk and Apsalliq "maintaining silence" among the Tigara. It was said that they wrapped themselves in rabbit skin blankets and lit no fire. Saityen and two other companions were in a women's hut away from the community together.

Saityen prayed for the departing spirit of Qatüya'aana, that he may not stay around in this earthly plain, but join the creative forces of the greater universe, and onward to another life.

Somehow word got around on the middle Kobuk River that Saityen was up Ivasaaqtignillik ambushing unsuspecting hunters from the Kobuk. A man by the name of Aakałukpak from the Akuniġmiut people of the Qalugruaq area began to get a group of men together. This was a serious threat. Reportedly they were from the Igliqliqsiuġvik area. They intended to kill Saityen and his men.

They traveled up the Kobuk and as they got near Qalugruaq (Salmon River) they came upon a woman and her son, whose name was Uularaġuaraq, and they conscripted him. If he did not agree to come with them, they would have killed him as he stood. His mother was against this and told him, "You have nothing against those people up there (meaning no relative of his were killed there), therefore you may only use three arrows." It was agreed Uularaġuaraq would come along and use only three arrows, no more.

They traveled on up the Kobuk through an unnamed pass to the Noataaq headwaters and through Ivisaaqtignillik. Since Saityen was in seclusion and in mourning, there was no one there to stop them. As they came over the pass to the Aalaasuk they saw the womens' hut and instructed Uularaġuaraq to dispatch the woman who was within and they proceeded to the settlement. They attacked the villagers in their sleep.

When Uularaġuaraq entered the hut, he was expecting a lone woman, but he became alarmed to see three warriors sleeping around the central hearth. He shot two men dead, but the other being Saityen jumped up and grabbed a wooden bucket as a shield. In that moment, Saityen and Uularaġuaraq recognized each other from their youth. They feinted a few times then Uularaġuaraq shot Saityen in the groin, and since he was out of arrows he ran towards the settlement and his other companions.

Meanwhile the Igliqliqsiuġvik men had killed everyone in the settlement and were in the process of taking down their cache of caribou and sheep meat from a high platform. Uularaġuaraq warned them that he had only wounded Saityen.

Saityen was crawling in the willows and brush with his arrows and killed one man on the platform, but the other man was safe. The men then turned their attention to Saityen and started shooting at him. He was able to avoid a few arrows until one hit him in the upper lip and nose. Saityen then put down his bow and arrows and turned away from them. In the old days when a man did this it meant that he was done fighting. Aakałukpak and his companions could see that he would die anyway so they left him.

Before Saityen Kkohkkee went into seclusion, he had instructed his wives to hide away from the community. They came out after the Igliqliqsiuġvik men had left and were nursing their husband. According to Stephen Peter Ch'igiioonta' he spent three days in a coma before he revived and came back to consciousness.

He wished to die on a small, elevated knoll, so his two wives packed him up to that site.

It was reported by Panniaq that Sannik/Satnik (Saityen) composed a dirge (which Panniaq could sing, music notation in Bergsland) for his younger wife, Ilikuq and died upon that knoll, which is called by the

Nunamiut, Sannikmik, in honor of Saityen. He was said to have left two young wives. The dirge was of a man lamenting leaving two beautiful young wives behind to fend for themselves. The arrows could not be extracted, and scabs formed around them. As Usisan Justus Mekiana said, "it was a sad moment because he was not going to be able to take care of his wives…It was a sad moment." Saityen died within a few days upon that knoll.

* Music notation in "Iñupiat Unipkaaŋich/ Iñupiat Stories, as told by Elijah Kakinya and Simon Paneak collected by Helge Ingstad, Edited and Translated by Knut Bergsland 1987, North Slope Borough Commission on Iñupiat History, Language and Culture Barrow, 1987," pages 350-352.

Then Saityen's wives obeyed his last wish and went to join Ditsiigiitł'uu Drit Khehkwaii at the mouth of the Eł tseeyh no'. Drit and Saityen were of an age, and Saityen knew then that his wives would live.

The Akuniġmiut meanwhile had secured their objective, they could go through Ivasaaqtignillik without hinderance. Notice however that it was not the newly established Kuuvaum Kaŋiaġmiut people who dealt that final blow to Saityen. Many Saaqił and Nendaaghe hut'aane people were left traumatized by the final raids and confrontations that caused their respective movements eastward, westward, and southward. Remember, they had all been related by family. My father, through his mother Soozun, said that many old people never talked about those times.

Nach'aatsan Jessie Aldzak and Ilikuq Lucy Shijuu Tr'oonii then became two of Drit's six wives. Saityen had two children who survived, with Jessie Nach'aatsan, Andrew Gaasheek'yuu Saityen and with Ilikuq Lucy he had John Neeshooch'it Saityen. Both Jessie and Lucy had many other children with Ditsiigiitł'uu Drit Khehkwaii. That will be covered in the next chapter.

Now because Saityen survived for a time after his fatal injury he was renamed Nitsihduu, which in Dzk means "Scab on the Nose." This reflected his last experience of this life and was consistent with Dinjii Zhuh naming practices. It is in that context that the story about him and his family was shared among the Dinjii Zhuh. When Aldzak, his father-in-law heard of Saityen's passing, he was deeply saddened. No longer Kkohkkee in his own estate, a refugee with no standing, it was truly disheartening. As for Aldzak he and his son Shiizin kept their Denaa names, as did a few others, like Aanaraq, Juuzii, and Ella (Aallaa). Regardless of his young age of death, Saityen's line did not stop with him. The line and legacy of Saityen continued through his two sons, Gaashiiky'uu Andrew Saityen, and Neeshooch'it John Saityen. This then is the household of Saityen.

The household of Saityen shows only the people who survived the move through four estates, two language communities, the scarlet fever epidemic of 1865, the 1898 famine, the influenza and measles epidemic of 1900, and the 1912/13 famine, the Spanish flu epidemic of 1926, and tuberculosis.

Andrew Gaashiik'yuu Saityen. (In Herbert Halvir Ginkhii Albert Tritt Drit Journal it is written Goodhichikyuu.) (ATJ). In modern Dinjii Zhuh K'yaa that would be Gaashiik'yuu, which means "I snowshoed in spite of extreme difficulty." Goodhaii means in desperate straits. That extreme difficulty may have been caused by age, hunger, exhaustion, or that the snowshoes became broken and he was unable to stop and fix them because of time or he didn't know how to fix them, or he didn't have the extra babiche. Andrew must have been born between 1837 and 1841. When his mother arrived among the Di'haįį Gwich'in within two or four years of his birth, she was still a young woman and had children with Drit. Andrew was raised in the household of Ditsiigiitł'uu Drit Khehkwaii. Andrew and his brother were considered orphans and as such could be

Saityen Vizhee K'aa

1st wife: Nach'aatsan Jessie Aldzak
    Gaashiik'yuu Andrew Saityen
        First partner: Emma Henry Gwats'oo Etchit, Draanjik
            Ch'itłee Khai' William Olim Sasa' Joseph Shuman Saityen
            1st wife Salina Shahnyaa, Draanjik Estate
                Eva, Charlotte, Esau
            2nd wife Fannie Gwandaii, Teetł'it Estate
                John, Peter
            3rd wife: Maggie Viłiyił'yo' William, Denaa
                Henry T'aaval, Hannah
        First wife: Name Lost:
            Phoebe Andrew Saityen Stevens h. Stephen Simon
                Sarah Stevens Malcolm
            Sarah Andrew Saityen Tritt Drith. Herbert Albert Tritt Drit
                Isaac, Martha, Paul, Abel, George
2nd wife: Ilikuq Lucy
    Neeshooch'it John Saityen   w. Ellin Vindeegwaazhraii Shit'iigwiłtthat
        William John Saityen   w. Mary Tritt Drit
            Elzee Ambrose William Saityen
        Katherine John Saityen h. Goozhiizhii Joseph Tsal Dzeegwaajyaati'
            Peter, Abraham, Sarah, Caroline
        (Sarah) Ellen John Saityen   h. Ch'ivera Thomas Shaaveezhraa
            Belle, Amelia, Joshua, Myra, Jonathan, John, Jennie, Jimmy, Charlie, Joe.

Fig. 21. Saityen Vizhee K'aa, Raboff, 2024.

given away at any time. At some point after his younger brother John Saityen was old enough to start training as a dinjii among the Dinjii Zhuh they were given to Dahjaltí' Khehkwaii. Young boys started training between the ages of 6 and 7 years of age. This would have meant that they left the Di'hąįį Estate shortly after the final ouster of the Too Loghe and Nendaaghe hut'aane from K'iitł'it/Naqsraq Pass in 1847. By the time Andrew was between 8 and 10 years old he went through three estates and became a resident of the fourth, the Neets'ąįį Estate. His maternal grandparents were Aldzak and his second wife, Deedzii Tragwaltsun Nach'aatsan Vahan, both Nendaaghe hut'aane Denaa from the Nendaaghe Estate.

Growing up in the upper middle Neets'ąįį Estate Gaashiik'yuu Andrew and Neeshooch'it John were often in contact with the Vuntut, Dagoo, Draanjik, and Gwichyaa Gwich'in Dinjii Zhuh people. Through trading ventures and gatherings he grew up knowing Emma Peter Gwats'oo. Whatever the circumstance, they had Ch'itłee Khai' William Sasa', who was a wanted child. He was taken and raised along with Thomas Suvera Chivera Siverzya Shaaveezhraa and his sister, Elizabeth Shaaveezhraa Moses Ch'igoozhrii and their half-sister Ellen by Joseph Shaaveezhraa and their stepmother Sarah Etchit. Thomas and Elizabeth were much older than William and Ellen from the marriage of Joseph with his first wife. Sarah Etchit was Joseph's second wife. Sarah Etchit was or became the sister-in-law of Emma Peter Gwats'oo Etchit. Emma Gwats'oo was Draanjik gwich'in. I think the bottom line was that Peter Gwats'oo Khaihkwaii did not want his daughter married to a Nendaaghe refugee.

The life of Ch'itłee Khai' William Sasa' Shuman Saityen will be covered elsewhere.

The first wife of Andrew, from this perspective is not known. My father did not know her name nor her lineage. They had Phoebe and Sarah and then their mother died. At the time it was not possible for a young father to raise young children by himself, so Phoebe was given to Robert John Ch'igiioonta' and his wife Virginia Jean Barber Flett. Robert John Ch'igiioonta' was a 1st half cousin of Andrew. That is their mothers were half-sisters. Phoebe's sister Sarah Ghoo was given to Gwichyaati' Gwichyaatsyaa Peter Roe Khehkwaii and his wife Eeshih Eshii Maggie Ch'igoozhrii. Peters' first wife and children died and he remarried a woman who could not have children. Gwichyaatsyaa and Eeshih raised many orphans together.

After the death of Dits'iigiitł'uu Drit Khehkwaii Andrew raised his younger half-brother Simon Drit and half-sister Joseph Vahan Drit. This often-caused people who did not know the family to assume that these were Andrew's biological children. Joseph Vahan may have been Ndik Dzeegwaajyaa's wife, and the mother of Goozhiizhii Joseph Tsal Dzeegwaajyaati', but we will never know for sure.

Phoebe married Stephen Simon and is the grandmother of the Malcolm family in Eagle. Sarah Ghoo married Herbert Halvir Ginkhii Albert Tritt Drit and is the grandmother of many Tritt family members on the Venetie Reservation. Both husbands were of Northern Denaa descent.

Neeshooch'it John Saityen married to Ellen Vindee Gwaazhraii Shit'iigwiłtthat. She was a 1st generation Neets'ąįį Gwich'in who was raised on the Neets'ąįį Estate. Her father was Simon Ralyil Shit'iigwiłtthat, Nendaaghe hut'aane Denaa and her mother Ellen Treenahtsyaa Dahjalti', Neets'ąįį Gwich'in. So far people of Nendaaghe Hut'aane heritage are intermarrying. They had three children, William, Katherine, and (Sarah) Ellen. When Ellen died, John was married to her sister Sarah, (ATJ), then still later to Eliza John Ko'nii'ak in the 1910 census and living with Henry Anazhrii Gwiiyati'. It appears that John had no children with these two other wives.

William John Saityen was married to Mary Edward Tritt Drit, second generation Nendaaghe. They had one child, Elzee Ambrose William Saityen. Katherine was married to Goozhiizhii Joseph Tsal Dzeegwaajyaati', second generation Nendaaghe. They had Avee Ndee Peter Weasel Eye Joseph, Abraham Joseph, Caroline Joseph Moses Ch'igoozhrii, and Sarah Joseph Abel Ch'idzii. (Sarah) Ellen Joseph was married to Thomas Shaaveezhraa, the son of Joseph (unknown) and his first wife also unknown. They were "found" so to speak among the Draanjik gwich'in. They had Belle who married Francis Adam Khyahtthoo. They adopted David and Simon Francis from two different families. Belle's other siblings were Amelia, Joshua, Myra, Jonathan, John Porcupine, Jennie Thomas William, Jimmy, Charlie, and Joe. This takes these families to recognizable descendants.

Now looking at these two stories from the Kuukpiġmiut/Nunamiut perspective Panniaq said of this build up to 1838:

Well, about the old Indians who were travelling quite a ways from the place where they had first settled. Nobody knows where they came from. <u>One group of the Indians</u>, *according to old Eskimos who talked about it,* <u>were Kobuk</u>; *they lived over in the headwater of the Kobuk and Noatak. This old Indian group was raised over in the headwaters of the Noatak and Kobuk, over in between there, nearby anyway. According to the story, we don't know how many years those Indians staying over in that area. This is a very, very long time ago but in… later on, somehow, there was a mix-up between the* **Kobuk Eskimos** *and the Indians because the Indians were jealous about the hunting grounds.* **Kobuk Eskimos** *can't stand that either, because they want to hunt too nearby; they were going to go. They became enemies of each other.*

Finally, they started to fight and killed one another. And then they began a big fight one time, fighting from generation to generation. They said that one time they almost killed all the **Kobuk Eskimos**, *one group almost. The Indian there are too many in those days I believe. Almost they kill them all off, the* **Kobuk people**, *but one fellow he jumped off the fence and got away from that group. The* **Kobuk Eskimos** *had their fences around all their tents during that time but too many Indians tried to pull the fences apart and found them. They were ready to fight with their bow and arrows; they had bow and arrows already that time. And then one boy jumped off the fence and run away to get other people from down below. And a bunch of* Kobuk people *went up to where the Indians are and the Eskimos fought them off. The Indians couldn't hardly stand it any longer and they beat it. That is why, I guess-not many men left.*

They don't want to stay over where they used to live in that area and over in upper Kobuk and Noatak, in the mountains there. And the Eskimos called them Uyaga(ġ)miut in the very old days. They love to stay in the rocks; they make rock house. My, it seems to be very hard to cut the trees. They don't have an axe and saw, that's why love to stay in the rocks during the summer time. Eskimos also like to make stone houses too, according to what the story was saying, but the Uyaga(ġ)miut love it very much.

—Panniaq Simon Paneak,
Transcript of Tape #842, E. Hall

Understand that Panniaq is telling the story one hundred and thirty years later. The Saaqił hut'aane Denaa had been Kuuvaum Kaŋiaġmiut Iñupiat for over 130 years. The Hulghaatne had been the Kobuk for its' whole length for over 130 years. The Denaa name for the region had been lost, buried in a placename along the upper Kobuk until Jenny Jackson meticulously related that placename. They were faithful, these old story tellers were so faithful.

This story firmly establishes that there were two groups of Indians, one of them "was Kobuk." At one point he says, as one Indian group, "they lived over in the headwater of Kobuk and Noatak." From there on the story confuses the Saakił Hut'aane Denaa with the "Kobuk Eskimos," whom I have put in bold type. The transition from the Saaqił hut'aane Denaa to Kuuvaum Kaŋiaġmiut Iñupiat had not occurred yet, however the transition was not fully understood or maybe difficult to relate clearly. There was a great deal of trauma in that transition. Peoples' lives depended upon their loyalties and family. Panniaq's story does differentiate the Akuniġmiut Iñupiat along the middle Kobuk who were called to assist, but in general terms as Eskimos (Iñupiat), not specific regional names. He did not say the Akuniġmiut. If he were speaking to people familiar with these regional ethnonyms, Panniaq might have been more specific. However, I still think this is about as clear a picture as a person could possibly visually draw, to shed light upon events so far removed. It completely brings into focus and vivifies the life and times of Kǫ'ehdan and Saityen Kkohkkee.

What old men knew and taught were knowledge systems which had power, qilya, and exerted qilya.

—Asatchaq Jimmy Kiḷigvak
In Ancient Land: Sacred Whale: The Inuit Hunt And Its Rituals
by Tom Lowenstein, 1993

Fig. 22. Chandler Lake, Too Loghe Estate. A Claude Fiddler Photograph.

Chapter 4
Too Loghe and That Dits'iigiitł'uu!

Too Loghe Estate is filled with narrow valley corridors, high elevation tundra, and mountains and hills. It is a land of abundance and starvation. It is a tough life filled with great joy and enormous sorrow. It is survival in an environment that cultivates humbleness and humility.

As Panniaq said, *"Then they stayed together some time over there in the upper Colville (Kuukpiq/ Kuukpik). Some young guys or women married or got wives from the Indians and Indians got a wife from the Eskimos. And they stay together for so many years; we don't know how long. Then they became unfriendly again toward each other. Sneaking, sneaking up on each other, killing one man, one another. Finally begin to fight in the fall after they build moss houses near the lake there. Ahtlik* (Atḣiq) *Lake they call it in the Eskimo name."* (Hall)

From this snippet we see the relationship of the Kuukpiġmiut before the long winter of 1816–1818, then shortly thereafter. Within five years after the catastrophic winter of 1816–1818 hostilities were in full swing.

After the circa 1822 attack on Atḣiq and the contraction of the Nendaaghe to the Itivluk Pass and the Aalaasuraq there followed a time of mutual agreement where relations could go on in a peaceful albeit watchful and suspicious way. The Kuukiġmiut in all three regions, the Kaniaŋiq, Killiq, and Qaŋmaliq Estates inched up their respective rivers (further south) into their estates and remained as cooperative as suspicious neighbors can be.

They resumed trade, messenger feasts, rights of way down their rivers, and otherwise conducted themselves in peaceful ways. The sixteen-year interlude between 1822 and the final ejection of the Nendaaghe in 1838 was a period of building the communities back up. Still nowhere near the original numbers which had been much reduced in territory, but still a vigorous community.

Let us review here a few comments about this life of the Too Loghe Hut'aane and the Kuukpiġmiut from the Iñupiat perspective.

Here then is Kunagnana Samual Kunaknana (in Puiguitkaat, 1981), *"It is said at that time long ago, those first ones who were subsisting there, these who were our ancestors, were subsisting down there; here along the Kuukpik, these, our ancestors were subsisting. And another thing, this Anaaqtuuvak, it had* as it's people Indians. It is said when it became spring those down there who are our ancestors, those living at Kuukpik, when it became spring they would go to the Indians over here. <u>To these their extended relatives who resided at Anaaqtuuwak.</u> Doing this because they had 'partners' among the Indians. Because it was just as if they were extended relatives to each other, the Indians and those who are our ancestors. We see that they behaved like extended relatives to each other. After first going over to them, then leaving them each time."* [possibly pointing to a map during the telling]

This is a clear view of the relationship between the Kuukiġmiut and the Nendaaghe and Too Loghe hut'aane before Atłiq and into the mid-1840s. Kunagnana and Panniq make it clear that the relationship between these groups was extended family.

Now we start to introduce the known families who were still in the Nendaaghe during that period of time. By family they are the Tłeevihti', Aldzak Kkohkkee, Ch'igiioonta', Gehikti', Ko'nii'ak families. These are families with genealogies. There probably were other families who either migrated out or were lost.

Of these families Tłeevihti' and his wife Tłeevih vihn were dedicated warriors. Tł'eevih Vihn died sometime in the 1820s. Their only known daughter who survived into adulthood, Tłeevih, also became a warrior and became the first wife of Aldzak. Their only known son's passing was not detailed by my father, only that he was younger than Tł'eevih. I estimated before that Tłeevihti' was born about 1760, his daughter Tłeevih born after circa 1780.

There are two Tłeevihti' stories told by Johnny Frank Drit in *Neeriihiinjik, 1995*. There are other Tłeevihti' stories, however these are readily available. Sarah Aldzak Shaaghan Dik Ch'igiioonta' Drit spent the last years of her life with her grandson Johnny Frank Drit and his wife, Sarah Ko'nii'ak Frank Drit. Sarah Aldzak told story after story and told the same stories many times. She would have told the stories of Tłeevihti' because he was her biological maternal grandfather and the great paternal grandfather of Johnny Frank Drit.

As stated elsewhere, story tellers usually prefaced a story by a short genealogy of the main characters, these stories clearly state that Tłeevihti' and his wife had two children, and the age relationship between those two were as an older sister and younger brother.

* * *

Synopsis of the Tłeevihti' Story

1. The setting: Open tundra with two small streams nearby. Nowhere to hide. On a clear day people and animals were visible for miles.

2. The participants: Tłeevihti' and two other men with their families. Tłeevihti' is described as quick and adept, and as a very small man. In one account the other two men had many children between them. Tłeevihti' had a wife and two children, an older daughter, and her younger brother. The daughter's name is Tłeevih, the son was not named because he did not survive into adulthood.

3. Two hundred Iñupiat warriors without their wives and children arrive and behave as if they are participating in a spring trade gathering. Play games, regale hosts, share songs and dance.

4. Tłeevihti' is suspicious and warns the other men about a possible attack.

5. Iñupiat warriors attack and kill the strongest man and then the other man. Tłeevihti' who was wary had kept his long knife, on his person, and hidden his bow and arrows. He escaped from the warriors using his long knife as a weapon. He remained at the periphery of the fighting.

6. Meanwhile his wife is killing warriors and although she is mindful of arrows she gets shot through both breasts and immediately runs to one of the small streams and falls face first into the shallow water with her torso in the water. Evidently feigning death. He instructed his children that in case fighting broke out to hide. They were by the bank of one of the streams barely able to hide in one direction. If someone had been on the opposite side they may have been visible.

7. Tłeevihti' taunts the remaining warriors and they shot arrows at him. He dodges the arrows and one by one the warriors run out of arrows and leave the scene. Finally, they are all heading home strung out in the distance, not walking as a group. Some of them already look like moving dots. Tłeevihti' retrieves his bow and arrows and follows them killing them one at a time as he catches up with them. The last three men run into the willows at the confluence of another stream and as it is getting dark, Tłeevihti' abandons the chase and returns.

8. Meanwhile his wife has been unable to remove the arrow. But the cold water has numbed some of the pain. Tłeevihti' returns, gathers up the spent arrows and builds a fire, boils up a lake plant poultice or tonic. The plant is called *vanchil dazhoo*. He removes the arrow from his wife's chest and rubs the area with the tonic he has brewed and wraps up her breasts.

9. The following winter Tłeevihti' goes to the camp of the Iñupiat. Their Umialik is his brother, *Khaiidhiiluu*. The warriors want to kill him, telling *Khaiidhiiluu* that Tłeevihti' has killed many men, but *Khaiidhiiluu* will not allow it. Tłeevihti' lives there all winter.

Discussion of Tłeevihti' Story:

Tłeevihti' was known as a very small man, maybe about or less than five feet tall. The average height of people during that time was probably much smaller than at present given hormones in modern foods and the diet of the times. There were two noted men who were evidently exceptionally small, Tłeevihti' and Ch'eekhwałti', in every story told about these two men their diminutive size was stated and reiterated.

Johnny Frank Drit was given to the exaggeration of numbers of people. For instance, thousands of people and hundreds of warriors. Given the estimated populations of people at the time, this would have been unlikely. The number of warriors was probably more like 20, perhaps 40 on the outside.

Atłiq is a community near two small streams. One stream joins the Ipnavik, the other stream joins the Itivluk. Located on the open tundra. It is a likely site. Between the Kaŋiaġmiut and Killiġmiut Estates and just south of the Kuukpik.

The most striking part of this story is that the Umialik *Khaiidhiiluu* is described as the brother of Tłeevihti'. How does an Iñupiat Umialik become the brother of a Nendaaghe hut'aane Denaa man? There are a few scenarios. 1. They may have been *Qataŋun*, co-siblings with the same father. 2. They could have been cousins, if the mother of *Khaiidhiiluu* was married to an Iñupiat man and was the aunt of Tłeevihti'. 3. *Khaiidhiiluu* might have been given to Tłeevihti's father during a time of famine and he was raised in the household but knowing that he was an Iñupiaq man returned to his relatives after attaining adulthood. This clearly demonstrates how closely these abutting groups interacted. *Khaiidhiiluu* as an Umialik was able to offer Tłeevihti' protection of a sort that no one else could have.

There are some questions as to the date of this event. The factors are 1. I have always assumed that the attack on Atłiq was after 1820. My reasons include the timing of the long two winters 1816–1818, and the estimated ages of my ancestors who were present during these events. 2. In making this assumption I neglected to include the internecine warfare that took place among the groups in regard to control of the trade routes. More on this in a bit. These internecine wars no doubt started earlier in the Northwest Arctic. This attack on Atłiq could have taken place in 1815/16. Or if we consider Burch's assertion that these conflicts could have taken place as early as 1790, but no earlier, then it's anyone's guess.

Returning to the estimated ages of Tłeevihti', his daughter Tłeevih and her daughter Dik Sarah Aldzak Ch'igiioonta' Drit and Tłeevih's stepdaughter Nachaats'an Natthaii Jessie Aldzak Saityen Drit, there is some wiggle room, but not much. In the story Tłeevih would have been a young woman almost of marriageable age during this event if it were 1815/16. In which case Tłeevih would have been born circa 1800 and married to Aldzak after 1816 then having Dik Sarah before 1820 and Shiizin Joseph after the birth of Nachaats'an Jessie circa 1821/22. Meaning Tłeevihti' was not married until later in his life which, of course, would not be unlikely. The upshot is the date of this event then is moved to an earlier date, circa 1815/16 and not 1820, a difference of 4 or 5 years. This particular Tłeevihti' story then predates the Ko'ehdan story. Ko'ehdan took place along the upper Nendaaghe River and the Tł'eevihti' story took place at or near Atłiq. The perpetrators were from western Iñupiat groups in the former and the Kuukpigmiut (and affiliated groups to the north) in the latter.

The mention of a "long knife," in this story further dates the story, but also is an indication of Tłeevihti''s status and or abilities as a hunter, trader, or warrior. Russian knives were traded within the Northwest Arctic since the 1640s minimally and knives were traded by Alexander MacKenzie (1789) and Sir Franklin (1826) along the lower Nagwichoonjik, and definitely by the time of Kotzebue's visit in 1816. To acquire a knife meant either being a good hunter, warrior, or a good trader. Certainly, he was an adept warrior. Since he was a warrior, he may have received the knife in payment.

* * *

Dik Sarah Aldzak and Ilikuq Lucy Saityen were two women who were oral historians. They kept the stories and genealogies directly from the Nendaaghe hu'taane Estate people to their Di'haii, Neets'aii, Draanjik, Vuntut, Dagoo, Teetł'it, Gwichyaa gwich'in, and Han Hwëch'in descendants who settled in these areas.

Johnny Frank Drit said that his grandmother Sarah, "talk all day long, just like radio." My grandmother Soozun Dahjalti' John Ch'igiioonta' also talked from morning to night. My father said he would wake up in the morning and she was telling stories. He would fall asleep listening to her stories. As the elder Trimble Gilbert said, "they train those girls from early on to tell those stories."

Aldzak married Tł'eevih then after 1815/16. They had two children who lived to maturity, Dik Sarah Aldzak and Shiizin Joseph Aldzak. Dik Sarah's original Denaa name has been lost. Aldzak's second wife was Deedzii Tr'agwaltsan (Dzk translation) Alice Aldzak, their two surviving daughters were Nach'aatsan Naathaii Jessie Aldzak Saityen and Mary Aldzak Khyahtthoo. Since wives were not married in succession Shiizin was reportedly younger than Nach'aatsan Jessie. There may have been other daughters or children who were married off in other regions, given away or abducted. Certainly, the mortality rate was high.

We know that Nach'aatsan Jessie Aldzak Saityen and her co-wife Ilikuq Lucy Saityen

Aldzak Kkohkkee Vizhee K'aa, Nendaaghe

1st wife Tłeevih:
   1.   Dik Sarah Aldzak
   1st husband: Ch'igiioonta' **Nendaaghe**
        a.   Ch'indeeghoo Vatroogwilts'ii Ch'igiioonta'
        1st wife Ch'iyikgwatthah Mary Vitsiik'iitł'aa Ch'iji'oonta'
        Dı̨'hạı̨ı̨ Estate, 1st cousin of Ditsiigiitł'uu Drit
        2nd wife: Lucy Vił̇iiyił'o' Ch'adzah, **Saakił**
            14. Alice Ch'igiioonta' Alexander Ch'ijinah'in
        Mary Ditr'ik, adopted
   2nd husband: Ditsiigiitł'uu Drit Khehkwaii, **Dı̨'hạı̨ı̨**
        b.   Dritzhuu Edoor Edward Drit
        Adaa vitsii ahaa Ann Ko'nii'ak
        c.   Drizhuu Frank Fraum Drit
        Wife: Ch'igwihch'in Lucy Gehik
   2.   Shiizin Joseph Aldzak, **Nendaaghe, Dı̨'hạı̨ı̨, Neets'ąı̨ı̨**
   Wife: Susan Tr'ootsyaa Drit, **Di'hạı̨ı̨**
        Myra Ch'itaiigwatrat John Drit Tizya Kykavihchik, **Vuntut**

2nd wife Deedzii Tr'agwaltsan Alice
   3.   Naach'aatsan Natthaii Jessie Aldzak, **Nendaaghe, Dı̨'hạı̨ı̨, Neets'ąı̨ı̨**
   1st husband: Saityen, **Nendaaghe**
        a.   Andrew Gaasheeky'uu Saityen, **Di'hạı̨ı̨, Neets'ąı̨ı̨**
        1st partner Emma Peter Gwats'oo Etchit, **Draanjik**
        1st wife: Name unknown
   2nd husband: Ditsiigiitł'uu Drit Khehkwaii, **Dı̨'hạı̨ı̨ Estate**
        b.   Gwah'aii John Drit,
        Wife: Nich'it Lal Mary (family not known)
        c.   Ditsii Ahndii Drits'ik Belle Ch'adzahvahan Drit
        married to Gok'eech'ahtthaii Gookahtthak John Ch'adzahti',**Tanacross**
        Brother of Alice, and maternal grandmother of Hester David Evan.
        d.   Drits'ik Mary Drit
        e.   Silas Drit, wife Eliza Dzeegwaajyaati',
        f.   Joseph Vahan, possibly married to Ndik Dzeegwaajyaa
        Gozhizhi Joseph Tsal Dzeegwaajyaati', **Neets'ąı̨ı̨, Vuntut**
   4.   Mary Aldzak m. Deek'an John Khyahtthoo, **Nendaaghe**

Fig. 23. *Aldzak Kkohkkee Vizhee K'aa, Nendaaghe*. Raboff, 2024.

*A note here: Myra Ch'itaügwatrat Aldzak John Tizya Kykavihchik is the only surviving child were married as young women to Saityen Kkohkkee on the Nendaaghe Estate and after his death moved circa 1839/41 directly to the Dį'haii Estate and Ditsiigiitł'uu Drit Khehkwaii.

Dik Sarah Aldzak meanwhile was married to Ch'igiioonta' (Dzk translation) and was in the midst of rearing a family. Her youngest child, Vatroogwiltsii John Ch'igiioonta' survived the transition. My father mentioned no other surviving family members in the Ch'igiioonta' line, and neither did Sophie Ch'eelil Khagooheenjikti' John Ch'igiioonta'. Mary Ditr'ik was adopted.

Aldzak Kkohkkee, after the 1838 ouster from Nendaaghe moved to the Too Loghe Estate along with his son-in-law Ch'igiioonta', Dik Sarah, Shiizin and other surviving family members plus the Gehikti' and Ko'nii'ak families. As stated earlier to be a Kkohkkee or Khehkwaii and move to another estate as a refugee is an absolute last resort. Aldzak Kkohkkee had no choice, he wanted his family and the extended family and community which depended upon his leadership to live.

Shit'iigwiłtthat Simon Ralyil (also Laryil) went directly from the Eastern Saaqił Estate directly to the household of Dahjalti' Khehkwaii on the Neets'aii Estate after 1838. The Shit'iigwiłtthat family were those who were in the Taah K'ehoolaanh area. They had closer ties to the Saaqił hut'aane community. Simon Shit'iigwiłtthat's sisters and or cousins were intermarried with the Saaqił hut'aane as we will see later. Going straight to the Neets'aii Estate had everything to do with Dahjalti' Khehkwaii. Make no mistake about it, Dahjalti' Khehkwaii was a major influence and shaped the lives of the Nendaaghe, Too Loghe hut'aane and the people in the Gwich'in Estates for generations.

Now we return to the Khyahtthoo family, which included the Gwahtłaati', and evidently the Isaac, Herbert and Simple families. There is no doubt that they represented an extended family community, as the Aldzak family did. I don't think they originated in the Nendaaghe Estate unless it was one of the northern most regions. My estimation is that they originated in the northern Too Loghe Estate, but it may remain to be seen. In which case they would have had to abandon the area immediately after 1822 and possibly after Atłiq (1815/16) and move to Eastern Saaqił region or to the Too Loghe Estate. This family was split up. Perhaps settling in the middle Too Loghe estate, gradually migrating eastward to K'iitł'it/Naqsraq and the eastern Too Loghe Estate. One trade route of the region went from the upper Hulghaatne/Kobuk right to and through K'iitł'it/Naqsraq going north. Going south they went down the Eł tseeyh no'/K'iitłuu/ Kiiñaqvak through the Dį'haii Estate and areas to the south. They identified as Saaqił or Too Loghe hut'aane Denaa depending on where they ended up. The extended Khyahtthoo family, is harder to place because as a group they were more separated, went to different regions, and then later recognizing each other as extended family and apparently re-grouped.

Between 1815/1822 and 1838 the Khyahtthoo family bonds with the Too Loghe hut'aane increased, assuming they were not Too Loghe to begin with. After 1838 the Too Loghe found themselves host to the remaining refugee Nendaaghe hut'aane and related Saaqił hut'aane. This also signaled a period of increased antagonism with their Killiġmiut and Qaŋmaliġmiut neighbors to the north. This also indicated a rise in population for the area. More mouths to feed caused extreme stress to the newly reorganized settlements. It took at least a year or two to get situated in the right location for themselves. Which takes us to 1842 at least.

The 1838 altercation between the Nendaaghe and Saaqił hut'aane split up the Shit'iigwiłtthat Simon, and some of the Khyahtthoo family members. However nowhere is it more apparent than in the person of *Khii Choo John Simon Nilthaati' Dzeegwaajyaati' Salmon*, the brother of Solomon Nideechi' Dzeegwaajyaati'. As young adults both brothers portaged for the Hudson's Bay Company, intermittently perhaps over a ten-year period probably after 1855+. Meanwhile being a cousin of Shit'iigwiłtthat Simon (later baptized John Moore), his descendants assumed that *Khii Choo* was a same mother/same father brother. Meanwhile Khii Choo was also later baptized John, so that he appears as **John Simon Salmon** in the Canadian census for 1891 and is estimated to have been born 1839 and 52 years old. In the Albert Tritt Journals he appears as "**Simon Adzee Alvee**." Also, he was very close to the Khyahtthoo family. Adam Ch'ik'i'tthankal Khyahtthoo was often a travelling companion. All this to say that it is difficult to follow family dispersal.

Then nature reared her head again with the eruptions of Agung in Indonesia, (1843), Helka in Iceland (1845), Fonualei in Tonga, (1846), and Sinarka in the Kuril Islands, Russia (1846) with the resultant interruption of normal weather flow, and caribou and food scarcity. On top of an exceptionally cold winter (1842), evidently Agung brought heavy rains to the Yukon in 1843 (Zagoskin, 1967). Heavy rains and high water make it very difficult to fish. Often the fish food supplies needed for the whole winter is not met during high water.

The Agung eruption had effects all across the north even to Nagwichoonjik (Han Gwachoo) in Canada. As a letter dated August 1844 by John Bell, HBC employee at Teeł'it Zhee (Peel River Fort) wrote, "*In general scarcity of provisions prevail throughout the District this season, and I tremble for our safety here ensuing winter...*"

In the mid-1840s then, it's no wonder that Panniaq said, "*And another time, Indians came again. The men only come for fighting but they are getting skinny and almost starving. They could not find any more Eskimos in that area. And then the Eskimos found them on the way to go out to the Colville* (Kuukpik), *late in the spring, sometime in April, and they told them not to come again anymore. If they want to come back to fight, at a later time, they could kill them all off right now. They told them like that. They would have killed them all the Indians that time if they wanted to; they said they don't* (want) *to kill them anymore but they tell them not come back again. If they are starving again, they will kill them all off. So the Indians never come back to fight with the Eskimos according to people who were talking about (it).*" (Hall)

Of course, this was not a one-way deal, the Iñupiat communities also suffered from the volcanic repercussions.

The Too Loghe were contracting and moving finally up the Qaŋmaliq and to the K'iitł'it /Naqsraq Pass.

Meanwhile the Khyahtthoo family got to know the brothers Drit and Ch'iji'oonta' quite well. That included Drit's son Ditsiigiitł'uu Drit Khehkwaii. The Too Loghe Hut'aane were already well acquainted with the Di'haįį gwich'in. Their relations were cordial, but cool. They were still Tl'eeyegga hut'aane Denaa.

So it was, that after 1838 and the Nendaaghe/ Saaqił hut'aane confrontations along the Hulghaatne, there developed a growing enmity between these two groups which shaped the course of out migration from the region. A family feud is hard to understand. Most of the Nendaaghe ended up on the Gwich'in Estates all the way into Canada and the Nagwichoonjik (Han Gwachoo) River delta, and most of the Saaqił hut'aane fled to the middle Yukon River valley between the Tozitna and Koyitł'ots'ina rivers, those who stayed became Kuuvaum Kaŋiaġmiut Iñupiat. The descendants of these two groups identified as two different groups, the Dinjii Zhuh of the Gwich'in Estates and as the Denaa people of the Middle Yukon. It has taken time to heal this deeply held pain and suffering, and knowledge. After 1838 the Saaqił and Nendaaghe hut'aane communities were shrouded in a mystery cloud and almost out of memory.

Then Elijah Kakinyah (in Hopson 1978). "*It is said that Indians lived there at Anaaktuuvuk Pass before; also there were the Eskimos* [Kaniaŋiġmiut and Killiġmiut] *who traveled down river through Kuukpik. The Qaŋmaliqs* [Qaŋmaliġmiut] *intermarried with the Indians in those days. After the older group marry some Indians they wouldn't allow their other relatives to marry Indians so they wouldn't become Indians. One of the younger ones got mad when they wouldn't allow him to marry an Indian* [Iñupiaq] *girl and attempted to begin a war with them. He made trouble among others and wanted to fight the Qaŋmaliġmiut. It is said that eventually the Indians were killed. After the fighting was over, the rest of the Indians fled up east. The others then stayed where Indians have lived before* [Dį'haįį Estate]."

In this excerpt it is evident that this is at a later date than the Kunaqnana story when both communities were stressed. This points to the shortage of young women of marriageable age. The order in which food was served and eaten favored young boys, therefore young girls and women were the first to suffer during food shortages and afterwards led to a shortage of young women for a period of time. Since both of these groups were subsisting in the same environmental setting there is every reason to assume that the eating order was probably similar and led to the same results. There is a strong undercurrent in Iñupiaq renditions of events that the conflict was in part caused by this shortage of women.

The Iñupiat were keenly aware of their growing dominance in this situation.

Following the volcanic eruptions of Agung in Indonesia in 1843, Sinarka in the Kuril Islands, Russia in 1846 and the Fontualei in Tonga also in 1846, weather was unpredictable and hunting and gathering was turned topsy-turvy. Not only were the Too Loghe hut'aane and Kuukpiġmiut afraid of raids and attacks they had to struggle to survive this unpredictable period of hunger and want. It is no wonder than that the Iñupiat ran into starving Denaa warriors, who most likely ran out of food which they thought would be available in route.

In the spring of 1847, the Kuukpiġmiut as a combined force of Kaniaŋiġmiut, Killiġmiut, and Qaŋmaliġmiut then were congregated as they were for the spring trade at Kongumauk, in the region of Tulugak Lake in K'iitł'it/Naqsraq Pass. They seized their opportunity to evict the Too Loghe hut'aane for good from K'iitł'it/Naqsraq Pass. This final confrontation was swift and the surviving Too Loghe hut'aane fled the area to the south, southwest, and east.

Although Iñupiaq renditions of these events were far more detailed, it is important for people to know some of the participants because some may have living descendants. The men were Aguaqutsit, Amoquiq, Aanaŋuluk, Angukak, Aqsiataujaq, Ilawaguluk, Kaunulak, Kiatsaun, Makkalik, Pamiulak, Suvlu, Tatpana, Ula, and Ularjuaq (Panniaq, Ingstad 1954). As unlikely as it may seem even at this date stories were passed along family lines and there may still be a story of that provenance still out there.

The Indians that Panniaq named were Qawatik, Tajutsik and Tullik. Two Indian women were captured Hirshi and another who remains unidentified. Hirshi was married first to Ula and then to Suvlu/Suwlo, the grandfather of Panniaq. Panniaq did not say if Hirshi had Iñupiat descendants.

Now before I start writing about the dispersal of the Too Loghe Tl'eeyegge hut'anne Denaa in more detail, I must introduce Ditsiigiitł'uu Drit Khehkwaii and the Dį'haįį gwich'in Estate.

Ditsiigiitł'uu Drit Khehkwaii

Before 1847, the Dį'haįį community was in an almost constant state of warfare. Starting in the 1820/30s there were a series of internecine conflicts within the Gwich'in Estates. These internecine conflicts were brought on by the khehkwaii who wanted to dominate the trade routes within a given region and were exacerbated by the introduction of new trade items. Twenty to fifteen years before Indigenous peoples actually met the European traders, they were reacting to their coming arrival. Alexander Hunter Murray, William Lucas Hardisty, Strachen Jones, and other Hudson's Bay Company (HBC) traders did comment about these internecine conflicts which, they state, took place some 20 years before they arrived. The Native community in the Yukon Flats commented on this and declared that they were more numerous before these conflicts.

If anyone had commented on extreme weather in the past, the HBC men did not comment on it. It is my opinion that they thought food scarcity was endemic among Native American people. They did write about food scarcity in their journals, but no comments about past extreme weather events.

Although I say that the desire to dominate the trade routes brought on these internecine conflicts the eruption of Tambora (1815–1816) and its aftermath in the region may have been a strong contributing factor. It is not possible to say for sure, but neither is it possible to discount this since the weather patterns of the whole northern hemisphere at the time was unusually cold. As brought to light by William K. Klingaman and Nicholas P. Klingaman in "The Year Without Summer: 1816: And The Volcano That Darkened The World And Changed History, (2013)." This pattern of unusual and sudden cold weather is attested to all across Northern Canada and specifically in the Barren Lands (p.c. Chris Cannon). Closer to home, eastern Japan had low rice yields during this time period. (manuscript, Chisato Murikami, 2021)

Since there were no written records of those years in the Yukon Flats or among the Western Gwich'in estates we cannot say positively that Tambora's lasting weather effects influenced these internecine conflicts. It would be unlikely that weather events did not occur in the Western Gwich'in Estates considering Tambora's effect on the rest of the world's written climatic accounts.

I would like to visit two stories. One is from my paternal grandmother, Soozun Dahjalti' John Ch'igiioonta' and the other from the accounts of Ellen Treenahtsyaa Dahjalti' Shit'eegwiłtthat through her grand-daughter Maggie William Ch'iji'oonta' Ch'igiioonta' Gilbert. Soozun's grandmother Ilikuq Lucy Saityen knew about the two winters of 1816–1818. She heard firsthand accounts from older family members in the upper Hulghaatne River valley. Ellen Treenahtsyaa lived through the double winter on the western Neets'ąįį Estate.

Soozun said two things that point to this story. 1. There were only 6 true Gwichyaa gwich'in families living in Gwichyaa Zhee at the turn of the last century. Given the mortality rate and the diseases that had swept through the region that could be a total of 40 people (including children and seniors) on the outside. 2. the elders said that in the future the seasons would go back and forth and spill into each other. In the first instance, Soozun was an adult at this time and knew that the Yukon Flats was being and had been repopulated not only by Denaa from Nendaaghe and Too Loghe estates, and the Dį'hąįį, but by other peoples from the south and east. When the Hudson's Bay Company Traders came into the region in 1847 this influx had been going on for at least an estimated ten or fifteen years. Even with the internecine wars it simply is not possible to explain a population of 40 people in 1900 without taking into consideration that a severe famine was likely the result of the Tambora eruption. Secondly, people always talked about the weather. However, present elders from the Yukon Flats have not heard of two winters back to back. The elders in 1900 did not doubt that that sort of weather event could happen. It probably happened in the lifetime of their parents or grandparents.

In 1851 the HBC traders write about only 6 people remaining in the community of the "lower Indians" meaning the Taghachwx xut'aana Denaa people. There was a man named Peter Kaii at Gwichyaa Zhee around the turn of the last century. Kaii means left over, a gift from the deceased, and in this case the last member of his family left alive. These are oral and written accounts of significant loss.

Ellen Treenahtsyaa Dahjalti' was a firsthand witness of the double winter 1816–1818. She said that springtime had come, but that it hadn't really set into summer and then it became winter again (p.c. T. Gilbert). Keep in mind that early springtime was always a time of food scarcity. Migratory birds arrived by the thousands and fish were on their migratory routes through the waterways. Winter came again after a brief thaw. Treenahtsyaa said that all the animals died including the caribou. People scrounged for anything to eat. It was helpful that her father Dahjalti' Khehkwaii was already a community leader and a good provider, but still it was a difficult period to endure and people did die.

If the year without a summer hit the people of Kauwarak at the end of June 1817, then it was a matter of days before the weather in the Yukon Flats was affected. This would have caught people at their fish camps just before the first king salmon came up the river. The fish that would have provided food through most of the winter was not there. They stayed in place, hastily prepared for winter and gathered all the waterfowl that did not fly. Fortunately, they had carried out the yearly trade and had plenty of hides to make winter clothing, but these things had to be made immediately since winter was upon them. As in other areas of the north, they could not pick berries or medicinal plants. The men had to be fully clothed along with their snowshoes to carry out what hunting could be done. They emerged from two winters back-to-back in the spring of 1818. It would be hard to know how many people perished during that interval. There is no doubt that depopulation did occur.

After the regrouping of survivors, a major conflict erupted in the area north of the Ch'oonjik between the Teetł'it, Dagoo, Vuntut, Draanjik, Gwichyaa, Denduu, and Neets'aii Estates. The Taghachwx xut'aana were probably drawn into the fray to some extent. These conflicts lasted well into 1844 among the Dagoo who were known to the HBC as the "Rat Indians," and also entered the Teetł'it Estate region.

Dahjalti's adopted son Googhwaii (and his brother) committed fratricide when they killed their uncle Olti' and were forced from the region of the upper Ch'oonjik. Olti's family and relatives threatened reprisal and told Dahjalti' (and his family) not to return to the region. Dahjalti and Olti' were raised together in the household of K'aiiheenjik. They were regarded as brothers, but they may not have been biologically related.

Since the Di'haii Estate is the furthest western Gwich'in Estate they had less to do with the conflict further east, but everything to do with the conflict as it presented in their region of the upper Koyitł'ots'ina area trade routes.

We can see from the trade map that the Di'haii had access to the North through the Qaŋmaliq and the Itkillik rivers on their western borders and the Vyàh K'it/Kuugruaq River, Ivasaak, and Saġvagniqtuuq on their eastern borders and possibly the Hulahula to their preferred trading sites, Niġliq, Łihteeraadal (Łeeridiidal)/Qaaktuġvik, and Nanjyuughat/Qikiqpagruk. Their southern trade routes took them down the Koyitł'ots'ina to the Yukon and upriver to the Tozitna, or conversely over Ch'aataa down the Ch'aataanjik (Tseet'o' Huno') and down the Yukon to Noochuu Loghoyet or up the Yukon to Gwichyaa Zhee. Yet another route was up the Neek'eklehno' and down the Teedriinjik and up the Yukon from there to Gwichyaa Zhee.

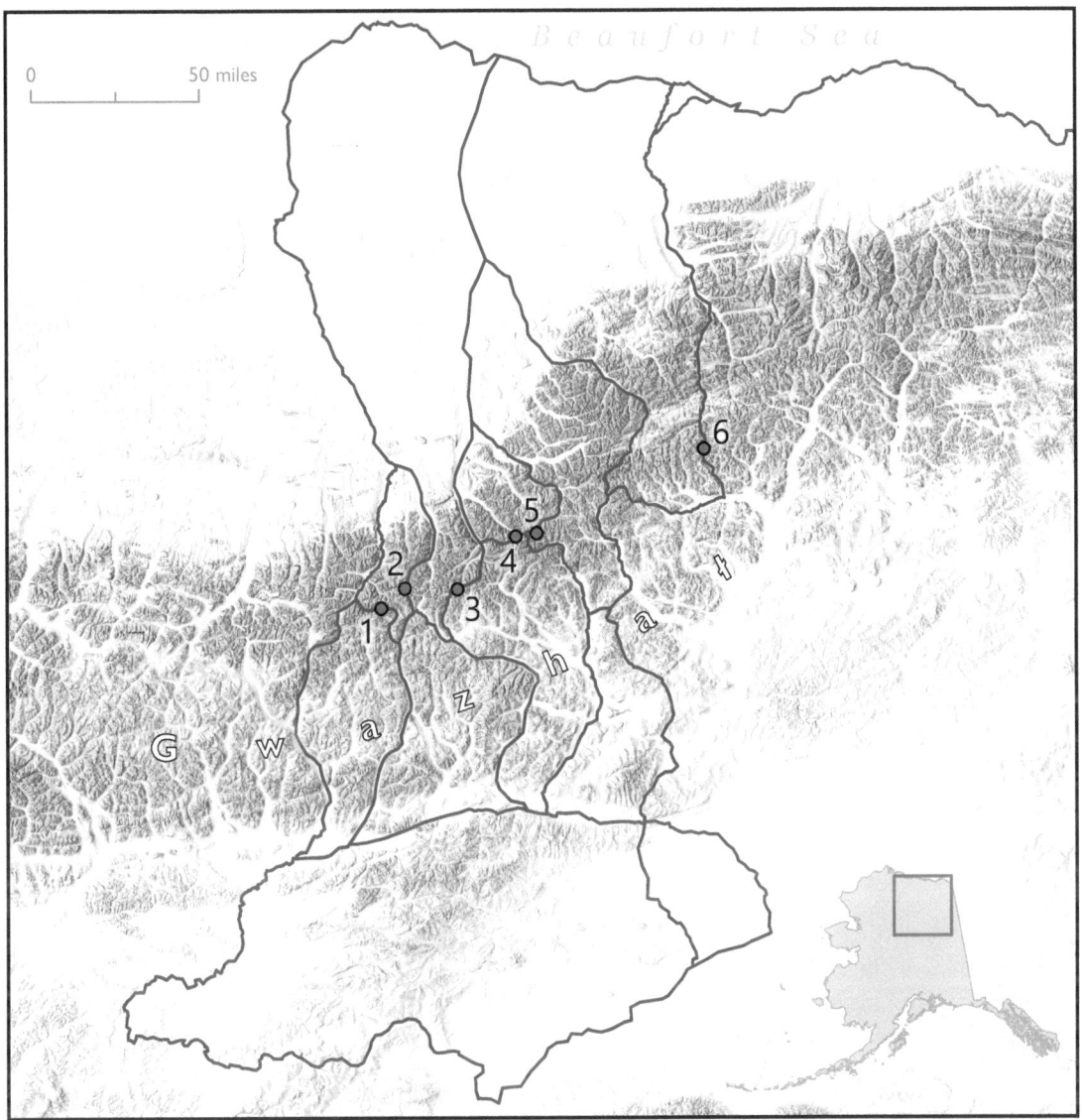

Fig. 24. Dį'hąįį Trade Routes. Raboff, 2024. Map by Haley McCaig and Adam K. Freeburg.

K'iitł'uu, which my father reported was below the mouth of the K'iitł'uu, was centrally located for all the trade routes to the north, south, and west. The Too Loghe, Saakił hut'aane, and maybe a few Iñupiat traders would go through the region on the way to Niġliq, Nochuu Loghoyet, and Noolaaghe Doh trade fairs. Chehłee Van for trade routes in north, south, and west. In former times the Neets'ąįį, Denduu, and Gwichyaa gwich'in along with the Taghachwx xut'aana would pass through going north either going to Niġliq or Łihteeraadal (Łeeridiidal)/Qaaktuġvik, perhaps even to Nanjyuughat/Qikiqpagruk. The Chehłee Van route also went west down the Bettles River, up the Dietrich River and up the Koyuktuvuk Creek to the headwaters of the Itkillik River and down the Neek'eklehno' to the Koyitł'ots'ina.

Ditsiigiitł'uu Drit Khehkwaii grew up hearing and later speaking, Denaakk'e, Dinjii Zhuh K'yaa, Lower Tanana, and at least one Iñupiat dialect. As a contemporary of Saityen he was born circa 1820.

We have no way to estimate the father Drit's age, but his brother, Ch'iji'oonta' (baptized William) on the 1891 census for Rampart House is listed as 70 years old, in the 1900 US census he is listed as 72 years old. Now considering that census takers guessed at peoples' ages and that those guesses were almost always an underestimation of peoples real ages, it would not surprise me if the original estimate of his age was 10 years off, he might have been 75 to 80 years old on the first census at Rampart House. I would estimate that Ch'iji'oonta was born circa 1816 give or take a few years. Drit (II) was the older brother. In large families the older siblings could be as much as 20 years older than their youngest siblings, and it was not uncommon then for uncles and aunts to be younger than their nieces and nephews. Coupled with this is the fact that Dinjii Zhuh men, depending upon their circumstances, had from 1 to 8 wives during the course of their lives. Drit (II) could have been born circa 1800.

That places Drit (II) right in the midst of the battles to gain control of the trade routes. It is my opinion that the internecine wars as they presented in the Upper Koyitł'ots'ina were not carried out to the scale of the conflict along the Choonjik or on the Nendaaghe Estate. Considering the estimated population of 180 people in the Koyitł'ots'ina, and the total of 40 men in 1867, it's hard to imagine that this community would want to lose any male members if they could help it. In former times there was a small settlement at Chehłee Van with perhaps 30 to 40 people. Still the Dį'haįį could also not afford to be passive observers. If any members went out to join in these territorial and trade raids it would have been the young men who hired themselves out as mercenaries and men closely related to the Nendaaghe and Too Loghe hut'aane Denaa.

The Nendaaghe, Too Loghe, Saakił, Dį'haįį, Neets'aįį, Vuntut, and Dagoo being mountain Indians married each other and also intermarried to the Kuukpiġmiut, Akuniġmiut, and other neighboring Iñupiat groups. They were all year around residents of the Gwazhał Cordillera. What happened in one area of the range had a direct impact on people throughout the range in one way or another. When the Nendaaghe were attacked every one of these family groups and regions joined in the fray choosing sides, joining either as mercenaries or as a group, contributing something.

To hire oneself out as a mercenary among the people of the Gwich'in Estates meant that one would be paid, in beads, dentalia (shells and currency), feathers, or in material goods, such as skins, hides, fur pelts, and ts'aih (red ochre). For instance, one unit of feathers was called a ch'aataa, the whole wing of typically a Bald or Golden eagle, peregrine or other falcons, loon wing, or an owl wing. Beads and dentalia which were traded in strands were paid in strands. I am sure there were other ways to make payment but will not conjecture about those means since I do not know.

There is an area about the making of weapons that was considered personal. Arrows were made and designed by the user and therefore considered as a part of "his medicine." This may have extended to other weapons, for instance, the ch'anghwarh or anaullaun, but there I am uncertain. However, this did not extend to ready-made items like long knives and rifles traded from Europeans sources. Since arrows were "his medicine," if an enemy picked up his arrow and shot it back at him, it was more likely to hit him since it would be considered as the arrow going back to its owner. In other words, the makers' thoughts, intentions, and energy were a part of his weapons and therefore highly personal items. Other people were discouraged from handling or becoming familiar with his personal weapons or especially his medicine pouch.

Ditsiigiitł'uu Drit Khehkwaii, born circa 1817, then grew up in a community full of activity.

Brothers: Drit (II) and Ch'iji'oonta' Gozhee K'aa, Di'hąįį Estate

Drit II: circa 1800–unknown, wife or wives: unknown
1. Gokąąhtii Koxki with unknown wife or adopted.
2. Ditsiigiitł'uu Drit Khehkwaii (in separate family box)
3. Younger sister: m. Deets'i' Khagooheenjikti, **Nendaaghe**
    a. Shrahzhitgwach'aa John Deets'at Leviti' Ditsiizeeti' Tsiigalti' Khagooheenjikti'
       m. to Jennie Ch'idił, Taghchwx
    b. Levi, Robert, James, Sophie, Collin, Caroline, Elijah, O, O, Myra, Sarah, Silas, and Jimmy.

Ch'iji'oonta' William circa 1817 died after 1910
1st Wife: Eliza Shaaghan Zhrai' Dahjalti' (real or adopted unknown)
1. Ellen M. to John Whiteface Ch'ikhai'kyuuti'
   Eva, Mary (s. Alfred White), Phillip (s. Jim-jim Felix)
2. Martha Natthaii
   m. to Archibald Anderson Tthulthaikui Bikkuinchati' Atshintsyaa
       Adopted Harriet and her brother David Itrik children of Mary Ditr'ik Drit and Tr'ootsyaa Juuzii John Drit.
3. John Ch'iji'oonta' m. Mary
   a. William, Julia, and Birch Creek Jimmy
4. Peter Tee'ho'haa M. Mary Kookotunatit
   Adopted stepdaughters Rachel, Edith, and Annie Kookotunatit
5. Mary m. to Deeghoozhraii Vatr'oogwiltsii John Ch'igii'oonta'
   a. Paul, Peter, Robert, Henry, Jimmy, Collin, Annie, Horace, Charlie, Ellen, Margaret, Emma, and Laura.
6. William Ch'igiioonta' 1st wife: Christine Christy Vi'tsi'ik Ozhriichinkaii, widow, 2nd wife: Maria Ch'igoozhrii
   a. Stepchildren: Salina (Christy), and Johnny Ross and Jacob (Maria)

2nd wife unknown:
7. Mary m. to Vich'i'nintaii Joseph Khyahtthoo, Too Loghe, Neets'ąįį, Danzhit
   a. Calib Joseph Kellum Khyahtthoo.

Fig. 25. Brothers: Drit (II) and Ch'iji'oonta' Gozhee K'aa, Dį'hąįį. Raboff, 2024.

He grew up participating in caribou drives and the fall salmon fishery along the Koyitł'ots'ina. Later he went hunting for sheep with the men and as he got older to trade fairs throughout the region. He knew everyone in the region who traded with his community and he became fluent to varying degrees in all their languages. He made contacts with his contemporaries, young men his own age. Ditsiigiitł'uu Drit became a khehkwaii about the same time as Saityen, in his early 20s. Ditsiigiitł'uu Drit Khehkwaii was born circa 1817 he died 1855. We see then that he lived into his mid-30s. Ditsiigiitł'uu Drit was Khehkwaii for about 14 or 16 years of his life.

Ditsiigiitł'uu Drit Khehkwaii Vizhee K'aa, Dį'hąįį, 1817–1855

1st wife: Łihteerąhdyaa Shiłihteerąhdyaa Gehik Dzeegwaajyaati', **Nendaaghe**
    No children
2nd wife: Nach'aatsan Natthaii Jessie Aldzak Saityen Drit, **Nendaaghe**
    John Gw'ahaii, Belle, Mary Drits'ik, Joseph Vahan, and Silas Drit
3rd wife: Ilikuq Lucy Saityen Shijuu Tr'oonii Shiigyaa Tr'oonii Drit Khyahtthoo, **Saaqił**
    Tsineveh Shohvatt'oo Robert Gamun, Juuzii John, and Shaanaavee Vahan Drit
4th wife: Dik Sarah Aldzak Ch'igiioonta' Drit, **Nendaaghe**
    Dritzhuu Edoor Edward and Drizhuu Fraum Frank Drit
5th wife: Jaandii, Njaandii, Njaa ahdii, **Dį'hąįį**
    No known children
6th wife: Neeshih Shit'iigwiłtthat, **Saaqił**
    No known children with Ditsiigiitł'uu

Ditsiigiitł'uu means that he had the same name as his grandfather specifically, and in this case perhaps his father. In other words, Drit the third.

No order to enumeration of wives.

Łihteerąhdyaa and Jaandii had no children, Neeshih was an older woman.
Notice that five of his wives were Tl'eeyyee hut'aane Denaa.
Note: ten children lived into adulthood.

Fig. 26. Ditsiigiitł'uu Drit Khehkwaii Vizhee K'aa, Dį'hąįį. 1817–1855. Raboff, 2024.

Ditsiigiitł'uu Drit Khehkwaii inherited Nach'aatsan Natthaii Jessie Aldzak and Ilikuq Lucy Shiijuu Tr'oonii from Saityen between 1839 and 1841. He may already have been married to Jaandii. After the final battle of Kongumauk in Naqsruq/K'iitł'it pass in 1847, he was joined by the surviving members of the Aldzak, Gehik, and Ko'nii'ak families. That included Łihteerąhdyaa and Dik Sarah Aldzak Ch'igiioonta' and her son Deeghoozhraii John Ch'igiioonta'. This meant that his five younger children, Joseph Vahan, Silas, Shanaavee Vahan, Dritzhuu, and Drizhuu were born between 1847 and 1855.

As a khehkwaii Ditsiigiitł'uu had a lot of work to attend to. He had to organize the fall and spring caribou drives, the autumn sheep hunt and ts'aih gathering, the summer fishery, oversee the preparations for trade fairs and messenger feasts, and consider the defenses of the Dį'hąįį Estate. The defenses of the estate meant, an espionage and information gathering network from all other estates which affected his own estate and particularly for trade items and where they originated. He would have known who carried what and the quality of their goods. Ditsiigiitł'uu knew how to comport himself well and orate at trade fairs and gatherings. He also organized raids and carried out revenge killings and paid mercenaries. On top of all of this he saw to the organization of his household, circumcisions, rites of passage, marriages, burials, and cremations. His knowledge of where and when to gather the resources on his estate were a part of his daily life. Ditsiigiitł'uu was not laying around wondering what to do next, he was a busy man with a workload.

Through this trade/espionage network, Ditsiigiitł'uu would have known about the disposition and behavior of the Kashaverov trip members along the Taġiuq shores in 1838, the activities of the Russian American Company (RAC), and the arrival of the small pox epidemic at the mouth of the Yukon, the adventures of Zagoskin 1842–1843 along the Yukon and lower Koyitł'ots'ina, the trips of the Plover (1848–1854), the wintering in Kotzebue Sound, and their trips and wintering in Nuvuk/Utgiaġvik (Journals of Rochfort Magurie, Bockstoce, 1988)), the Enterprise at Nanjyuughat / Qikiqpagruk and the HBC activities along the Nagwichoonjik and the early arrivals of Sir Alexander MacKenzie (1789) and later, Sir John Franklin (1826). The stories of these encounters were repeated from group to group, particularly of the entitlement, audacity, and the unabated airs of superiority with which many of these encounters took place. At first these encounters were cause for amusement, until it became obvious that the behavior that was expected in return was one of obsequious compliance, obedience, and fear.

It was during the winter of 1843 that Russian Naval Lt. Lavrenty Zagoskin was up the Koyitł'ots'ina hoping to go further north to Kotzebue Sound. At that time no one reported to him of major altercations taking place in the region to the northeast. He reported illness and death up the river, but it was not smallpox, and furthermore his translator and informants were not inclined to describe the upriver inhabitants in any detail. They did say, among other things, that the upper Natives spoke a different language. The members of his expedition were Grigory Nikitin (Nikitun), Pakhomov, Kurochkin, Bazhenov, and Ivanov. This was three years from the forced ejection and evacuation at Naqsraq/K'iitł'it.

Their guide, Tatlek, a native of the Noolaaghe Doh area was inclined to abandon the expedition, when Zagoskin threatened that he (Tatlek) would then have no access to his wife until their return to Nulato, and that he would not receive the wages agreed upon. This little tidbit of information did not fall on deaf ears.

Ditsiigiitł'uu was also aware of the new religion that the Europeans brought, of their conflicting denominations, the abhorrence of polygamy, and their desire to change the appearance and clothing of each community they encountered. The Europeans brought with them their own list of taboos, and practices, and demanded varying degrees of adherence to religious precepts. The absolute rejection of the practice of male circumcision among the Dinjii Zhuh of the Gwich'in Estates was unexpected. All these observations and reports made deep impressions.

From these observations, the Di'haii and Neets'aii men decided first to have their young men learn everything possible about these intruders, especially their ability to read and write, and secondly not to bring their women to trade fairs where non-indigenous people might be gathered along the shores and waterways.

The routing of the Too Loghe hut'aane Denaa from Naqsraq/K'iitł'it Pass and the Too Loghe Estate was followed by the arrival of the Hudson's Bay Company traders at Gwichyaa Zhee shortly thereafter in June, 1847. This ejection caused chaos among the surviving Too Loghe hut'aane, and within the Di'haii and Neets'aii Gwich'in communities. If we recall the final confrontation between the Saaqił and Nendaaghe hut'aane caused a deep schism within the Tl'eeyegge hut'aane community circa 1838. The Saaqił hut'aane community was split into those who stayed and became Kuuvaum Kaŋiġmiut Iñupiat and those who fled mostly to the lower reaches of the Koyitł'ots'ina and westward, and the area between the Meloghezeetna and Tozitna and the hills along the north side of the Yukon River. The Nendaaghe hut'aane moved eastward into Too Loghe, Di'haii and Neets'aii estates.

The Too Loghe Denaa in 1847 consisted of refugee Saakił and Nendaaghe hut'aane and original Too Loghe hut'aane people. Since the Too Loghe, Dį'hąįį and Neets'ąįį Estates abutted their intermarriage and trading ties were well established. They identified as only one group, Denaa or Dinjii Zhuh, Too Loghe or Dį'hąįį or Neets'ąįį. In this context Aldzak and his extended family group had no choice but to join the Dį'hąįį since his daughter was married to Ditsiigiitł'uu Drit Khehkwaii. The Dzeegwaajyaati' and Shit'iigwiłtthat families were related and also related to the extended Khyahtthoo family. The Khyahtthoo family moved almost directly on to the Neets'ąįį Estate under the sponsorship of Dahjalti' Khehkwaii. That sponsorship was a lifeline.

This left the Too Loghe hut'aane people who were mostly related to the former Saaqił hut'aane people now living along the northside of the Yukon River to the south and groups of whom now lived around the mouth of the Aalaasuk/Alatna and along headwaters flowing out of the hills to the north of the Yukon River. These Too Loghe hut'aane Denaa were loath to leave the high alpine mountains of the Gwazhał Cordillera. They were primarily mountain people. However, they had to go somewhere. We will return to them in the next chapter.

The population of the Dį'hąįį Estate was never very high, (180–220), and after years of warfare and conflict and the hardship of inclement weather brought on by the eruptions of mounts Agung, Helka, Fonualei, and Sinarka in the mid-1840s, the Dį'hąįį were in an extremely vulnerable position.

The arrival of Alexander Hunter Murray and the British trading firm, Hudson's Bay Company in Gwichyaa Zhee in 1847 was something that was anticipated in the Dinjii Zhuh community. The establishment of the fort at Gwichyaa Zhee was a welcome event. It meant that the bottleneck to European goods along the Teetł'it and Nagwichoonjik was finally broken. The Teetł'it and Dagoo people lost their middlemen status as traders. Their dominance of this trade route had been a source of complaint for the Hudson's Bay traders at Teetł'it Zhee well into the 1840s (HBC, 1844). Although their trade in guns to these groups probably exacerbated this situation. Upon their arrival the HBC had an almost immediate demand for guns in the Yukon Flats. Mr. Murray was very judicious in determining whom he traded these guns to.

The introduction of guns in the Yukon Flats up-ended traditional warfare and retaliatory skirmishes in the surrounding regions within the year, 1847/48.

* * *

It is now necessary to present the Ko'nii'ak and Khyahtthoo Kkohkee families as they transitioned into the Dį'hąįį, Neets'ąįį, Vuntut, Dagoo, and Teetł'it estates, after 1847. The Ko'nii'ak family is predominately Nendaaghe hut'aane Denaa in origin being a part of the Aldzak extended family group. The Khyahtthoo family has been harder for me to place, because my father knew this family only distantly since we have no direct line of descent from this family, so that beginning to understand their relationships, family interactions, and place of origin has taken years.

The Ko'nii'ak family as stated earlier is a part of the Aldzak family group who originated on the Nendaaghe Estate. We have followed this family as they transitioned from the northern Nendaaghe Estate region to the area around the headwaters of the Aalaasurauq, Alatna, and Killik for some 20 years before the final altercation with the Saaqił hut'aane Denaa which caused them then to relocate to the Naqsraq/K'iitł'it region of Too Loghe Estate in the years before their final ouster in 1847 from that region. As a group they lived on the Too Loghe Estate probably less than ten

Ko'nii'ak Vizhee K'aa, Nendaaghe

Wife: Nitch'it Tr'oonii
1. Vats'ach'arahthan Vats'at Ch'araathan Vit'ishitr'ijahthan Thomas Ko'nii'ak
   1st wife woman from Fort Good Hope, Canada.
   - a. Peter Thomas, **Teetł'it**
   - b. Son
     1. Jim Thompson, **Teetł'it**
        daughter Elizabeth Thompson Wells
     2. Christy Thompson
     Others at Teetł'it Zhee
2. Vitsii Deeyuunyaa Ko'nii'ak
3. Vindeegwiizhii John Ko'nii'ak, **Nendaaghe, Dį'hąįį**
   1st wife Toh Val'i' Gehik, **Nendaaghe, Dį'hąįį, Neets'ąįį**
   Phillip, Eliza and Lucy
   2nd wife Mary Ch'idii Khyahtthoo, **Too Loghe, Neets'ąįį**
   James, Sarah, Peter, Christian
4. Adaa vitsii Ahaa Anna Joseph Vahan Ko'nii'ak Drit, **Dį'hąįį**
   Married to Dritzhuu Edoor Edward **Drit, Dį'hąįį, Neets'ąįį**
   Joseph, George, Herbert/Albert, Rachel, Mary, Lucy, Myra
5. Nitsih ghaih gaii Louise Ko'nii'ak, **Dį'hąįį, Neets'ąįį**
   Married to Oozhriikaii, Fred Anaaraq (K), **Too Loghe, Neets'ąįį**
   Deetreech'yaa Simon, Deetreezhuu Robert, Daniel/Donald,(**Vuntut**) Enoch, Ellen, Mary Dzan, Lucy Esau Crow, Jimmy, Zhoh Gwats'an Fred.

Please note I have used (K) to show extended Khyahtthoo family. Further explanation of personal names in Personal Names Glossary.

Fig. 27. Ko'nii'ak Vizhee K'aa, Nendaaghe. Raboff, 2024.

years. Now we follow them as they transition into the Dį'hąįį, Neets'ąįį, Vuntut, Dagoo, and Teetł'it Gwich'in estates by family.

This family chart reflects where the family members came from and their various regional identities in transition. Keep in mind that in a community with only oral tradition (not written), information is like sand, it can be lost very easily. For instance, someone who went to the south for a period of ten years upon his return to the region can be mistaken as someone who actually came from south of the region instead of someone who was just away for an extended period of time.

A person's relationships had everything to do with survival. Partnership, marriage, and adoption were ways to establish relationship outside of direct family.

Evidently, at the time of their flight from Naqsraq/K'iitł'it, Ko'nii'ak and his wife Nitch'it Tr'oonii had three surviving children. Vindeegwiizhii John Ko'nii'ak told a descriptive tale of being on his mother's back during that flight and enduring tearful hunger. It was a desperately cold, wet, hungry retreat to safety and life thus people fell behind and were left.

A portion of a cranium was found near Hunts Fork and archaeologists and communities in the area wonder which people it could have belonged to. Meanwhile it sits on a shelf in a museum.

Ko'nii'ak and his wife may have been anywhere from their late 20s to their early forties during this period of time. Women had children into their late 40s and early 50s. After they joined Ditsiigiitł'uu Drit Khehkwaii they had two surviving daughters, Adaa Vitsii Ahaa Ann Ko'nii'ak Drit, and Nitsih Ghaih Gaii Louise Ko'nii'ak Khyahtthoo.

The Khyahtthoo family included eleven "brothers," and one sister who was the only daughter to survive, Ch'idii Mary Khyahtthoo Ko'nii'ak. Of these "brothers," a few were cousins of the Khyahtthoo brothers, in other words more of less stating that they were extended family as in the case of the Aldzak family. Later John **Kyahtho** is listed in the Robert McDonald Journals (entries 1863, 1864, 1866) and his brother who evidently did not convert to Christianity or McDonald was too tired to mention his conversion or his name.

I view Khyahtthoo John as a true kkohkkee/khehkwaii, but due to his recent arrival into the Gwich'in Estates and his Denaa character and aspect, he was never acknowledged as a khehkwaii among the Dinjii Zhuh of that era nor in the present. However, it should be acknowledged that it was his true role. He took his extended family out of the Nendaaghe or Too Loghe Estate and onto the Neets'ąįį Estate intact and after the passing of Dahjalti' in 1847 established and maintained his own tthal. It was his extended family who later moved into the Vuntut, Dagoo, and Teetł'it estates during and after his passing. He should be honored as Khyahtthoo Kkohkkee.

The further away from our family's direct lines of descent, the less my father was able to distinguish brothers from cousins in the genealogies. This was the case with the Khyahtthoo family. McDonald's journals (RMc) often do not distinguish cousins from brothers, and sometimes he did not know or care.

Understand that this extended family chart was pieced together over many years. Their subsequent dispersal in the 20th century added to the difficulty. At best I view this as a skeleton version of this family genealogy. However, I might add that DNA websites have borne out my father's comments and my research into written records to date.

This family will of necessity be presented in several sections. First the Vitsii'ik/Vi'iits'ik brothers, Vi'etr'ik/Vi'eets'ik (McDonald's handwritten r and s often hard to tell apart) Wilson and Dhindeegwaazhii Thomas (as written in Albert Tritt Journal, ATJ) are brothers reportedly not cousins in McDonald (RMc) as Vihtseik/Vihtsiik/Vihttseikk aka John Black.

1. Vitsii'ik Vi'iitr'ik ts'à' Dhindeegwaazhii Gozhee K'aa

Vi'iitr'ik Wilson, (aka John Black in RMc), **Nendaghe, Neets'ąįį**
w. Deedzii
    a.   Natthal William Vi'iitr'ik, w. Maria Viłiiyiłyo', **Too Loghe, Draanjik**
            Albert, Enoch, Levi, Emma, Margaret, Maggie, Mary, Lilly, Johnny, T'aaval
              Henry, Samuel, and Hannah
    b.   Jinjyah
    c.   Christina Vi'iitr'ik h. Orzhriichinkaii Archie (K) **Neets'ąįį Draanjik**
            Mary Firth, Ch'akal Jonas, Arabella, Selina Ross, Martha Crow, David
    d.   Andrew Vi'iitr'ik, **Neets'ąįį, Dagoo, T'eetł'it**
            Went to Canada. Descendant, Vitrekwaa family.
    e.   Sophia Vi'iitr'ik h. Peter Adam Brule Khyahtthoo **Neets'ąįį, Vuntut**
            Charlotte John Khyahtthoo, Margaret John Khyahtthoo Carroll

Dhindeegwaazhii Thomas Vi'iitr'ik, (aka T. Black) **Nendaghe, Draanjik**, died 1913
1st w. Ilikaq Lucy Shigyaa Tr'oonii Saityen
    a.   Raised Lucy's granddaughter, Soozun Dahjalti'
2nd w. Eliza

Fig. 28. Vitsii'ik, Vi'iitr'ik ts'à' Dhindeegwaazhii Gozhee K'aa. Raboff, 2024.

Then there is the family of the brother of Khyahtthoo John. Two of his brother's sons survived, but there is no mention of a daughter.

2. Khyahtthoo Kkohkkee Vizhee K'aa; Brother's sons Gozhee K'aa

1.   Gwizhoo Frizzy James William Hardisty Khyahtthoo
1st wife Jane, family unknown
      Beatrice Khyahtthoo, 1878
2nd wife Ann, family unknown
      Zeh Gwitee'aa Henry Khyahtthoo, adopted by uncle Deek'an
      1st wife Julia Roderick Khyahtthoo
          Paul Henry Khyahtthoo
          Sarah Henry Khyahtthoo, **Gwichyaa, Danzhit**
      2nd wife Tsuk Kyaht'oo Nilii Tsik Maria Gwats'oo Thomas
          Adopted Ben Thomas and Charlie Jyahts'u' Brawna Henry the children of Maria with her 1st and 2nd husbands respectively.

2.   Teech'i'tsoo Vich'i'nintaii Gwalul Stronghead Joseph Khyahtthoo
1st wife Christina
2nd wife Mary Ch'iji'oonta' (adopted daughter of William and Eliza)
      Calib Galuke Calif Kellum (one person)
3rd wife Ann, the widow of his older brother
      Andrew Joseph Khyahtthoo
4th wife Katherine John Ch'adzahti'
      Saa Emma Joseph McDonald Felix, Myra Joseph David K'aii Adams
5th wife Laura Shit'eegwiłtthat Ch'iji'oonta, widow
      No children together
      Grandchildren: Charlotte Shahnyaa, Edward, and Annie, others

Fig. 29. Khyahtthoo Kkohkkee Vizhee K'aa and Brother's Sons. Raboff, 2024.

Khyahtthoo family continuation: 3. Ch'iki'tthankul Adam Rotika Khyahtthoo. In McDonald (RMc) as Tshitshikul.

3. Ch'iki'tthankul Adam Khyahtthoo Vizhee K'aa

Ch'iki'tthankul Adam Rotika Khyahtthoo, **Nendaghe, Neets'ąįį**
1st wife Maria, family unknown
- a. Emma Iłlil Vihn Adam Khyahtthoo Netro **Neets'ąįį, Vuntut**
    1st husband Charlie Netro
    Rachel, Caroline, Eliza, Abraham, Alice, Mary, Joseph, Sarah, Lazarus
- b. Ch'itishgaii' Francis Adam Khyahtthoo **Neets'ąįį, Draanjik**
    1st wife Belle John Dahjalti', **Neets'ąįį**
        No children
    2nd wife Belle Shaaveezhraa
        Adopted David Collin Ch'igiioonta' Francis
            And Simon Porcupine Shaaveezhraa Francis (her nephew)
- c. Marazhiz Marcis adopted by aunt Maggie Eeshih Ch'igoozhrii and Peter Roe
- d. Adopted Jacob Collin Ch'igiioonta'
- e. Joseph Adam Khyahtthoo
    1st wife Myra Joseph Gwalul Khyahtthoo
        David Adam, Neil Adam, Ellen Adams Tritt
    2nd wife Maggie Eshih Ch'igoozhrii, **Neets'ąįį**
        Maggie had no biological children

Fig. 30. Ch'iki'tthankul Adam Khyahtthoo Vizhee K'aa. Raboff, 2024.

In my opinion, Ch'iki'tthankul had three natural brothers, Vach'aa Alexander, Eetsoo/Itsoo (Vihtsoo in RMc) Charlie and Dek'an John Khyahtthoo. Since his brothers had small families they will be included as one family in the next chart. The reason McDonald encountered this family in the 1860s is because by that time the brothers had a Tthał (caribou coral) up the Khiinjik/Sheenjik River valley and they were supplying the HBC with meat.

Dek'an John Deacon Khyahtthoo (Tikyin (RMc) was a person who performed cremations. This was an important community role. The church did not view this practice as Christian, so people became ashamed of his name, and somehow his name became John Deacon on the US census.

4. Vach'aa Alexander, Vihtsoo Charlie, and Dek'an John Khyahtthoo Gozhee K'aa

1. Vach'aa Alexander Murray Khyahtthoo w. Maria, **Nendaghe, Neets'ąįį**
    a. Ch'itł'eh John Alexander m. to Caroline Kykavichik, **Neets'ąįį, Gwichyaa**
    b. Agnes Alexander Khyahtthoo m. to Ch'akal Jonas Oozhriichinkaii
    c. Ch'aa David John Khyahtthoo m. to Charlotte Pruie Brule Khyahtthoo
    d. Peter Cadzow Khyahtthoo m. Shinahshii Annie Horace, **Neets'ąįį, Vuntut**
    e. Alice Alexander Khyahtthoo m. William Khii Choo Salmon Dzeegwaajyaa
    d. Enoch John Khyahtthoo m. Mary Loola Gwats'oo John, **Neets'ąįį, Draanjik**
2. Vihtsoo Charlie Khyahtthoo m. to Emma, **Nendaghe, Neets'ąįį**
    a. Laura Vihtsoo Khyahtthoo, **Neets'ąįį, Hant'ee**
       1st husband Nakal Sam John Nakal
       (K) **Too Loghe Neets'ąįį, Hant'ee**
          Adopted Sammy John from cousin Rachel Adam Khyahtthoo,
          Because of census records later known as John Sam.
       2nd husband Edward Gwankaiitii
    b. James Charlie Vihtsoo Khyahtthoo
3. Deek'an John Khyahtthoo w. Mary Aldzak, **Nendaghe, Neets'ąįį**
    John and Mary raised orphaned children who were mostly relatives.
    a. Peter, Jacob Collin Ch'igiioonta', Gabriel Ch'adzahti', Margaret, and Henry Zeh Khyahtthoo

Fig. 31. Vach'aa Alexander, Vihtsoo Charlie, and Dek'an John Khyahtthoo Gozhee K'aa. Raboff, 2024.

This brings Gwahtłaatii John (K) into the mix. Kwatlatyi in McDonald. He was regarded by Ch'aa David John Khyahtthoo as a very close relative. Perhaps it was through Maria, but we will never know unless there are family who do know on the Canadian side. Chart 5 then is Gwahtłaatii John.

5. John Gwahtłaatii (K) Vizhee K'aa

1st wife Annie Bluefish
   Laura, Yenuiyit Elias Gwahtłaatii, Elizabeth, Hannah, Jane, David, Phillip, William, John, Ephram Mary and twin, Alfred, Emma, and Charlie Tsal.

Note: Gwahtłaatii may or may not have been born before the transition to the Neets'ąįį Estate that temporarily places him as originating on the Too Loghe Estate. He may have been adopted into Alexander Vach'aas' family as an orphan.

Fig. 32. Gwahtłaatii John Khyahtthoo (K) Vizhee K'aa. Raboff, 2024.

Chart 6 will include the Ozhriichinkaii Archibald, Ozhriikaii Fred Anaaraq, and the Simple brothers. Both names mean that Archie and Fred were the last of their line when they entered the Gwich'in Estates. Chinkaii means he carried (in this case) the name out with him.

6. Ozhriichinkaii, Ozhriikaii, and Simple Goozhee K'aa

1. Ozhriichinkaii, Archie w. Christine Vi'iitr'ik, **Too Loghe, Neets'ąįį, Vuntut**
     Mary Firth, Ch'akal Jones, Arabella, Selina Ross, Martha Crow, David
2. Ozhriikaii Fred Anaaraq w. Nitsih ghaih gaii Louise Ko'nii'ak, **Too Loghe, Neets'ąįį**
     Deetreech'yaa Simon, Deetreezhuu Robert, Daniel/Donald,(**Vuntut**) Enoch, Ellen, Mary Dzan, Lucy Esau Crow, Jimmy, Zhoh Gwats'an John Fred.
3. Simon Simple, w. Natso Lucy, **Too Loghe, Neets'ąįį, Vuntut, Dagoo, Teetł'it**
     Elizabeth, others unknown
4. Peter Simple w. Ann
     Philomen, Effie, others unknown

Note: Ozhriichinkaii family was orphaned and dispersed most descendants in Canada.

The Simple/Semple family appear on the 1891 Canadian Census for LaPierre House. It appears that Simon was the original person into the region, coming as a HBC porter in (RMC) as early as 1864. He went through 5 estates in 17 years. Peter and his brother Samuel may have been his older sons. Unable to take this family any further.

Fig. 33. Ozhriichinkaii, Ozhriikaii, and Simple Goozhee K'aa. Raboff, 2024.

We see then that there are 12 or 13 Khyahtthoo extended family members, depending on whether Gwahtłaatii family truly fits into the Vach'aa Alexander Khyahtthoo family or not. Here then is Teek'i Oonjik Roderick Khyahtthoo in table 7 and Ch'idii Mary Khyahtthoo in Table 8.

7. Teek'i Oonjik Tikionjik Roderick John Vihts'oo Khyahtthoo Vizhee K'aa, Too Loghe, Neets'ąįį, Vuntut, Han

1st wife Mary's family unknown
    Martha, Jack, Jacob, and Matilda
2nd wife Emma Adam Khyahtthoo
    Julia Henry Khyahtthoo, Bella Beiderman

Fig. 34. Vihtsoo Teeki'oonjik Roderick John Khyahtthoo Vizhee K'aa, Too Loghe, Neets'ąįį, Vuntut. Raboff, 2024.

8. Ch'idii Mary Khyahtthoo Johnson and Sister, Myra Gozhee K'aa. Neets'ąįį

1st husband Joseph Dzeegwaajyaati'
    Laura Dzeegwaajyaati' Drit, Albert, and Charlie
2nd husband Vindeegwiizhii John Ko'nii'ak
    James Jimmy John, Charlie, Sarah Frank, Peter, and Christian Ko'nii'ak
Ch'idii had a much older sister later called Myra. No known children. D. Circa 1900.

Fig. 35. Ch'idii Mary Khyahtthoo Johnson and sister, Myra Gozhee K'aa. Neets'ąįį. Raboff, 2024.

This then concludes the dispersal of the Khyahtthoo extended family.

The Simple/Semple, Tsiiteelyaa Isaac, and Herbert families are a part of the Khyahtthoo extended family. Because I am less familiar with these families their charts will not appear here. However, it is necessary to mention them here because of their extensive connection to the area and they will appear in another writing.

Neets'egwich'in, they were the only ones who had a school, they trained us. They are the university of Dinjii Zhuh.

—Paul Solomon Dzeegwaajyaati', Sr.

Hillside along Marsh Fork of Canning River, 2010. A Claude Fiddler Photograph.

Chapter 5
The Last Eight Years

The years from 1847 until the passing of Ditsiigiitł'uu Drit Khehkwaii in 1855 were also the last eight years of not only his life, but of the Dį'hąįį Estate in the mid-1800s.

The ouster of the Too Loghe hut'aane in 1847 effectively reduced the Dį'hąįį Estate to just the area of the upper Koyitł'ots'ina region, about 1/3 of its former size. To lose 2/3rds of the estate meant curtailment of travel, trade, and seasonal access to much needed food resources.

Before I launch into this very storied eight-year period it is necessary to pay homage to Shininduu K'eezhiizhal Dahjalti' Khehkwaii since he died in the first half of 1847. His passing was not only a blow for the Neets'ąįį gwich'in, but for the whole of the Dinjii Zhuh community of the time. He was raised in the household of *K'aiiheenjik Khehkai'* a major khehkwaii/khehkai' of the eastern Dagoo or Teetł'it estates before and shortly after 1800. From the Neets'ąįį gwich'in perspective there are only a few highlights that remain about his life as a khehkai', but nothing about his family life, lines of descendent, or exact place of origin. K'aiiheenjik Khehkai' became a legendary figure. K'aiiheenjik Khehkai' was the person who raised Dahjalti' into adulthood, a responsible human being.

Shininduu was a sickly child who became a phenomenal young man known as K'eezhiizhal. He was nothing short of brilliant as evinced in his very name, K'eezhiizhal. K'eezhiizhal means, "he walks and breathes expanded awareness and presence into every step." He had gravitas and the bearing of a leader. He matured into an exceptional leader.

Shahnyaati' Khaihkwaii relayed his passing to Alexander Hunter Murray in June 1847, and caused him to write, "*He often spoke of his father, and with great affection and sorrow, and sometimes so agitated that he could scarcely articulate his words. The old chief, he said, was once a great man and a great warrior…that before his death he spoke good words to his sons…*"

In his household Dahjalti' Khehkwaii raised most of the Western Gwich'in Estates khehkwaii of the latter half of the 1800s. It is because of the decisions that he made during his lifetime that thousands of Dinjii Zhuh people live on today. Dahjalti' was ceremoniously cremated along the upper K'aii'eehchu'njik near the mouth of Tryahtsi'njik. So yes, we respectfully honor Shininduu K'eezhiizhal Dahjalti' Khehkwaii. Hąį'.

* * *

The events in Naqsraq/Kiitł'it in 1847 put Ditsiigiitł'uu Drit Khehkwaii in a desperately vulnerable position. The population of his estate was at an all-time low, basically himself and perhaps 60 to 90 family and extended family members on the estate. No doubt community members who were inadvertently at Naqsraq for trade lost their lives including the mother and father of *Passak*, the young boy raised by Umialik *Omigaloon* in Nuvuk reportedly about 10 years old in 1852 (Maguire 1852–1854, Bockstoce). The weather was terrible and unpredictable due to the recent volcanic activity miles away and subsisting off the land was almost random. There were few marriageable women and times were difficult, and the resource base was diminished. Considering the recent routing, it was dangerous to go out onto the open coastal plain to gather migrating freshwater fish and waterfowl and eggs, and to follow the caribou herd to their summer feeding grounds. This was an enormous loss. There was starvation.

The very decisions and actions that Ditsiigiitł'uu Drit Khehkwaii made during this eight-year period resulted in the consequent re-distrubution of the people in the upper Koyitł'ots'ina all the way to the Teetł'it Estate in the east.

It is necessary to point out a few facts about this man, Drit. The first is that in a time of few women, Ditsiigiitł'uu Drit Khehkwaii had at the end of 1847 five wives, and later 6 wives. This no doubt engendered jealousy and resentful envy. Secondly, there are very few stories about him or his life. Considering that he is the forefather of many people and a husband of two of the most exceptional oral historians of the time, this shunning of the stories of his life stands out. The only thing my father would say was that Ditsiigiitł'uu made a mess of things.

Drit had a real or adopted brother who was raised with him known as Gookąąhtii also written as Kooceatii, Koongahte, Kooeeawtee in HBC records. According to my father and Isaac Tritt Drit, Gookąąhtii was a man with no wife or known children. Isaac Tritt Drit thought that Gookąąhtii was Drit Khehkwaii's son and the son of Dik Sarah Aldzak, but I think that unlikely considering that in 1847 Drit was in his late 20s or early 30s. My father had said that Gookąąhtii was the older brother of Ditsiigiitł'uu. It appears that I misunderstood Isaac assuming he was talking about Drit the younger when he was referring to his father Drit II, perhaps with a different mother. Gookąąhtii Koxki, then was the real, adopted, or older half-brother of Drit III and the son of Drit II. That would be more in line with probability. Gookąąhtii Koxki lived on the Taghachwx Estate at or near the mouth of the Tseet'o Huno'. Back to him shortly.

* * *

Who lived along the Kk'oonootne in the 1840s? To answer the question, the ethnonym for the people who lived along the Kk'oonootne was Kk'oonootne hut'aane. The question now becomes who were these people in the 1840s?

In reiteration, please note that the Denaa naming of regional estates followed the names of rivers as among the Iñupiat communities, not by regional proximity or comparative land features as among the Dinjii Zhuh.

I have briefly mentioned the **Taghachwx Xwt'ana Lower Tanana** Estate and will cover them again in more detail. I must, however, mention here the language and make up of this small group. They were a mixed group of Denaa, Dinjii Zhuh and Lower Tanana who spoke a mixed language with words from Denaakk'e, Dinjii Zhuh K'yaa, and Lower Tanana languages (p.c., Peter John, Isabelle Charlie, wordlist in Dall 1870 and Whymper, 1868).

Too Loghe, an eastern Kk'oonootne Estate settlement, was very close to the meeting of borders with the Di'haii and Taghachwx xwt'ana Lower Tanana estates which makes it very likely that they were also a highly intermarried community of the three regions, but because they were in the Koyitł'ots'ina valley spoke a Denaakk'e dialect.

Let us reprise what happened in the Upper Kobuk in circa 1838. The Saaqił people and the Akunigmiut Iñupiat routed the Nendaaghe hut'aane (who were living on the eastern Saaqił Estate) displacing them from the Nendaaghe and Saaqił estates for all time. Survivors moved east. Then the Saaqił found themselves faced with an ultimatum to either become Iñupiat or leave the Saaqił Estate as Denaa; many of them moved south. It was not an organized flight for safety. Much as the Nendaaghe hut'aane, they left in groups of extended family units. It was after these events that the very mention of Nendaaghe and Saaqił estates went out of usage by all the surrounding peoples, they were no longer Denaa estates. The Saaqił Estate became an Iñupiat estate and the Nendaaghe Estate was probably renamed briefly before the abandonment of the region after the caribou crash of the 1880s. Subsequently, as seen in the writings of Burch and the oral traditions of the region, the people who survived the ensuing famine, and moved away from the former Nendaaghe Estate were not able to perpetuate the name for the region, they did not pass it on (except maybe in "Maniilaq.") However, the Kuuvam Kaŋiagmiut Iñupiat consistently used Nunataaq for both the river and the region of the forgotten estate to this day (also Beatrice Vincent of Tikigaq in Puiguitkaat 1981).

There are three routes out of the Upper Kobuk River to the south. First: the first route would be to the Aalaashuk and down to the Koyitł'ots'ina then overland to the Meloghezeet No' or conversely up the Kk'oonootne. As a means to identify the groups this will be the **Aalaashuk group** and **Aalaashuk route**. Second: the second route would be down the Ts'eeteetna to a low pass that connects to the Hugaadzaat No'. This will be the **Ts'eeteetna group** and **Ts'eeteetna route**. Third: the third route is up the Selawik to the headwaters of the Huslia, Dakli, or Kateel rivers or conversely up the Kk'otsoh No' to the Tleek'edetlnaa' headwaters leading to Norton Sound. This is the **Selawik group** and **Selawik route**. All these routes were used to flee the Upper Kobuk to varying degrees of welcome, indifference, hostility and/or outright confrontation.

Considering that these dates coincided with the smallpox epidemic on the lower Yukon and the disease travelled up the Yukon in 1838/39 and up Norton Sound to the north, the Saaqił hut'aane with extended family and trading partners in these regions were more likely to find refuge. The survivors along the Hugaadzaat No' or Kodeel Kkaakk'e, for instance, were hard pressed to gather let alone process resources to carry on and no doubt welcomed those who were able to gather and process food for the coming winter. All of these displacements were colored by the practice of *senh* and the *deyenenh* (deyenh) of all the communities involved, which is described thoroughly by Miranda Wright (unpublished Thesis 1995).

The **Aalaashuk group** who went south, was forced to travel further in hopes of finding an estate on which to stay. The Saaqił hut'aane were primarily a riverine people. During the winter they hunted caribou which over wintered in the surrounding foothills and during the summer the men hiked north to the open tundra in the latter half of June to hunt caribou while the women stayed behind and harvested the salmon fishery. They could have stayed near the Neek'eklehno', but this was not an option because of their recent ejection of the Nendaaghe whose members now formed a part of the Di'haii and the Too Loghe estates. One could not safely make a livelihood in enemy territory since revenge killing was very much in place. At that time Neek'eklehno' was tacitly a part of the Di'haii Estate. This left the lower reaches of the Aalaashuk, the Kk'oonootne, and upper reaches of the Meleghozeet no', and the Yukon River open to various degrees of resettlement by the now former Saaqił hut'aane. These were members of the **Aalaashuk** and **Ts'eeteetna groups**. The Ts'eeteetna group settled in areas west of the Meloghezeet no' to the mouth of the Koyitł'ots'ina, whereas the Aalaashuk group settled to the east of the Meloghezeet No' all the way to within miles of the Yukon and Tanana River confluence. The Saaqił became absorbed among the Kodeel Kkaakk'e, Yookkene, Noghee, and Kkaayuh estates at the onset. The **Selawik group** who left via the Selawik and Kk'otsoh No' and Tleek'edetlnaa' went west and south. These routes also reflected the existing trade routes of the times. These routes were familiar to the Saaqił hut'aane who choose these routes, and they knew trading partners and extended relatives in route, if they had survived the smallpox epidemic.

The **Selawik group** had the most confrontation and conflict, although the Aalaashuk and Ts'eeteetna group conflicts seemed to drag on. The turmoil of the smallpox epidemic cannot be underestimated. Every region was blaming the Russians and each other for bringing about this conflagration. So many people died the survivors were regrouping as quickly as possible and outsiders or those further away from the trading center at Saint Michaels' became viewed as aggressors. This **Selawik group** was in transition (at Khutulkaket village, also Kerotyet, Kelroleyet, and Kelroteyit) when they were confronted by a combined group of surviving Ulukagmiut Denaa and Unaliq' Yupiit people (Zagoskin, Andrew Sunno, C. Lucier, M. Wright, K.L. Pratt 2012). However, this repulsion resulted in the breakup of this group with some members fleeing back up north and ending up near the mouth of the Kk'otsoh No' (where they met Kashaverov 1838) before re-entering the Upper Kobuk decades later (Q.B. Atoruk, Burch, Andrew Sunno, C. Lucier). The others meanwhile went across the Yukon River to the Innoko River and up its' headwaters into the Kuskokwim drainage and settled in a community called Ohagmiut. Ohagmiut was a mixed community of Denaa and Yupiit people. This community suffered through epidemics and was finally disbanded during the 1940s and 1950s when a school was established at St. Mary's along the Yukon River. (p.c. Ellen and Pius Savage, Elizabeth Barents).

The clearest telling of this transition is in Ticasuk Emily Ivanoff Brown, "Roots of Ticasuk: An Eskimo Woman's Family Story, 1981." Ticasuk relates through her stepmother, Nee Appangak (Mrs. Carrie Soxie);

Our ancestors migrated here from the Kobuk Valley, they were Kuvunmute [Kuuvaum Kaŋiaġmiut] Kobuk people, and they were Indian Eskimos. The Kuvunmute moved southward passing through Seelvik, Kaŋġik, and Immitchak. Some settled in Kayak along Norton Bay. Indeed, my parents celebrated festivals with your grandfather Qunigruk's parents in Koyuk. But more of the Kuvunmute moved on than stayed, for their leader thought it unwise to live so far from the main ocean and sea mammals.

They moved north to Pastolik, but as they could not speak the language of the natives there, they moved again and settled on the west sandbank of the Unalakleet River. Their descendants are the Unalakleets.

Ticasuk Emily Brown goes on with genealogies that go back to the original "Indian Eskimo" ancestors and relates through historical fiction the major events of the transition into the area of Unalakleet, Shaktoolik, the Koyuk River, and area of eastern Norton Sound.

This is a very brief summary of a far more complicated and nuanced set of circumstances involving these transitions and how they transpired.

Keep in mind that all three of these groups were entering estates that were moderately or severely depopulated by the smallpox epidemic. For instance, Zagoskin found 11 survivors in Noologhe Doh in 1842, on the Kaiyuh Denaa Estate. Wherever they found themselves they followed the customs of the times and adopted the language of the estate they were living upon. In most cases they were adapting to and changing Denaakk'e dialects. But this is important because it led to the die-off of the Saaqił hut'aane dialect along the Yukon River within a generation.

A few families of the **Aalaashuk group** joined the Kk'oonootne hut'aane along the north side of the Yukon River hills and at the headwaters at **Too Loghe** (also spelled Talowa), a small lake and settlement near the Kk'oonootne headwaters. Going down the Kk'oonootne from Too Loghe a small group moved to the settlement of **Sełyee Menkk'et** and yet a few families settled at **Dobendaatłtonh Denh**. The location of Dobendaatłtonh Denh was a mystery to this writer. According to Donald Clark (MS. 2012) it is to the south of Caribou Mountain, which is to the west of Too Loghe settlement. *Dobendatltonh* means a lake without an outlet, a kettle lake at a high elevation. There are many kettle lakes in the Koyitł'ots'ina Valley. I wrongly assumed it was one on the North side of the Koyitł'ots'ina. There is a small kettle lake directly southeast of Caribou Mountain (high elevation) and near the end of a small tributary of the Kk'oonootne. A few members of the **Aalaashuk** and **Ts'eeteetna groups** joined members of the *Todaatłtonh* settlement at its outlet *Mendenaadletno'* (E. Simon tape, Clark 2012, Schrader 1899) into the lower Kk'oonootne. Edwin Simon called these people "*Tadaeatantahoddaena*" (not in modern orthography).

By 1847 some of these refugees had been in the middle and upper Kk'oonootne, the Hugaadzaat No', Kodeel Kkaakk'e, Ohagmiut, and the Lower and Middle Yukon River for almost 10 years. They no longer self-identified as Saaqił hut'aane, but as residents of the estate upon which they lived.

These movements to the south were noted by Russian American Company employees Malakhov (Selawik group) and Deryabin (Ts'eeteetna and Aalaashuk groups) as they transitioned and traded in Nulato by 1838.

The upshot is that after 1838, there were a few long term Kk'oonootne residents who were joined by a few families of the former Saaqił hut'aane in the **Aalaashuk group**. It is my opinion that there were never many people along the Kk'oonootne to begin with, because the food resources in the area simply cannot sustain a large group of people.

* * *

According to the Koyukon Athabascan Dictionary *Too Tleekk'e Hut'aane* and *Too Loghe Hut'aane* are the headwaters people. Too Loghe Hut'aane is a specific group ethnonym whereas ***too tleekk'e hut'aane*** is any group that lives in the lowlands near water, it usually is a generic term, no specific group ethnonym attached. Not being a Denaakk'e speaker this initially was confusing since then I assumed that **Too Tleekk'e Hut'aane** was a specific ethnonym because it was also capitalized. This convinced me even more that this was an ethnonym and not a generic term for 'lowlands people.' This is confusing, since how then do 'headwaters people,' and 'lowlands people' get to be the same people? In my mind, there is only one scenario where this could have happened. It is this: After their 1847 ejection from Too Loghe Estate (high elevation places), some surviving families find themselves living in 'the lowlands' of the Neek'eklehno' and when asked who they are by people around the mouth of the Aalaashuk and Koyitł'ots'ina rivers, they say, **Too Tleekk'e Hut'aane**. Comparatively speaking yes, they moved to the lowlands from the highlands, and called themselves 'lowlands people.' By the time these surviving families were recorded some 40 years had passed, long enough for a younger generation to forget altogether or not know about the former Too Loghe Estate and claim **Too Tleekk'e hut'aane** (of the Neek'eklehno') as their ethnonym. Interestingly they created an ethnonym out of their shared circumstances.

Normally I regard ethnonyms as quite ancient, but this current writing up-ends this view. Instead, it seems to be that the estates themselves, as economic units able to sustain a group of people, are the ancient ones.

These same people taken from the Dinjii Zhuh understanding were known as **K'iitł'it gwich'in**, "residents of the headwaters of the K'iitł'uu river.' Before 1847 these people were known as K'iitł'it gwich'in by the Dinjii Zhuh community and **Too Loghe hut'aane** by Denaa people, as **Tagagavik** by the Nunamiut of Naqsraq sometime after 1847 (N.J. Gubser 1965) and as **K'uytl'ohut'ana** (upper Koyitł'otsina people) by the Menhti xwt'ana Lower Tanana people. After 1847 there was perhaps an uneasy agreement that the Too Loghe may occupy the area of the Neek'eklehno' and areas to the south which were unoccupied because of the severe weather. Which suggests that the two groups were equally manned, and the Di'haii estate being traditionally Dinjii Zhuh territory, the incoming group agreed and were grateful. The Too Loghe had nowhere else to go.

In a 1971 interview, Edwin Simon also suggested that the Too Tl'eekk'e may also have been known as, **Sayhin hut'aane**. Although Edwin was not certain (he repeated a name which he had heard at sometime during his life), and when further interrogated by Annette MacFayden-Clark, he later attributed the name to 'Eskimo' people. According to the dictionary, **Sehno hut'aane** are, "Eskimo people from several inland drainages to the west and north, lit. 'side stream people', *Jettè applies the term to the Kobuk people (s-12);* **also used for Eskimo people of Anaktuvuk Pass.**" From my view this appears to be a dialect variation between Too Tl'eekk'e hutaane and the former Saaqił hut'aane along the Yukon River who were Jettè's main informants. Sehno appears as a place name in the Internet map, "Dena Atlas," 2023 by G. Smith and J. Kari for the area of Anaktuvuk Pass. The questions are: 1. How old a name is Sehno? 2. Was it a place name bestowed by the Too Loghe? And 3. Who were the informants that led Jettè to the above conclusions?

The composition of the "**Too Loghe Denaa, Too Tleekk'e Denaa, K'iitł'it gwich'n, Tagagavik, K'uytl'ohut'ana**" group before their displacement was, a genetic mixture of all the other groups abutting their estate, but who self-identified as Denaa people. They evidently had Denaa, Iñupiat, and Dinjii Zhuh names or at least Iñupiatized and Dinjii Zhuh influenced names such as Qawatik, Tajutsik, Tullik, Doyuk, K'eeldzeettl, Shaht'aii, Ch'ooghwałzhii, Senaaneyo', and Viłiiyiłyo'. Furthermore, there were a number of refugee Nendaaghe and Saaqił Denaa who had been resident with them for close to 10 years. Too Loghe hut'aane Denaa were mountain people. As caribou people living in the "lowlands" it was not an easy fit for them. The ways of the lowlands people had to be learned and comprised a different tool kit, and mindset. There were two caribou herds in the hills to the southeast which were easily accessible, however they were on the Kk'oonootne and Taghachwx estates. To the west of K'iitł'uu the caribou from the Western Arctic Caribou Herd (WACH) and the Central Arctic Caribou Herd (CACH) overwintered to the north of the Koyitł'ots'ina. This was accessible safely only in its easterly range because of the altercation with the former Saaqił hut'aane along the upper Kobuk some ten years hence, now the Kuuvaum Kaŋiaġmiut Iñupiat community.

As has been noted, the upper Koyitł'ots'ina

was not an area that could support large numbers of people. The vulcanism of Tambora (1815–16) (and Zavarskii) no doubt affected the Koyitł'ots'ina ability to sustain people. The river literally froze to its bottom to such an extent that fish did not return for several years, evidently well into the 1820s and 1830s. (Sidney Huntington 1993). By the end of 1847 there are two communities of people living in close proximity in the upper Koyitł'ots'ina, the now former Too Loghe Denaa and the Di̲'ha̲ii̲ gwich'in. The Di̲'ha̲ii̲ Estate as it was encountered in 1847 accommodated the Too Loghe along the Neek'eklehno' and its uplands to the south of that river and for some distance to the west.

* * *

We return to the Taghachwx Estate. The Taghachwx estate had two koxki whom we know of so far, Gooką̲ą̲htii Koxki and Ch'idził Koxki. Gooką̲ą̲htii was raised by Drit II Khehkwaii on the Di̲'ha̲ii̲ estate, and Ch'idził Koxki was raised by Dahjalti' Khehkwaii on the Neets'a̲ii̲ estate.

This estate has been the most difficult estate to weave into the narrative of the 1800s displacements because it happened very quickly and was complicated by the number of groups involved. By the end of 1865 all the former residents were killed, died of starvation and/or epidemic, were abducted and/or displaced.

This rapid displacement is reflected in the known former names of the present Ray River. In Whymper 1869 as *Shtehaut (Ch'ataa'at)*. On the Whymper map 1870 it is spelled *Tseet'o*, and in Raymond map 1871 it is spelled *Chetaut (Ch'ataa'at)*. Robert McDonald in 1877 wrote *Kitli-Kutchin River*. White in 1901 gathered two names for the river from Sam (Pitka) as *Sawtauquanah (Ch'ataa Huna')*, and from Adam as *Sataut (Ch'ataa'at)*. Jules Jette's 1904 map with Charlie Tema'anyułta the river is called *Tseet'o Huno'*, and in Jette 1910 mistakenly referred to it as the former *Tlaa Ts'oonesh No'*, which is a different river altogether.

Each of these names were elicited from Denaakk'e and Lower Tanana speakers in three different dialects (Kodeel Kk'aakk'e, Saaqił, and Yookkene, maybe Too Loghe) in different time frames, a Denaakk'e/Lower Tanana speaker, and three Dinjii Zhuh K'yaa speakers. All of whom had various degrees of understanding or none about who had been displaced in the region.

The brief biography of Charlie "Kali" *Tema'anyułta* aka Isaac *Yerontoradit'o* in Jettè leads from the *Naaheh dote Denh* settlement about 2 miles below the present location of Louden to *Hududodedtlaatl Denh* a settlement 3 miles below the confluence of the Yukon and Tanana Rivers. This informs me that he was of the Ts'eeteetno' group of refugees. His wife Lucy was born in the early 1870s and died in 1910. In a Jettè census, his stepdaughter was known as Jennie Isaac, which is significant in that he may also have been known as "Old Isaac," in other locations and oral story telling. Charlie then was, at the time of working with Jette, 45 years old. According to Jettè, Charlie, *"resided for many years at Fort Hamlin."* Charlie was certainly old enough to have heard of the placenames in the area firsthand, since he was well traveled in the region. Which from the other place names he named suggests his familiarity with the rivers and creeks in the Lower Ramparts and all the way to the Taghachwx Estate eastern border. Therefore, when he called the river **Tseet'o Huno'** it rings true. That would have been the Taghachwx xwt'ana name for that location. A *Menhti xwt'ana* speaker of the time would have known that. His familiarity with the regional placenames bear out his long term residence in the area. His repertoire of placenames was vast.

Here is where the comparative geography of the Dinjii Zhuh comes to the fore. To the Dinjii Zhuh estates the mountain ranges to the north are known as **Gwazhał** "a swelling", the

Fig. 36. Charlie Tema'anyulta', Malina Collections, Anchorage Museum of History, B2000.014.283.

mountains to the south were known, in Murray, as "Big Beaver Mountains," ***Tsee Choo Ddhah***. As the range moves westward toward the Lower Ramparts they lose elevation and become known as ***Tsee Kon'*** "Beaver House Mountains". The Yukon River splits the range of mountains apart right below the Tseet'o Huno'. The Tsee Choo Ddhah/kon' mountains then become Tseet'o Dleła', (Lt) and hook to the southwest and then to the North northwest all the way to the settlement of Too Loghe. Along with ***Łel'one*** to the southeast this creates a circle of mountains in the whole Tseet'o Huno' uplands, which is known as Tsee t'o. ***Tsee t'o*** being, "Inside The Beaver House," or the "Beaver Sitting Up In A Ball." The name of the range creates a visual story for its whole east/west length and strengthens its memorization. ***Huno'*** is consistent with the mixed language of the region, where ***hun/han*** is the Dzk name for river/creek and ***no'/na'*** being the Lower Tanana and Denaakk'e name for river/creek.

The *Ch'ataanjik* was also a Dinjii Zhuh K'yaa name for the river. It could mean, in its older form, ***Ch'ataa***, a whole bird wing and feathers usually of eagle, hawk, or owl used in payment for services and *njik*, river/stream. It also means "This River Leads To A Pass Through The Mountains." At the very end of the river known as *Tseet'o Hutl'ot* (Dn) (Tseet'o headwaters) it goes over a pass to a stream known as *Mekk'e Tsoł Hoolaan No'* that feeds into the ***Kk'eeyh Degheleetno'*** which in turn feeds into the Kk'oonootne. The last three streams form a part of the winter trail that connects to the Tozitna. And in former times the headwaters region was a meeting and feasting place (Kari 2011).

When we meet the Taghachwx in 1847 they had Dinjii Zhuh leadership, the residents were multilingual, and had been creating a **Dene Creole** as such demonstrated by the word, Huno'. Dene languages being very conservative, the 'framework' of the language was Lower Tanana/Denaakk'e, however fully 1/3rd of the wordlist was in Dinjii Zhuh K'yaa, and some of those words were recent trade items (Dall, Whymper). Denaakk'e and Lower Tanana are mutually intelligible languages, more so near the mouth of the Tanana. Dinjii Zhuh K'yaa is a more divergent language and is considered to be one of the hardest Dena languages to learn. This multi-lingual community self-identified as Taghachwx xwt'ana Lower Tanana people.

Where exactly the borders were on the south banks of the Yukon can only be hinted at, but one giveaway is that the Menhti xwt'ana immediately to their south considered the upper ***Draydlaya Chaget*** (Chatanika) as the extent of their estate (Peter John of Minto). There was a settlement above the Lower Ramparts Rapids called ***Xulenh Kayeh***, which was a mixed community regarded as a part of the Taghachwx Estate. In investigating hydronyms (names for waterways) we find the names; han, hun, kon, k'oo, and njik (Dzk), chaaget, nik'a, no', na' (Lt), and neek'e, njek, kaakk'et, na', ne' (Dn). The strong kaakk'et of Denaakk'e is not present in this area. The result is very much like this; Tsogho Nik'a, Tsogho Neek'e, Tsojege Tso Neek'e, Tsonjek, and Tseenjik for the present Beaver Creek. Tsogho Nik'a was formerly firmly within the Taghachwx Estate. Tsogho Nik'a "Beaver Fur Stream," (Lt) is the south eastern border and following that to its headwaters (not far from Draydlaya Chagat) would show the full extent of the southeastern border of the former Taghachwx Estate.

Comparatively speaking, Chatanika (Lt) and Ch'ataanjik (Dzk) are very similar names in two different languages and in two different locations. In this case Chatanika is in the ***Toghotili Tu Tl'ot*** dialect of the Lower Tanana which was elicited in 1904 (Kari 2012). Chatanika was never re-elicited from a Menhti xwt'ana speaker in whose region it represents a border, their name for the old mouth of the Chatanika river is ***Draydlaya Chaget***.

All these names reflect the knowledge of the

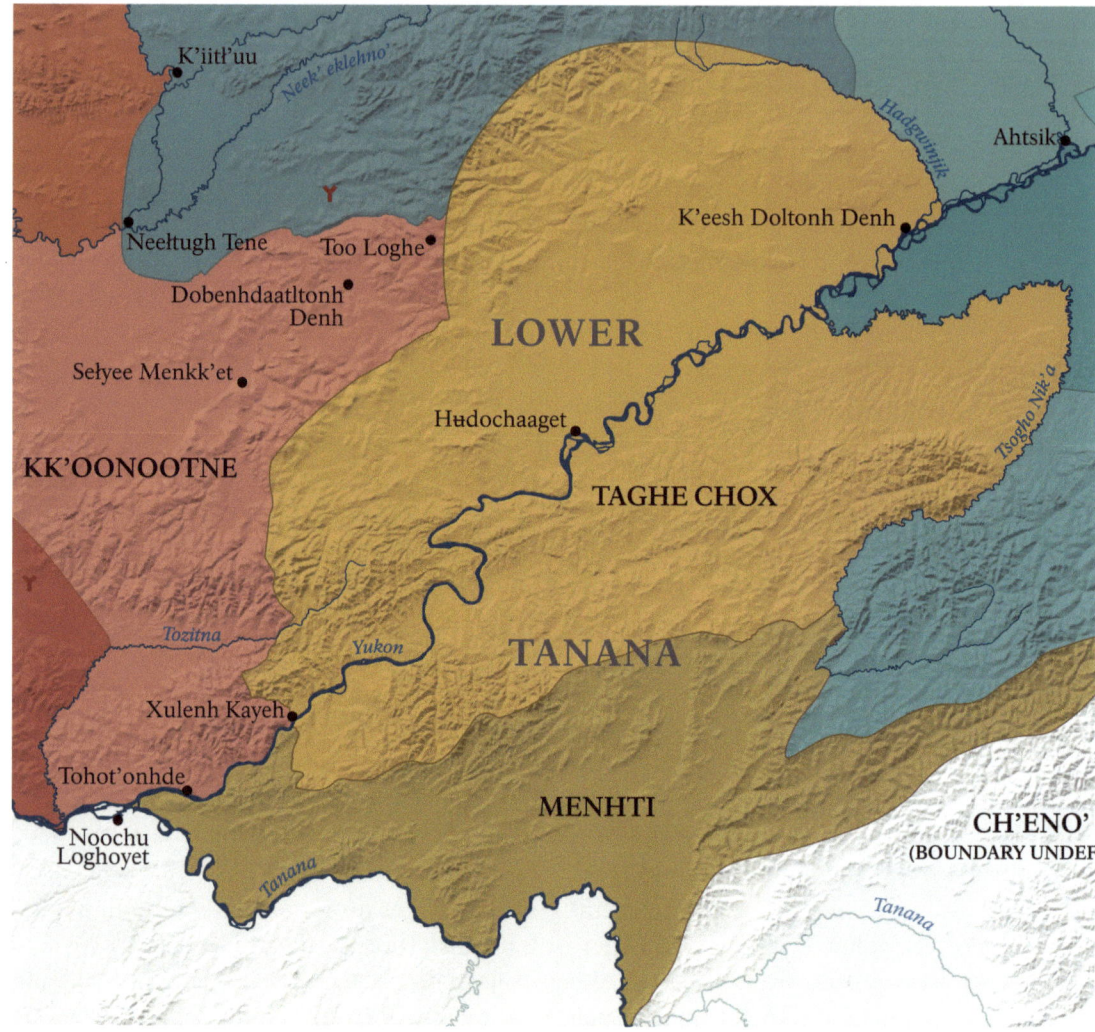

Fig. 37. Taghachwx Lower Tanana Estate. Raboff and GANPP, 2024

informants, where they were from and when they came into the country. I am taking the Charlie Tema'anyułta/Isaac Yerontoradił'o (1904) place names as the authority for this region of the river from Noochu Loghoyet to the Tsogho Nik'a on the south and Hadwinjik on the north side of the Yukon River.

Where the Taghachwx border is along the Lower Ramparts can be deduced by the names for the Lower Ramparts Rapids, a common meeting spot. The location was called Taaghe Choh and Taghekoh (Dn) and Teetsii (Dzk). The *teetsii* in this instance may refer 1. to logs or debris piling up on the rocks in the rapids during low water or if the rocks have been shifted by ice and catch floating debris, 2. a 'cache' under the water since caches were covered with rocks if available, or 3. it could be the point at which the Teetsii gwich'in lands begin, as interpreted by a Dzk speaker. Robert McDonald traveled with Dzk speakers, so almost any place name could be in translation from Taghachwx Lower Tanana into Dinjii Zhuh K'yaa. It must be remarked here that Taghachwx looks close to Taaghe Choh, and if this does signify a border, there is no one available at this point to verify. However, in Menhti' xwt'ana Lower Tanana we have Taghachwx xwt'ana (current orthography) as a placename for the rapids (p.c. Kari). This in my view is proof positive of the Lower Ramparts rapids as the Taghachwx/Menhti xwt'ana border on the east side of the river.

The northern border of Taghachwx abutt the southern border of Di'haii Estate, where the Hadwinjik is the northeastern edge, and the headwaters of the Hodzana and the Hudochaaget form the northwestern abutment. The western border hugs the ridegeline of the Ray Mountains to the headwaters of the Ts'eet'o Huno' and then to Xulenh Kayah.

Here we need to have a discussion about the river Hadwinjik on the northwestern border. Jettè through Kali Charlie *Tema'anyutta*/Isaac *Yerontoradit'o* wrote the name of this river as Hadwinjik, which I will maintain here and a small tributary to the north as Heegwinjik. Heegwinjik may have been a route taken to access the Di'haii from the Hadwinjik. Subsequently the Hadwinjik has been called the Ureenjik "Moon River," Urenjik, Uree Gwits'ik "Mouth of Moon River," Heegwinjik, Oozriinjik by Dzk speakers. It is presently on maps as Hadweenzic.

At present this would be the best delineation of the former Taghachwx xwt'ana estate that can be mustered.

* * *

Before reconstructing the displacements and the movements of people between 1847 and 1851 it is necessary to discuss likely alliances, and the survivor's perception of who was perpetrating actions during various conflicts which occurred, and all the people who participated and their reasons for involvement.

All the participants by group are; 1. Too Tleek'e Denaa, 2. Di'haii gwich'in, 3. Kk'oonootne Denaa, 4. Taghachwx xwt'ana, 5. Menhti xwt'ana (group to the south of Taghachwx), the 6. Yookkene Denaa, and 7. the Deenduu gwich'in. The outliers were the Toghotili Tu Tl'ot Lower Tanana Estate. The individuals who are known participants are; 1. Ditsiigiitl'uu Drit Khehkwaii, 2. Khyahtthoo Kkohkk'ee, 3. Gookąąhtii Koxki, 4. Ch'iził Koxki, 5. Xodalttheyh Kwska, and 6. Shahnyaati' Khehkwaii. Passive participant Doyuk K'eeldzeettl, later Old Alexander, who was too young but was a witness to the results. Although they participated wholeheartedly, I am unfamiliar with possible Menhti or Yookkene headmen, outside of Xodalttheyh Kwska of the late Hester Evan of Nenana or the headmen among the Too Loghe outside of Khyahtthoo Kkohkkee, although Ch'ooghwałzhii (McDonald Choowhulhzi 1867) who was an elder Too Tleekk'e leader in 1867 may have participated as a younger man.

One silent participant was the Hudson's Bay Company who entered the Yukon Flats in the summer of 1847.

Then we look at the informants, 1. Edwin Simon (relation of Doyuk K'eeldzeettl Alexander), 2. Lee Simon, in Clark 2012, 3. Joe Williams (a grandson of Doyuk K'eeldzeettl, 4. Robert William, grandson of Doyuk K'eeldzeettl Alexander, 5. Leonard John of Stevens Village, and 6. Silas Me-too John Khagooheenjikti' of Venetie (p.c. 1991), and the informants via White, Raymond, Whymper, Dall, Robert McDonald, Jules Jettè, the HBC records, Osgood and McKennen.

Because of the rapid displacement of the Taghachwx Lower Tanana, people were often misidentified, the assumption being that there were only Lower Tanana on the Tanana River and not along the Yukon River by more distant or longer time-lapsed informants. Therefore, they assumed it was the Menhti and/or other lower Tanana groups in the region who were the attackers. Furthermore, since the Taghachwx had Dinjii Zhuh educated leadership it was assumed that it was the Dinjii Zhuh who were leading certain raids. Then there was the issue of the many names of the former Too Loghe hut'aane Denaa, which hence forth shall be called **Too Tleekk'e hut'aane**.

As we will see likely alliances occurred between 1. Too Tleekk'e/ Dį'hąįį, 2. Too Tleekk'e, Dį'hąįį and Taghachwx Lower Tanana, 3. Taghachwx and Menhti Lower Tanana, and possibly 4. Yookkene and Menhti Lower Tanana. Among the leadership Ditsiigiitł'uu/Too Tleekk'e leadership, Ditsiigiitł'uu/Khyahtthoo, Ditsiigiitł'uu/ Gookąąhtii, Gookąąhtii /Ch'idził, Ch'idził/ young Neets'ąįį, Draanjik mercenaries, Ch'idził/Shahnyaati', Shahnyaati'/ Ch'idził,and Shahnyaati'/ Menhti leadership. As yet its' impossible to see what alliances were made by Xodalttheyh Kwska of Toklat. Keep in mind that a large number of the Yookkene were former residents of the former Saaqił Estate (both Aalaashuk and Ts'eeteetna' group) and had enemies among the Too Tleekk'e and Dį'hąįį, many of who were former Nendaaghe hut'aane.

Now we may try to ascertain what happened between 1847–51 in the upper Koyitł'ots'ina and specifically the Kk'oonootne.

* * *

We return to the Too Loghe and the Dį'hąįį estates people. After their ejection from the Naqsraq Pass, their desperate situation sinks in, and they react quickly. It simply is not possible for two communities of people to make it through the coming winter in the upper Koyitł'ots'ina especially without access to the resources on the open tundra. They decide that they must 1. have more access to the Kk'oonootne flats lands, which as noted is partially abandoned and/or now occupied by members of the former Saaqił people (Aalaashuk group) and the resident Kk'oonootne hut'aane, and 2. they must get access to the two caribou herds to the south currently known as the Ray Mountain Herd and the Hodzana Herd.

Since Dį'hąįį is Ditsiigiitł'uu's estate, he most likely organizes the Too Loghe and the Khyahtthoo family group to attack the ***Todaatłtonh*** settlement near the mouth of the Kk'oonootne. This will not only gain them safe access to more of the Kk'oonootne Flats, but various members of the group had scores to settle with the former Saaqił among this group. The only problem with this plan is that they are mountain and high tundra fighters not riverine area fighters. They underestimate the defenses of Todaatłtonh and perhaps the weather and terrain of the area. According to informants in the region, they were soundly defeated and the survivors fled, and that they did not have guns at this time (Edwin Simon, Donald Clark). Clark thought this might have happened about the same time as the Nulato event in 1851. That would have been unlikely considering that by 1851 the Taghachwx, Too Tleek'e, and Dį'hąįį had guns and would have used them, plus, at that time, they would have been travelling through hostile territory.

It was after this raid that Khyahtthoo Kkohkkee, seeing the state of his family, and fearing the coming winter and the scepter of starvation, and at the invitation of Dahjalti' Khehkwaii, moved onto the Neets'ąįį Estate. This was not an easy call, but when it came to the life of his extended family, the only possible decision. Khyahtthoo Kkohkkee was a denaa, he had a responsibility to his family to keep them alive. Up to this point it was uncertain as to the estate he originated upon. After this decision on his part, I would say he was an original Nendaaghe hut'aane Denaa, a true Tl'eeyegge hut'aane. His decision did call into question the tactical leadership abilities of Ditsiigiitł'uu. After spending a year along the Ahtr'ąįįnjik and the Tryahtsi'nik, (along the middle K'aii'eehchu'njik) the Khyahtthoo family moved into the Khiinjik/Sheenjik river valley where very shortly they became the main providers of meat and skins for the Hudson's Bay Company situated in Gwichyaa Zhee.

The Todaatłtonh settlement was the first

target since it allowed for access to more of the Kk'oonootne Flats. Even though this raid was a major setback, it still achieved the goal of getting more access to the Kk'oonootne Flats. It was a red flag that said, "enter the Kk'oonootne Flats at your own risk," to the Kk'oonootne hut'aane. However, make no mistake, to lose a large number of men from a reported 25 man raiding party was a major blow.

Realizing that without the young warriors of the Khyahtthoo Kkohkkee extended family, they would need more help, so Ditsiigiitł'uu and the Too Tleekk'e hutaane leadership enlisted the help of Gookąąhtii Koxki, the Taghachwx koxki in the Tseet'o Huno' area, and brother or half-brother of Ditsiigiitł'uu Drit Khehkwaii.

Here is where it seems apparent that the settlements of Too Loghe, Dobendaatltonh Denh, and Sełyee Menkk'et were not overrun once, but **twice**. This initial attack is where Doyuk Alexander's father (a most likely Too Loghe hut'aane person originally from Naqsraq) was left as the resident kkohkkee. This informed later Denaa story tellers to assume that Doyuk K'eeldzeettl's parents were then Dinjii Zhuh because his father sided with this combined community of agitators. As with all incoming refugees they immediately started speaking the mixed language of the Taghachwx, which further identitified Doyuk K'eeldzeettl Alexander as Dinjii Zhuh. Since Dobendaatltonh Denh and Too Loghe are so close, it too was razed and all food resources taken. This accomplished their second objective, to have access to the Hodzana and Ray Mountain caribou herds.

However, looking down the line, they see that what was initiated with the first failed attack now must be finished if the Too Tleekk'e are to have any semblance of peaceful access to an estate of their own. Furthermore, winter is fast approaching, and adequate provisions had not been made for the coming winter. Be that as it may they have no choice but to push on. This time the goal is to take over the whole of the Kk'oonootne Estate.

During the fall and winter of 1847/48 then these people went over the Tseet'o Huno' pass and attacked **Sełyee Menkk'et** and probably made attempts at pushing people out of the upper Meloghezeet no'. The Meloghzeet No' part of the action was vague to Clark's informants. It is equally unclear from this perspective. This is where the participation of the Yokkene and the former Ts'eeteetna' group below the mouth of the Meloghozeet No', in my view, could not possibly have been avoided. The Too Tleekk'e are left as the new resident owners.

It was during this part of the attack phase that Ditsiigiitł'uu Khehkwaii took Neeshih, (the sister of Shit'iigwiłtthat Simon) and her son Ch'ijinjaa John Di'chi' Zhyaa Shitiigwiłtthat. Ch'ijinjaa was just old enough that it was doubtful that Ditsiigiitł'uu would allow him to live. His mother hastily sent him off to his Uncle Shit'iigwiłtthat on the Neets'ąįį Estate. She gave him exact instructions on how to find his uncle. With snares and a knife, she sent him off into the wilderness alone. He arrived at his destination. Ch'ijinjaa's story is a very well-known local story. Keep in mind that these people knew each other and their extended families. Once again, they were not fighting and abducting strangers.

The attack over Tseet'o Huno' Pass was carried out by Too Tleekk'e, Di'hąįį, and Gookąąhtii Koxki for sure. They were all within the immediate region of the upper Kk'oonootne'. What role was played by Ch'idził Koxki is not as clear. He occupied the eastern most Taghachwx region in the Yukon Flats west of Tsogho Nik'a and below the mouth of the Teedriinjik. According to Murray the Taghachwx xwt'ana had a total of 20 warriors and two leaders in 1847. It is my view that both Gookąąhtii and Ch'idził Koxki were whole heartedly involved during the Tseet'o Huno' attack on the middle Kk'oonootne. This takeover of access to both caribou herds aligned with their interests. It is easy then for later informants along the Koyitł'ots'ina to identify these people as 'Tanana Indians.' The Taghachwx were a Lower Tanana speaking group.

As in all conflicts mercenaries were actively recruited probably from among the Menhti xwt'ana and the Deenduu gwich'in. Shahnyaati' Khaihkwaii, who was leader among the Deenduu gwich'in, had other objectives at the time and was not initially involved at this point. As Murray wrote in 1849, "*Four of the middle band (Taghachwx xwt'ana) are with them (the Deenduu) trying to get some of them with guns to go to war with them against the men of the shade (Kk'oonootne hut'aane), but Antoine (Houle, interpreter) thinks only one or two of our Indians will go although they are offered plenty of beads for payment.*"

* * *

During the first winter of occupation Murray's journal and daily records are very descriptive of the habits of the residents, the resources available to them, the furs available, the environmental setting and the items available for trade and the availability of meat and fish to be bought. The Russian activities in particular occupied Murray's interests and his main lines of questioning of not only the local community, but those who lived further afield and who traded with the Russians. He enumerated surrounding groups and their estimated numbers, what supplies he had available to trade, and the number of guns he had available for trade. Murray had a limited number of guns and had earmarked these for among others, Shahnyaati' who was at the time the best hunter in the Yukon Flats. As of 1849 he said 12 people had guns and that they vastly preferred HBC guns to any others referring to Russian firearms. He was selling mostly ammunition and powder through the winters of 1847–50.

Several people in each group already had guns and saluted each other with a volley of firing their guns in greeting.

It is pertinent to point out that the HBC and Murray knew well that they were encroaching upon Russian Territory before they came into the Yukon Flats. Murray was always on the lookout for Russians and wary of possible encounters. Hence his extensive questioning of both local and distant Natives.

The arrival of the Hudson's Bay Company also brought colonized women of Native American descent and European women into the country for the first time. This introduction led to the confrontation in which, "*One of them in the fall wished to enter Mr. Hope's house while his wife was alone, she shut the door in his face, and he again tried to force it open and to effect this draw his knife on the woman, as he said afterwards, only to frighten her, and I believe he meant nothing more, still it was requested that he should have a particular* **blowing up** *which he got, and with orders never to enter the house again. The poor fellow was frightened almost to death about it, he has not been here since. Except that one instance I can say nothing against them.*" According to the Collins English Dictionary, a *blowing up* means a reprimand, a <u>reproof</u> or formal admonition; <u>rebuke</u>. Severe rebuke. Also means berating in the Thesaurus.

In regard to provisioning of meat to the HBC employees there seemed to be an expectation that the local community would provide this service of being 'fort hunters,' as a show of appreciation to them (the HBC) for being in their midst and trading with them. The rate of exchange for meat, fowl, and other edible meats and fish, was tobacco, ammunition, and powder, or perhaps credit for future goods. This was not entirely clear cut. It was for his service as the "best hunter," that Shahnyaati' was allowed to have one of the few guns available in 1847 in trade.

In further observations Murray writes, "*Dancing and singing are their favourite amusements, and they excel any other Indians that I have seen in both, leaping wrestling, and other feats of strength and agility are often practiced, particularly when different bands meet who are on friendly terms. They are inveterate talkers, everyone that arrives makes a speech which we must listen to, before he moves from the door, explaining where he has been, how hard he has worked to get so and so for us, that he ought to be well paid, the news from the other hand, etc. etc., and they will not be interrupted until it is finished, though it should be the coldest day in winter."*

Murray wrote about the manner of dress for men, women, and children, the order of food consumption, who cooked, and including the confinement of feet, "…*the child's legs hang on each side, encased in boots, the feet are confined to prevent them growing, they have all short and unshapely feet, but this with them is considered handsome.*"

From an ethnographic perspective these observations were most accurate and although some aspects of these observations have been watered down over the years, they were recognizable features of my own upbringing.

Alexander Hunter Murray was an educated man, he was not an individual one would describe as a 'mountain man.' When he came out into the Yukon Flats it was the second year of his employment with the Hudson's Bay Company. He was recently married and his wife spent the first winter at La Pierre House at the headwaters of the Teetł'it. He was not a seasoned employee inured in years of company habituation and understanding of relations with the Native American communities. His writing was concise, clear, and brief, but thorough.

* * *

Now we turn to Shahnyaati' Khaihkwaii, the young Deenduu leader, whom Murray referred to as "Little Chief," although Shahnyaati's exact height is not known. Gwi'eech'it Shahnyaati'. In that personal names were often a brief biography of a person's life we start with his name. Gwi'eech'it was not an original Dinjii Zhuh person, he came from the region known as Tanacross. During the late 1820s and 1830s when this group was involved in internal conflicts revolving around who would control trade and trade routes through their country, Gwi'eech'it as a young boy escaped with his life with a group of other refugees from the area. Gwi'eech'it means, "He was thrown towards us." He had no choice but to leave the Tanacross country. Dahjalti' Khehkwaii was at the height of his physical and mental abilities. He took those refugee boys and trained them and raised them. Now this group included Gwi'eech'it's cousin Shreeveeya (Saveah in Murray). When they grew up Gwi'eech'it became khehkwaii among the Deenduu and Saveah became khaihkwaii around *Shoo*, some 25 miles to the northwest of Gwichyaa Zhee. When Gwi'eech'it had his first child with Too'at, his second wife (Strachen Jonas, HBC), he named his son Shahnyuu (Shahnyaa) and then became known as (Shahnuuti') Shahnyaati', "The Father of Shahnyaa."

In naming systems this practice of renaming the father after the child and adding "The father of," is known as a **teknonymy**.

Robert McKennan (1964) and Fredrick Hadleigh-West (1959) were both told by Neets'ąįį informants, Hareedzee Joseph "Joe Number 6" Khagooheenjikti' and another un-named source in Arctic Village that Shahnyaati' came from Kuhel li (in McKennan) and *Kwohelin* (in Hadleigh-West). This is very close "**Xulenh Kayeh**", the mixed settlement above the Lower Ramparts Taghe Choh that Peter John identified. There are two reasons why it is Neets'ąįį gwich'in informants who had this information. The first reason is that Gwi'eech'it Shahnyaati' was raised on the Neets'ąįį Estate and the community would have shared those stories with Joe Number 6 Khagooheenjikti'. The second reason is that Shahnyaati' had something to do with the killing of their forefathers.

As the original Gwichyaa gwich'in died off

the language changed, as seen in Shahnuu and Shahnyaa. The uu and oo sounds were replaced by aa sounds in the Yukon Flats, but not in all of the Dzk speaking area. The language shifted.

In 1847 when Murray came into the country, it was much to the benefit of Shahnyaati' and he took full ownership of this unexpected "boon." Shahnyaati's first objective was to acquire guns and the second was to set himself up as a middleman, and then thirdly to exact revenge upon those who massacred his parents, siblings, and extended family. He acquired his first gun in 1847 and got several more between 1848 and 1851. Between 1847 and 1849 he traveled to the Arctic Ocean and then went southwest into the Menhti xwt'ana lands along the Lower Tanana River during the fall of 1849 and spent several spring times among the Menhti and Yookkene.

It is here necessary to clear up a bit of confusion that has taken place over the years. There is a location at the Lower Ramparts Rapids along the Yukon River known in two languages as, *Taaghe Choh* (Dn) and *Teetsii* (Dzk). This location marks the meeting point of the Menhti xwt'ana and the former Taghachwx xwt'ana boundary. At the lower end of the rapids there is a small creek that comes in from the northside of the Yukon River, known as *Tlaa Chux No'* "**Big Rock Creek**". At this very spot was a camp said to belong to Senito. Senito and Shahnyaati' are two different men, Senito was an original Saaqił hut'aane of the Ts'eeteetno' group who came into the country near Kokrines. After his daughter, Margaret, was married to Alfred Mayo, he became a river man and traveled as far up the Yukon River as Fort Reliance, Dawson City, Mayo, and all the way to St. Michaels in Norton Sound. He was also a witness in Sitka, Alaska during the trail of the murder of Archbishop Seghers (1886). His last fish camp was at **Tlaa Chux No'** at the western foot of the Lower Yukon River Rapids.

The upshot is that both Shahnyaati' and Senito occupied this location at Tlaa Chux No' in different time frames. Senito was the last to occupy this location, hence the name of the location, "Senito's Camp."

After Shahnyaati's excursion north and southwest in 1849 Murray wrote, "*None of the lower band (Deenduu) were here since April, they are passing the spring with the 'Tannin-Kootchin' (Menhti xwt'ana, Yookkene Denaa) on the other side of the mountains to the west of this,* **and I have heard, have disposed of many of their furs to that band for beads**…*I fully expected to have prevented the Indians here from meeting them, and it was my policy and is still, however repugnant to my feelings to encourage [rather?] than otherwise the enmity between the Kootcha-Kootchin and lower bands.*"

Murray's expectations of a cooperative, well-armed fort hunter who will be attentive to the needs of the HBC, an aggressive influential informant, and person who will "bring strange and lower Indians" to the fort to further the trade are quite thoroughly reversed by Shahnyaati's behavior.

In 1849 Murray wrote in company notes, "*The little chief and five men arrived. These lower Indians (Deenduu) are becoming very troublesome and difficult to please. The little chief in particular has been down among the Russian Indians since summer and has continued to go there and trade unless he gets things his own way here. He may go for I will not I've (give) more to the Indian than to the other Indians.*"

To further identify Shahnyaati' we have Katherine Arndt in 1996, "*the party led by Little Chief, very likely the twelve flintlock-armed strangers whom Vasilii Deriabin met among the Native traders below 'Lake Mintokh' that summer.*" Most likely near or at the mouth of the Nowitna River.

Shahnyaati' was known to Murray of the HBC and to Deriabin of the Russian-American Company by the summer of 1849. He was strengthening his trading ties and at the same time doing reconnaissance and lay plans to make his first revenge attack against the Middle Tanana people.

By the summer of 1850, after three winters

of warfare, the eastern most Taghachwx Koxki, Ch'idzil Koxki, is exhausted. He is barely gathering the necessary food for the winter and he needs to do more preparations for raids, but his resources are depleted, and it is now necessary for him to hire mercenaries. As a means to get resources however, he hires himself out to Shahnyaati' Khaihkwaii, along with his second in command Deets'i' Khagooheenjikti' (p.c., S. John Khagooheenjikti', 1991), and a few others of their men. The agreed exchange was payment in furs.

Meanwhile Shahnyaati' hires mercenaries from among the Draanjik, who are now swelling with Khyahtthoo Kkohkkee's men, and a few recently immigrated Di'haii and Neets'aii gwich'in. He's hired enough men to make his move against the settlement of **Troth Yeddha' Bena'** at the base of Troth Yeddha' on the Toghotili Tu Tl'ot Lower Tanana Estate. The ridge of Troth Yeddha' became "College Hill" of the University of Alaska Fairbanks (UAF).

The story of this raid is a well-known story in the Yukon Flats. Shahnyaati' was able to hire enough mercenaries to accomplish his objective. They arrived at Trothe Yeddha' Bena' and proceeded to kill all the residents, men, women, and children. Why this story stuck out in the memory of so many was because of the actions of Chidzil Koxki. Chidzil deliberately threw a live infant into the water. Shahnyaati' was horrified and furious. After the raid was complete, he harangued Chidzil in front of everyone present. Since all believed in shan, senh, and in reincarnation, the manner of death was very important to the living and then deceased, especially concerning an infant. This raid would have been impossible to place if it had not been for this one incident.

The back story of this raid which actually took place at the settlement at the base of Troth Yeddha', which in the Toklat dialect of the speaker was **Tsoł Dlela'** (Hester John Evan Interview with J. Kari 2003). This is a summary of Hester's telling, "*A group of Dotnayi men (Deenduu men) raided the village due to food shortage during the fall. They killed a few people and burned down the structures. An old married couple and a young man survived. The old woman was in plain view the whole time. The warriors decided to let her be since, they reasoned, she could not survive for long on her own. The old woman had hidden her husband in the meat cache, and the boy hid by his canoe under a cut bank. After the raid the survivors went up to **Beyada' Tene** near the present Cantwell area. This boy became a grown warrior known as Xodalttheyh.*" He later took part in a war at **Tohot'anhde**. Hester also stated that this event took place in late fall.

It was sometime after this event that the Menhti gave a name to Shahnyaati', **Dray Chiito'** or **Draichiiatat**, "The Man who made treaty at Draydlaya Chaget." Shahnyaati's raid at Troth Yeddha' Bena' evidently settled a long-standing dispute between the Menhti and Toghotili Tu Tl'ot Lower Tanana. Chief Charlie K'aatele' X'aateelea' "Something concealed in his pocket" recanted his name for Shahnyaati' to Peter John. Chief Charlie died in 1923. His full name then became Gwi'eech'it Dray Chiito' Draichiiatat Shahnyaati'. It is apparent how names of people varied from region to region and how the names of these people could become misidentified or lost altogether.

Murray's comments in 1849 about Little Chief reveals more than he lets known in print. He omits this raid altogether and two others which took place shortly before and/or after these events in the area of Minto flats at **Dextso degho** along the lower Draydlaya Chaget and the other at **Menok'oget**, at the present site of Minto (Peter John interview, Kari 1999). Who the participants were in these raids is unknown at present, they did not directly involve Shahnyaati' Khaihkwaii and in the meanwhile he turned his attention elsewhere.

The constant activity between the Too Tleekk'e, Di'haii, Taghachwx Lower Tanana, and Kk'oonootne hut'aane did not escape his notice. By spring of 1850 it was apparent that their combined effort to take over the Kk'oonootne basin was not proceeding well. Disease and starvation were among them and things did not look good. So Shahnyaati' shifted and decided to tip the scales because it was in his interests to do so.

* * *

We return then to the major conflict between the Too Tleekk'e, Dı̨'hąįį, Taghachwx Lower Tanana, and Kk'oonootne hut'aane. During the winter of 1847/48 this group managed to take control of the settlements of Too Loghe, Sełyee Menkk'et, and Dobendaatltonh Denh. They killed everyone that they did not take hostage and replaced them with people from their own communities, which in this case meant mostly Too Tleekk'e.

It was at this time that Ditsiigiitł'uu Khehkwaii took Neeshih and her son Ch'ijinjaa John Di'ch'i' Zhyaa since he knew her brother Shitiigwiłtthat Simon Ralyil.

In November 1848 Murray wrote that Gookąą̨htii arrived with 12 other men, and by December 1848, both Gookąą̨htii and Ch'idził arrived with 11 men. Altogether they were down to 13 warriors including themselves in December of 1848.

In the following winters of 1848, 1849 and 1850 many of them starved to death. As Murray reported in June 1850, "*Eight of the middle band (Taghachwx), the Indians immediately below the Kootcha Kootchin arrived today…This band had intended going to the meet the Russians as usual, but they were disappointed last year and are now afraid of the Indians, farther down, with whom they have been at war.*" As of 1850 then the 20 warriors of the Taghachwx are now down to eight warriors.

Ordinarily the Taghachwx Lower Tanana occupying the middle ground of the Lower Ramparts would hold the key to trading with all the surrounding groups, the Denaa, Dinjii Zhuh, and Lower Tanana, but no Shahnyaati' made himself useful to Murray. Murray traded the first guns with Shahnyaati' knowingly handing him the upper hand in trade, warfare, and intimidation within the region. As Murray said, "*however repugnant to my feelings to encourage [rather?] than otherwise the enmity between the Kootcha-Kootchin and lower bands.*" In this sense it was in Shahnyaati's interest to establish good relationships with the Menhti xwt'aana and the Yookkene hut'aane and to this end he resided at *Tlaa Chux No'* below Taaghe Choh.

The Yookkene hut'aane, having been joined post 1838 by the Aalaashuk group of former Saaqił hut'aane were no longer passive observers of the conflicts immediately to the north of their estate. This takeover of the upper Kk'oonootne temporarily interrupted the peaceful time-honored tradition of the Yookkene and Menhti xwt'ana seasonal hunt of the Ray Mountain Caribou Herd. The actions of the Too Tleekk'e, Dı̨'hąįį, and the Taghachwx had their full attention. During the assault along the upper Meloghezeet No' these people were participating in the conflicts at some level. To what extent, this writer does not know. This is a part of the telling of these events that will have to come from those communities.

I might mention here that Frederica de Laguna reported assaults happening "from the Kobuk" via Mrs. Coulombe. This is so vague a reference that it would have to be connected to other events or story tellers to get a fuller idea of what happened when and where.

The Taghachwx xwt'ana then, instead of paying attention to their role as the middlemen for the region, are caught up in warfare, that is debilitating to their community and destroys the good relationships that they probably had before 1847. Shahnyaati's presence at Tlaa Chux No' and Taaghe Chux troubles Gookąą̨htii Koxki and his followers, but they are not only struggling to provide for themselves, they are also in constant fear of retaliations, and making further plans for one raid or another.

The alliances of the Taghachwx are colored by who the Koxki were and where they came from. Gookąąhtii Koxki was born and raised on the Dį'haįį Estate, his father was Drit II, his half-brother was Ditsiigiitł'uu Drit Khehkwaii. Ch'idził Koxki was raised in the household of Dahjalti' along the middle *K'aii'eehchu'njik*. This suggests that Ch'idził was either an orphan whom Dahjalti' took to himself or that Ch'idził's father deliberately and voluntarily gave him to Dahjalti' to raise into a man. Dahjalti' Khehkwaii in this sense ran a very private exclusive school for the rearing of young boys and men. My great, great-great aunt recounted those days fondly with her descendants. Gwii'eech'it (Shahnyaati') was raised in the same household, so they grew up knowing each other. Furthermore, Shahnyaati' bound Ch'idził through marriage to his daughter thereby placing a filial responsibility upon him. The two men were not directly related otherwise, but they knew each other very well. By hiring Ch'idził Koxki, Shahnyaati' furthers his own interests and allowed Ch'idził to continue his efforts.

In 1849 Antoine Houle, a fort interpreter did not think that the Deenduu would join the Taghachwx in a planned raid even though they were offered plenty of beads in payment. Come March of 1850, Shahnyaati' had already decided it is time to enter the fray and allowed several of his warriors to participate on the raid on Sełyee Menkk'et and Too Loghe.

As Murray wrote in March 1850, "*three Indians from below (Deenduu), two of them belong to them is called the middle band (Taghachwx). They two brought a good many furs…they got the two old guns I bought from the men last summer, some beads, ammo and tobacco. They said some (of) them trade about two days journey below this and intend to convince them to try and kill some and send him for the (tans.?). There has been a great fight between them with middle Indians and another band (of) Indians there and the run in which 20 (15 men and 5 women) of the latter were killed.*" Murray was not sure of group identity in the area of the Lower Yukon Ramparts and the Tanana River confluence, so it was impossible for him to be exact about groups in the region. This, unbeknownst to Murray, was the attack at Too Loghe and then Sełyee Menkk'et. It is questionable if anyone was left at Dobendaatltonh Denh after the initial raids.

* * *

How or why the Too Tleekk'e, Dį'haįį, and Taghachwx break their alliance is a subject upon which I can only conjecture. The Too Tleekk'e are Denaa, Tl'eeyegge hut'aane to the bone. They made agreements with the Dį'haįį gwich'in and the Taghachwx xwt'ana Lower Tanana because they had to eat, the means to their livelihood was paramount, so as much as they may not have trusted either group, they understand the need to carve out a place for themselves to make a living, to have the means to feed themselves. Once they are established in 1847/48 in the upper Kk'oonootne however and see the threat of the Yookkene just to the south of their area of occupation. They had reason to have second thoughts about what side they needed to be on. By being in the Kk'oonootne they have more access to the Ray Mountain Caribou Herd than the Yookkene hut'aane and Menhti xwt'ana who also had a tradition of hunting seasonally in the region. After the winter of 1848 then they are loath to participate in further raids which drain their resources and manpower and which they no longer see as serving their interests. This inaction registers with the Dį'haįį and Taghachwx like an arrow, a direct affront, because these raids had led to loss of lives not only during the raids, but at the home front where people were starving to death. They risked their lives for the occupation of the upper Kk'oonootne which now is occupied by the Too Tleekk'e. In March of 1850 the Dį'haįį, Taghachwx xwt'ana, and Deenduu gwich'in mercenaries

Viłiyił'yo' Vizhee K'aa

Name of parents unknown, same mother for all. Too Loghe Estate
1. **Hudughyenee**: est. 1835/40–1907
1st husband unknown:
2nd husband Doyuk K'eeldzeettl Old Alexander
    Yeyelthudodolno Eva Jack adopted Little Beatus and Kathleen, Nedo'edaadle'
Unnamed daughter, husband David, only child
    Yerełno Sam Joseph
2. Unnamed Sister, only surviving son, Peter Tsal, b. circa 1865 raised by Thomas Teegoogeetsii
    Peter Tsal
    1st wife Kitty Ch'idził
        Moses, Abraham, Lucy, Mary, Sampson, Margaret
    2nd wife Louise Gwankaitii, her second husband
        Albert, Peter, Samson, and Titus.
3. Maria
1st husband Unknown Denaa man
    Maggie and Lucy
2nd husband Henry Gwats'oo
    Alice, Charlie, Paul, Charlotte, and Lucy
4. Viłiyił'o' Beaver Creek William, (father Grigorii Nikitun, Tungus/Evank)
    Circa 1851–1910 +. Wife: Khagooheenjik Nich'it Gwileįį Agnes Hishinlai'
    Kenneth, Edmond, Ann Joseph Senaaneyo, William, Belle, and Ellen.

Fig. 38. Viłiyił'yo' Vizhee K'aa. Raboff, 2024.

(other mercenaries might have been involved as well) wiped out the settlements of Sełyee Menkk'et and Too Loghe in the upper Kk'oonootne.

This is in accord with the accounts of Too Tleekk'e descendants along the lower Kk'oonootne, especially with the Lee Simon account.

Ditsiigiitł'uu Khehkwaii took Doyuk K'eeldzeettl's sister, (later Ch'ichi'tsoo vahan), and two brothers, George Chukasi and Thomas Teegoogeetsii along with their mother at Too Loghe. During the ensuing winter of starvation, he is not able to keep them. He hands over George, Thomas, and their mother to Ch'idził Koxki near the present location of White Eye. He kept their sister, Ch'ichi'tsoo vahan. Whatever happened next is not clear, but the upshot was that George (the older brother) was raised with Ditsiigiitł'uu until Ditsiigiitł'uu passed in 1855 and eventually ended up in Stevens Village as an adult. George knew the Dį'haįį and Neets'aįį quite well. He grew up with Vindeegweezhii John Ko'nii'ak. Thomas Teegoogeetsii was eventually given to Shahnyaati' and spent most of his life among the Deenduu and later in the area between K'iidootin Gwitsik and Tsegho Nik'a and nearer to George. He was married to George's stepdaughter Harriet (the daughter of Grace, one of Georges' many wives).

At Sełyee Menkk'et Ditsiigiitł'uu takes the younger siblings of Hudughyenee (Hotoyeni in Clark), the grandmother of Eva Jack. She was married and living in her husband's estate when her siblings are reportedly abducted and/or killed. This was a Too Tleekk'e family of Too Loghe Estate origin. One of her sisters died (the mother of Peter Tsal), and Maria and Viłiyił'o' were taken probably by someone who was somehow related to them or it may have been Chooghwałzhii. Viłiyił'o' turned up in 1867 as a teenager traveling with the senior, Chooghwałzhii and another lad, Sahtaii (Sa'taii or Shaht'aii) in the upper K'aii'eehchu'njik. At that time, he was living in the upper Koyitł'ots'ina along with other surviving Too Tleekk'e hut'ane. According to McDonald there were at least 180 people in that group.

As for the family of Doyuk K'eeldzeettl Alexander then we see they are George Chukasi, Ch'ichi'ts'oo Vahan, and Thomas Teegoogeetsii. George had many wives and children who came mostly from Stevens Village. Thomas had children and most of his descendants now live in Birch Creek. Ch'ichi'ts'oo Vahan Ch'igiioonta' was the first wife of Deegoozhraii John Vatrogwiltsii Chi'giioonta. She died with her infant daughter during an epidemic before 1865.

* * *

We return to the journal entries and HBC records for further developments. Murray wrote on June 6, 1850, *"(Suffering amongst the Indians to the west) one band I believe of the Tchukootchi (Taghachwx) have all except two men died of starvation and these only survived by eating their dead comrades."* In this case it could not have been a band of people, but a settlement. Also, this is after the raids in March, so it might have been people who were away at the time of the raids and only came back later and find themselves stranded. Or it might have been a group of Dị'haịi to the north of Too Loghe. There is no doubt though that this was one of the direct results of continued raids in the region.

Murray *believes* that they are Taghachwx, but it could have been Too Tleekk'e or Dị'haịi who found themselves in this position. Even during the 1850s the upper Koyitł'ots'ina corridor was a hard place to eke out a livelihood.

One statement about cannibalism was that after awareness of such activity these people or persons were often shunned. People showed compassion but treaded lightly around them.

Then the fallout from Shahnyaati's raid on the **Toghotili Tu Tl'ot Lower Tanana** began to make itself known. Murray writes on June 13, 1850, *"Twelve Indians and families from opposite side of river (Deenduu)…The reason they have come so soon is that they are afraid the lower Indians are up in search of them…traces of strange Indians have been seen in the woods night before last… (Antoine) Hoole saw a stranger when going to visit the nets in the lake behind. The Black River Indians will not come from their camp for fear of meeting some lower Indians…"* This basically says outright that the Draanjik gwich'in were also participants as mercenaries in the Troth Yeddha' Bene' raid.

On March 1, 1851, Murray writes; *"Four Indians from the mountains west of this arrived… These poor fellows live by themselves in the mountains, being all that remains of a large band: While these four (two men and two boys were off hunting, all their friends were killed by the mountain Indians from below…this is the first time they have visited the fort."* Now this comes across as Too Tleekk'e or Dị'haịi who were stranded. There is no doubt that both groups were being systematically reduced in numbers either through famine or retaliatory raids from the mountains to the southwest. This, I believe, made the Too Tleekk'e live mainly along the Nekk'eklehno' and areas to the west of the region after 1850. Meanwhile, the Dị'haịi were moving incrementally further to the east towards the Upper Teedriinjik in the area of Chehłee Van. The 'mountain Indians below' could be referring to the Yookkene and Menhti or just the Yookkene to the southwest, not the Taghachwx.

On March 10, 1851, Murray writes, "*WLH (William Lucas Hardisty), Hoole, and Indians to Lower Indian camp. The distance is rather great but the Indians have promised to come nearer to us.*" This narrows down these four men to the Dį'hąįį, who up to this point had not gone to Gwichyaa Zhee. Murray sends these two men, Hardisty and Hoole, to accompany the men back to their region. Antoine Hoole was an interpreter. Hardisty, I believe, went along also to learn more of the language and to make an exact determination of where these people resided.

At this point Ditsiigiitł'uu Drit Khehkwaii is down to his immediate family, Ko'nii'ak family, Gehikti' family, Aldzak and his family, and his in-laws. They abandon the upper Koyitł'ots'ina except on a seasonal basis and move to the area of Chehłee Van. The upper Koyitł'ots'ina becomes temporarily abandoned seasonally.

Neither the Too Tleekk'e nor the Dį'hąįį want to venture too far into the Upper Koyitł'ots'ina unless they are sure of egress and a rapid retreat and are familiar with the immediate area. It was only within a few years of the passing of Ditsiigiitł'uu that the Too Tleekk'e hunted further up the river and went on trading trips to Niġliq along the Kuukpik. In 1854 they were sighted by Maguire and identified by the Iñupiat. Evidently, they were on their way to Łihteeraadal (Łeeridiidal)/Qaaktuġvik to trade.

My grandmother Soozun said that her mother and mother-in-law grew up on the shores of Chehłee Van and often shared stories of their early days in the region. That means that even after Ditsiigiitł'uu was gone at least some families stayed in the area for an indeterminate number of years as Dį'hąįį families appear on an early census for Fort Hamlin. My paternal great-uncle, Robert Ch'igiioonta', learned some English and could read and write having been around that fort and learning from the Fort men.

* * *

Now we get into an area of the raids that cannot be drawn out or revealed with clarity from this end. The action took place at Xulenh Kayeh, the settlement on the north side of the Yukon River just above Taghe Choh. This was the Taghachwx settlement at the very south end of their estate near the Lower Rampart Rapids, Taghe Choh. It is the boundary between the Menhti and Taghachwx estates. It is also nearer to the Yookkene Estate.

In March of 1850 when the Too Tleekk'e were displaced from the upper Kk'oonootne, this disrupted for a second time the traditional hunting of the Ray Mountain Caribou and Hodzana Caribou herds. It also triggers an immediate reaction from the Yookkene and Menhti, who annihilated everyone who happened to be at Xulenh Kayeh at the time. There is no way to know if this happened in the spring or during that summer of 1850.

The retaliation was equally swift with Taghachwx and Di'hąįį, and mercenaries in canoes. This may be the raid at **Toht'onhde** that Joe John recounts in Tanana in 1973. Toht'onhde is above the confluence of the Tanana and Yukon rivers along the northside of the Yukon River. It was the site of another massacre with three survivors. Hester Evan stated this raid took place in the fall. Although Joe John was not sure of where the protagonists came from, he knew they were from the headwaters of some drainage far away. The headwaters of the Koyitł'ts'ina are far away if you walk, hike, and canoe the distance. He was sure of where one of the survivors ended up, in Dawson, Yukon Territory, Canada. The other two, Joe John said, were an old shaman and his female assistant.

The two incidents at Xulenh Kayah and Toht'onhde occurred within the same summer.

This is the occasion in which Shahnyaati' gathered, according to Murray, thirty warriors and took off down river ostensibly on a revenge killing or payment mission, but along the way he had occasion to run into five Dį'haįį warriors on their way down to join a raid. Murray labeled these men as being "*Teytse-Kootchin,*" and although he had good interpreters, Teetsii gwich'in also just means any group down the river. At that time, the Dį'haįį would have qualified as 'teetsii gwich'in.' Why Shahnyaati' decided to intercept and kill these men is a mystery. Perhaps his relationship with Ditsiigiitł'uu was not to his liking. Maybe knowing the weakened position of Ditsiigiitł'uu he decided to rid himself of a potential rival. Or maybe he did not wish for the Dį'haįį mercenaries, to move onto the Taghachwx Estate. Most likely he did not wish for the Taghachwx to regain their position as middlemen in the region. He was already aware of their vulnerable situation, what he did was shove the knife into an already deep wound.

One of these five warriors was Deets'i' Khagooheenjikti', the Uncle of Hareedzee "Joe Number 6" Khagooheenjikti' and the father of John Leviti' Khagooheenjikti', who was the father of Ch'eelil Sophie and Silas John Khagooheenjikti'.

Meanwhile Gookąąhtii Koxki lived on and is on HBC records well into 1855 traveling with Yookkene denaa or most likely the Menhti' xwt'ana to trade in Gwichyaa Zhee. Ch'idził Koxki maintained his Taghachwx residence until his passing in the mid-1890s. The eastern region of the Taghachwx estate remained multilingual well into the 1950s.

By the summer of 1852 traders from the region of the Yukon/Tanana confluence come up to Gwichyaa Zhee for the first time, as noted by Chief Trader William Lucas Hardisty, who took over the fort when Murray left that summer.

The Too Tleekk'e who are now fully resident along the Neekk'eklehno' and upper Koyitł'ots'ina came to the fort for the first time in 1853. This is significant in that they made their peace with both the Taghachwx and Dį'haįį and traveled freely, at least seasonally, through their estates to trading sites.

When Ditsiigiitł'uu Drit Khehkwaii died in 1855, his family bought a "Death Outfit" from the Hudson's Bay Company. This selling of death outfits represents the first inklings of a new religion coming. He died between the ages of 35 and 38 years of age. His family and extended family gradually moved further east onto the Neets'ąįį, Eastern Taghachwx region, Draanjik Estate, Vuntut Estate, Teetł'it, Dagoo, and up the Yukon River to the start of the Upper Yukon River Ramparts.

This takes us to 1855 where I have decided to end this story.

"And Vit'eegwijyahch'yaa, the One whom we revere, is in all things, in every nth throughout all the eons, and in the present moment."

—Ch'igiioonta'

Glossary I
Regional Names

Dena

Aalaashuk Group: Group of Saaqił hut'aane who left the upper Kobuk River via the Aalaashuk or Alatna River, circa 1838.

Denaa: Dn Meaning "mankind" or "real human being" in the Denaakk'ee language.

Dinyeet hut'aane: Current residents of the former Taghachwx xwt'ana Estate.

Dołnayi men: Deenduu Estate men, in Toklat Lower Tanana dialect of Hester David Evan.

Khutulkaket Village: Also Kerotyet, Kelroleyet, and Kelroteyit. Lower Koyitł'otsina region.

Kkaayeh hut'aane: People of the Kkaayah Slough region. Also Kaiyuh Estate.

Kk'oonootne hut'aane: People of the Kk'oonootne River. Presently Kanuti River.

Kk'otsox hut'aane: Also Kkotsox xut'aane. Formerly Denaa residents of the Kkotsox, the Kaŋiq River, and now Buckland River.

Kodeel Kkaakk'e hut'aane: People of the Kodeel River region.

Kotsokhotana: Dn Group name in Russian Lt. Zagoskin after Kashaverov and on Russian Map 1842. In Kotzebue Sound, on northern shores of Seward Peninsula. Also Kkotsox xwt'ana. Presently Buckland River area.

Menhti xwt'ana Estate: Lower Tanana Estate at the mouth of the Tanana River.

Nendaaghe Estate: Inhabitants of the former Nendaaghe Estate, upper Noatak River, Upper Itviluk, Aalaasuaraaq, and Aalaashuk rivers.

Saaqił Estate: The area of the upper Hulghaatne, now upper Kobuk River. This is Saakił on map. I have changed the spelling to reflect local preferences.

Sayhin hut'aane: Inland Iñupiat people, possible Too Tl'eekk'e dialect Denaa. Also Sehno hut'aane.

Sehno hut'aane: Inland Iñupiat people. Yukon River dialect Denaa. Also Sayhin hut'aane.

Selawik group: group of Saaqił hut'aane who left the upper Kobuk River via the Selawik River, circa 1838.

Tadaeatantahoddaena: People of Taddaatltonh settlement, lower Kk'oonootne.

Taghachwx xwt'ana: A former Lower Tanana estate in the Lower Yukon Ramparts.

Tl'eeyegge hut'aane: Self ethnonym of the Denaa, presently known as the Koyukon in academic literature.

Too Loghe hut'aane: People of the former Too Loghe Estate. Also Too Tleekk'e.

Too Tleekk'e hut'aane: "People of the low lands." The new ethnonym for the former Too Loghe hut'aane after 1847.

Ts'eeteetna group: Group of Saaqił hut'aane who left the upper Kobuk River via the Ts'eeteetna River, circa 1838.

Ulukagmiut Denaa: Resident Denaa community up the Unalakleet River.

Yookkene Estate: Denaa estate on south side of Yukon River below Noochu Loghyet at the confluence of Yukon and Tanana rivers.

Dinjii Zhuh

Dį'hąįį gwich'in: Ones who live at the furthest edge or border (of known Dinjii Zhuh peoples' occupation). Formerly western most Dinjii Zhuh estate.

Dinjii Zhuh: Self-ethnonym of people known as "Gwich'in" in Alaska and Canada.

Dagoo gwich'in: A regional group. HBC called them "Rat Indians."

Deenduu gwich'in: A regional group. Also **Dołnayi** in Toklat Lower Tanana dialect.

Draanjik gwich'in: A regional group along the Draanjik River.

Gwichyaa gwich'in: A regional group in the Yukon Flats.

Gwitee gwich'in: A regional subgroup in the Yukon Flats.

Kiitł'it gwich'in: Dzk name for Too Loghe hut'aane.

Neets'ąįį gwich'in: Dzk regional group.

Teetł'it gwich'in: Dzk regional group.

Teetsii gwich'in: Dzk Generic name for the Tl'eeyegge Hut'aane Denaa and general name for those people who lived down river.

Vuntut gwich'in: Dzk regional group.

Iñupiat

Ïyaġaaġmiut: Kobuk River Iñupiaq dialect. 1. People who live among the rock cache. 2. People who live among the rock caches. Also Uyaġaaġmiut, Northern Iñupiaq dialect.

Kaniaŋiġmiut: Formerly residents of the Kuukpik headwaters area. One of three groups that constitute the Kuukpiġmiut, and presently Nunamiut.

Kaŋiġmiut: People from the Kaŋiq Estate. Presently the region of the Buckland River originally the Kaŋiq (river).

Killiġmiut: Formerly residents of the Killiq Estate. Middle Kuukpik.

Kivalliñiq Estate: Northwestern Arctic coastal area. To south of Tikiġaġmiut residence at Point Hope.

Kuuvaum Kaŋiaġmiut: Ethnonym of the people of the upper Kobuk River.

Kuukpiġmiut: Former residents of the Upper and Middle Kuukpik. Formerly the Iñupiat of the Kaniaŋiq, Killiq, and Qaŋmaliq Iñupiat estates.

Napaaqtuġmiut: People along the lower Noatak River from the Napaaqtuq Iñupiat Estate.

Nunamiut: Present people of Anaaqtuvuk, Alaska. Formerly the Kuukpiġmiut, made up of the Kaniaŋiġmiut, Killiġmiut, and Qaŋmaliġmiut.

Nuataaqmiut: People of the middle Noatak River. Also Nunataaġmiut

Nunataaġmiut: Former residents of the Nendaaghe Estate. Also Ïyaġaaġmiut and Uyaġaaġmiut.

Pittaġmiut: People of the Pittaq Estate. Northwestern Seward Peninsula.

Qaŋmaliġmiut: Formerly people of the Qaŋmaliq Iñupiat Estate.

Tagagavik: Nunamiut name for the Too Loghe hut'aane perhaps after 1847

Tikiġaġmiut: People of the Tigara Peninsula, presently people of Point Hope.

Tulugaġmiut: Formerly people of Tulugag Lake. Formerly Qaŋmaliġmiut.

Uyaġaaġmiut: In the Northern Iñupiaq dialect. 1. People who live among the rocks. 2. People who live among the rock caches. Also Iyaġaaġmiut: Kobuk River Iñupiaq dialect. Formerly Nendaaghe Estate.

Lower Tanana

Dołnayi: Name for Deenduu gwich'in in Toklat dialect of Lower Tanana.

Menhti xwt'ana: People of the Menhti Lower Tanana Estate.

Taghachwx xwt'ana: People formerly of the Taghachwx Lower Tanana Estate.

Toghotili Tu Tl'ot xwt'ana: People of the Toghotili Tu Tl'ot Lower Tanana Estate along the Middle Tanana to the east of the Menhti xwt'ana.

Toklat xwt'ana: People of the Toklat Lower Tanana Estate.

Yupiit

Ohagmiut: Former community in the upper Kuskokwim drainage.

Unaliq' Yupiit: Yupiit group to the south of Unalakleet River. Neighbors of the Ulukagmiut Denaa to their immediate north.

Other Group Names

Teetsii, Danzhit, Dagoo, Teetł'it, Han Hwëch'in, Yookkene, and Tanacross

Glossary II
Placenames by Estate

Dį'haįį Estate

Atigun Pass: I Presently a pass on the former Dį'haįį Estate.

Atigun River: I North Flowing River. Upper Dį'haįį Estate.

Dietrich River: River feeding into the upper Koyitł'ots'ina.

Dį'haįį Estate: Dzk Formerly western most estate of the Gwich'in Estates.

Chehłee Van: On maps as Chandalar Lake.

Ch'idriinjik: Dzk Enters Teedriinjik from the north.

Eł tseeyh no': Dn Windy river in Denaakk'e (also K'iitł'uu Dzk, Kiiñaqvak I)

Fish Creek: Enters the Neek'ekelno' from the south.

Hadwinjik also **Haweenzik:** A typo in the latter, interjected a Z where there should have been a J. On maps as Hadweenzic.

Hadwinjik: Enters the Yukon from the north. Between Teedriinjik and K'iidotin Gwitsik.

Heegwinjik: a small northern tributary of the Hadwinjik. A trade route between the Dį'haįį and Taghachwx estates.

Hudochaaget: Enters Yukon from the north. On maps as Dall River.

Hunt Fork: Western drainage into Eł tseeyh no', K'iitł'uu, Kiiñaqvak, John River.

Inukpasugruk: 1. Stream that flowed from the east at the headwaters of the Kiiñaqvak/Eł tseeyh no'/K'iitł'uu on former Too Loghe Estate.

Itqiliq: I: On map as Itkillik River.

Kiiñaqvak I: also Eł tsyeeh no': Dn, K'iitł'uu: Dzk. Presently the John River

K'iitł'it: Dzk The "Birch Bark shavings" River **headwaters** of the K'iitł'uu "Birch Bark Shavings" River. (also Eltsyeeh no' Dn, Kiiñaqvak I)

K'iitł'it Pass: Dzk 1. Birch Bark Shavings Pass. 2. Also Naqsraq in Nunamiut Iñupiaq. 3. On maps as Anaktuvuk Pass.

K'iitł'uu: Dzk 1. "Birch Bark Shavings River" Dzk, also Eł tseeyh no' Dn, Kiiñaqvak I., 2. The settlement below the mouth of the Koyitł'ots'ina and the Eł tseeyh no'. Settlement and river with the same name.

Koyitł'ots'ina: (Too Tleek'e dialect) Kk'uyetl'otsene (Middle Denaakk'e dialect), Kk'uy tl'otsine (current spelling) and Ooghe Kuh No'(Kkaayeh dialect): On maps as Koyukuk River. (personal communication, Virginia Ned) I will be using Koyitł'ots'ina throughout because that is what the former and present residents in the region call it.

Kuugruaq: I: See Vyàh K'it. On maps as Canning River.

Kuyuktuvuk Creek: I Creek entering Dietrich River from the west that leads to Oolah Pass.

Neek'eklehno': Dn On maps as South Fork Koyukuk River.

Neełtugh Tene: Dn Former settlement at the confluence of the Koyitł'otsina and the Neek'eklehno'.

Niġliq: Trading site near the mouth of the Kuukpik.

Noonekuh No': Dn Presently Jim Creek, Central Brooks Range.

Oolah Pass: Between the headwaters of the Ikillik River and Koyuktuvak Creek.

Saġvagniqtuuq: I Currently on maps as Sagavanirktok River.

Teedriinjik: Dzk "There is a heart (Chehłee Van) along this river." Enters the Yukon River from the north in the Yukon Flats.

Tootl'eets'ege: Little Dall River.

Vyàh K'it: Dzk: "The place where snares are set." Drains into Tagiaq. Also Kuugruaq in Iñupiat. On maps as the Canning River.

Kaniaŋiq Estate

Okpikruak: I, River along middle Kuukpiq/Kuukpik flowing from the south.

Killiq Estate

Okokmilaga River: I River flowing from the east into the Killiq/Killik.

Kk'oonootne Estate

Dobendaatltohn Denh: settlement on a small kettle lake to the south of Caribou Mountain. On Kk'oonootne Estate.

Kk'eeyh Degheleetno': Stream that feeds into the Kk'oonootne.

Mekk'e Tsoł Hoolaan No': Stream near Tseet'o' Hutl'ot, that is part of the pass to Kk'oonootne.

Mendenaadletno': Outlet of from a lakeside community known as Todaatltonh into the Kk'oonootne.

Sełyee Menkk'et: Settlement off the upper Kk'oonootne on shores of a lake.

Tadaeatantahoddaena: Edwin Simon name for residents of Todaatltonh region.

Todaatltonh: Lake side settlement lower Kk'oonootne.

Too Loghe: a settlement near the headwaters of the Kk'oonootne.

Menhti' xwt'ana Lower Tanana Estate

Dextso degh'o: Minto Flats along the Draydlaya Chaget.

Draydlaya Chaget: On maps as Chatanika.

Menok'oget: General location of Minto on maps.

Noochu Loghoyet: On Menhti Estate: Trading site.

Neets'ąįį Estate

Ahtr'aiinjik: On maps as Wind River.

Haweendzik: Enters the Yukon from the north. Between Teedriinjik and K'iidotin Gwitsik.

K'aii'eehchu'njik: "Willow Water River." On maps as East Fork Chandalar.

K'iidotin Gwitsik: Enters the Yukon from the south below Haweenzik. On maps as Birch Creek.

Kiits'al Tit: Carter Pass. "At the very tip of Kiits'al (the stream)"

Njuunjik: Dzk On maps as Juunjik River, "River of mountains without passes" or "Where we must crawl up over the pass."

Teedriinjik: Enters Yukon from the north. Temporarily Chandalar River.

Teeląįį Tthal: Dzk A caribou corral on the southern shore Van K'eedii. Last owner Juuzii Tr'ootsyaa John Drit.

Trail Creek: Enters the Teedriinjik from the south.

Trayahtsi'njik: "Ottertail Creek," On maps as Ottertail Creek.

Van K'eedii (K'ehdii): One lake on top of another. On maps as Old John Lake.

Yukon: Yukon River

Nendaaghe Denaa Estate

Aalaashuk, Aalaasuk: I: On maps as Alatna River. A re-shaped Nendaaghe Denaa word.

Aalaasuraq: I Presently the Nigu River.

Aneyuk: I Former settlement. Mouth of Anigaak River.

Aniġaak: I On map as Aniuk River in upper Noatak River.

Atłiq: I Former settlement in the middle of the Smith Lakes between the Ipnavik and Itivluk. Along the southern headwaters of the Kuukpiq.

Delong Mountains: Mountain range to the west of the Ipnavik.

Easter Creek: Upper Killik River region.

Etivolipar: I Howard spelling of staging area for group travel. Itivluk and Kuukpik confluence.

Itivluk: I River flowing north into the upper Kuukpik. Itivliim Kuuŋa. Itivluk, Etivluk as spelled on maps.

Itivluk Lake: I Also Narvaŋuluk and Etivluk Lake. Uncertain. Narvaŋuluk was once a settlement at Itivluk Lake. Or that **Narvaŋuluk** was the settlement and lake and then it became named Itivluk Lake. Uncertain. This should be ascertained by an Iñupiaq speaker.

Imailim Kuuŋa: I. The Imelyik River middle Noatak River area. Kuuŋa means "river." Imelyik and Imailum are basically the same work, but with the added Kuuŋa to the word the spelling of Imelyik is changed. Also Imelyik is in one Iñupiaq dialect up river from its mouth. Imailim Kuuŋa is in the Napaaqtuġmiut and Nuataaġmiut dialects.

Imelyik River: Also Imailim Kuuŋa

Innugararruck's Village: Camping site at Inyorurak Pass.

Inyorurak Pass: I Mountain pass to the east of Itivluk Pass.

Ipnavik: I. River at the headwaters of the Kuukpik/Colville.

Isheyak: Howard's spelling of Issakuq.

Issakuq: I. Settlement located at the Aalaasuraq and Itilyiurgiak Creek.

Itivliim Kuuŋa: I 1. On maps as Etivluk River.

Itivluk Naqsraq: I Itivluk Pass. On maps as Howard Pass.

Ivasaaqtignillik: I Presently Portage Creek, upper Noatak River.

Kalukruatchiak Point: I Bluff near the confluence of the Killiq and Kuukpik.

Kikitaliorak Lake: I 1. site about 20 miles to the east of Itivlik Pass and to the southwest of Narvaŋuluk.

Kinyiksukvik Lake: I Former Nendaaghe settlement.

Kikitaliorak Lake: I Settlement site about 20 miles to the east of Itivlik Pass and to the southwest of Narvaŋuluk

Kinyiksukvik Lake: Site of settlement

Kipmuk Lake: I. Site of Qupyuq settlement upper Noatak region.

Koolooguak: I Former settlement. Between Cutler and Imelyak rivers.

Kutuk: I Creek on east side of upper Aalaasuk/Alatna

Mount Papiġuq: Mountain at the headwaters of the Noatak River.

Narvaŋuluk: I Former settlement site along the Aalaasuraq at Itiviluk Lake.

Natmaqtuġiaq, Natmaktuġiaq and Nakmaktuak: On maps as Ambler Pass.

Nendaaghe: Dn Former Nendaaghe Denaa Estate and Denaa name for the upper Noatak River.

Ninŋuq: I Settlement along the upper Noatak.

Nunataaq: I Upper Kobuk River peoples' name for the former Nendaaghe Estate area and the river, Noataaq, Nuataam kuuŋa.

Okpikruak: I River along middle Kuukpiq/Kuukpik flowing from the south.

Pupik Hills: I Hills to the west of Aniġaak River.

Qupyuq: I Former settlement on Kipmuk Lake.

Quunġunaq: I On maps as Gull Pass in the Noatak headwaters

Sannikmik: A small elevated knoll to east of Ivaasaagtignillik where Saityen died.

Schwatka Mountains: Range between the upper Noatak and Kobuk rivers. A border range.

Shotcoaluk: Former settlement reported by Howard.

Smith Lakes: 3 small lakes between the Ipnavik and Itivluk rivers. Middle Lake former site of Atłiq settlement.

Tooloouk: I Camp or settlement below confluence of Itivluk and Kuukpik.

Tukuto Lake: Lake between the upper Ipnavik and upper Itivluk river. Former settlement/s site.

Tupilik: I Former settlement. Upper Noatak.

Ugpigruaq: I Former settlement.

Unakserok River: Eastern drainage into Aalaasuk River.

Qaŋmaliq Iñupiat Estate

Formerly an Iñupiat estate along the Kuukpiq/Kuukpik below the Killiq Estate entering from the south at the Qaŋmaliq. All names **are the same** as Too Loghe Estate.

Saaqił Denaa Estate

Hulghaatne: Dn. Former name for the upper Kobuk River.

Qala: Saaqił settlement, upper Kobuk.

Kobuk Kovak: Formerly Hulghaatne in its' upper reaches.

Nunataaq: I Upper Kobuk River peoples' name for the former Nendaaghe Estate area and the river, Noataaq, Nuataam kuuŋa.

Schwatka Mountains: Range between the upper Noatak and Kobuk rivers.

Taah K'ehoolaanh, Taah K'ehoolaanh Dehn: Dn Presently Walker Lake in the upper Kobuk River.

Taghachwx Lower Tanana Estate

Ch'ataanjik, Tseet'o Huno': Dzk, Lt Currently Ray River.

Hadwinjik in Jette: Dn, *Heegwinjik* in Stuck, Dzk: Hadweenzik River on maps. If this was with Charlie Tema'anyułta, I would be inclined to go with Jette for this name. The Hadweenzik might be a typo, instead of *jik*, they typed *zik*.

Hudochaaget: Enters Yukon from the north. On maps as Dall River.

Taaghe Choh: Lower Yukon Ramparts Rapids. Taghekoh, Dn, Teetsii, Dzk.

Taghachwx xwt'ana: Current orthography.

Teetsii: Also Taaghe Choh Dn.

Tsegho Nik'a: Beaver Fur River. Also Tsogho Neek'e, Tsojege Tso Neek'e, Tronjik in TX Lower Tanana and Tseenjik in Dzk. On maps as Beaver Creek.

Tseet'o Dlel: Mountains to southeast of Tseet'o Huno' ending on this ridge.

Tseet'o Huno': Also Ch'ataanjik. Ray River on maps.

Tseet'o Hutl'ot: Headwaters of Tseet'o' Huno'.

Xulenh Kayeh: Settlement just above Taghe Choh on the northside of the Yukon.

Yukon: Yukon River

Toghotili Tu tl'ot Lower Tanana Estate

Occupy the region along the Tanana River to the east of the Menhti' xwt'ana.

Troth Yeddha': Troth Yeddha' was renamed College Hill at the University of Alaska Fairbanks. Then in 2013 College Hill was renamed Troth Yeddha', its original Lower Tanana place name. Also Tsoł Dlela'

Troth Yeddha' Bena': Settlement at foothill of Troth Yeddha'.

Too Loghe Denaa Estate

Agiak Creek: I A creek that enters Agiak Lake from the south.

Agiak Lake: I Lake to the south of Chandler Lake.

Alatna Hills: Hills to the south of Endicott Mountains.

Amiloyak Lake: I To the north of Agiak Lake and south of Chandler Lake.

Anaqtuuvak Pass: I Formerly Naqsraq Pass.

Anaqtuuvak River: I Formerly the Qaŋmaliq.

April Creek: A creek on the former Toologhe Denaa Estate, Upper Killik region.

Ayiyak/Ayayaaq River: I Name of river from its mouth near Ayiyak Mesa along the Kuukpiq River to its headwaters to the west of current Little Chandler Lake.

Chandler Lakes: A group of lakes at the headwaters of the Maqpik River.

Eł tseeyh no': Dn "Windy River," and "Ochre Colored Spruce River" in Denaakk'e (also K'iitł'uu Dzk, Kiiñaqvak I).

Endicott Mountains: Range to the north of Alatna Hills.

Kanyuumavik: I A meeting place of Nunamiut and Too Loghe people which later became a place name.

Kaŋmalik, also Qaŋmaliq: On maps as Anaktuvuk River.

Kayyaavak: Area between Hunt Fork and Qaŋmaliq.

Kiiñaqvak: Also El tsyeeh no' Dn, K'iitł'uu Dzk: presently the John River

Killiq: I Presently on maps as Killik River.

Kiiñaqvak: I "Something that has to do with the face." On Map as John River.

Kiruqtagiak Creek: Small tributary of Maqpik River.

K'iitł'it: Dzk 1. "Headwaters of the Birch Bark Shavings River". Headwaters of the K'iitł'uu (also Eltsyeeh no' Dn, Kiiñaqvak I On maps as John River.

K'iitł'it Pass: Dzk 1. "Headwaters of the Birch Bark Shavings River" Pass. 2. Also "Birch Headwaters." 3. Also Naqsraq in Nunamiut Iñupiaq. 4. On maps as Anaktuvuk Pass.

K'iitł'uu: Dzk 1. "Birch Bark Shavings River," also Eł tseeyh no' Dn, Kiiñaqvak I., 2. The settlement below the mouth of the Koyitł'ots'ina and the Eł tseeyh no'. Settlement and river with the same name.

Kiruqtagiak Creek: Creek that ends to the west of Little Chandler Lake. Formerly the Ayiyak/Ayayaaq River.

Koyitł'ots'ina: (Too Tleek'e dialect, p.c., Virginia Ned) Kk'uyetl'otsene (Middle Denaakk'e dialect), Kk'uy tl'otsine (current spelling) and Ooghe Kuh No'(Kkaayeh dialect) On maps as Koyukuk River. I will be using Koyitł'ots'ina throughout because that is what the former and present residents in the region call it.

Kutuk: I Creek on east side of upper Aalaasuk/Alatna.

Kuugruaq: On maps as the Canning River. Formerly Vyùh K'it in Dį'hạįį dialect Dzk.

Maniïlaq: Upper Kobuk. Maunluk River on maps.

Maqpik River drainage: I River draining which enters the Ayiyak/Ayayaak River from the south near Tuktu Bluff. Currently written as Chandler River on maps.

Naqsraq: I 1. a ridge that divides watersheds of rivers; a pass, a valley or passage in the mountains; 2. low point of a hill; (i) to travel via the lowest point; 3. (t) to travel via its lowest point. On maps as Anaqtuuvak Pass. Also Dzk K'iitł'it.

Naqsraġlugiaq: I A mountain in the middle of Naqsraq Pass. Represents the middle of the pass from whence the rivers flow in opposite directions.

Okokmilaga River: I River flowing from the east into the Killiq.

Qaŋmaliq River: On maps as the Anaqtuuvuk River.

Tulugag Lake: I A lake about 5 miles north of the present community of Anaktuvuk Pass.

Uluskuk Bluff: I Bluff at the confluence of the Qaŋmaliq and Kuukpik rivers.

Unakserok River: Eastern drainage into Aalaasuk River.

Other Estates and Communities

Auksaakiaq: I Campsite near Tigara and former settlement of Nuvuġaluaq. Tigara Estate.

Gwichyaa Zhee: Dzk Otherwise known as Fort Yukon.

Hududodedetlaatl Denh: Former settlement three miles below the confluence of the Yukon and Tanana rivers.

Kanianiq Estate: Formerly an Iñupiat estate in the headwaters of the Kuukpik, west of the Killiq Estate.

Kauwerak: I Presently Port Clarence/Grantly Harbor region of Seward Peninsula.

Killiq Estate: I Formerly an estate between the Kanianiq and the Qaŋmaliq estates along the Kuukpik.

Kivilina District: I The Kivalliñaq Estate.

Kodeel Kkaakket: Settlement at mouth of Kodeel No' and Koyitł'ots'ina.

Kutulkaket Village: Also Kerotyet, Kelroleyet, and Kelroteyit. Former settlement reportedly along the lower Koyitł'ts'ina.

Naaheh dote Denh: settlement along the Yukon River 2 miles below Louden.

Noolaghe Doh: On maps as Nulato.

Nuvuġaluaq: I Former community about 7 miles north of Tigara. Tigara Estate.

Nuvuk: Former settlement on Spit near Utgiaġvik.

Qaŋmaliq Estate: I Formerly an Iñupiat estate east of Killiq Estate and north of Too Loghe Denaa Estate.

Saaqił Estate: Dn Former Denaa estate of the upper Kobuk River.

Teetł'it Zhee: Dzk Fort McPherson along the Teetł'it River.

Tigara: I Community on the Tigara Peninsula. Presently on maps as Point Hope.

Too Loghe Denaa Estate: Dn Former Denaa estate to the east of Nendaaghe Estate, north of the Saakił Estate and west of the Di'haii Estate.

Glossary III
Placenames

Rivers and Creeks

Aalaasuk, Aalaashuk: I Presently the Alatna River.

Aalaasuraq: I Presently the Nigu River.

Ahtr'ąįįnjik: Neets'ąįį Estate, "Wind River."

Aniġaak: I On map as Aniuk River in upper Noatak River.

Agiak Creek: I A creek that enters Agiak Lake from the south.

Anaqtuuvak River: I Formerly the **Qaŋmaliq** River.

April Creek: Upper Killik region.

Ayiyak/Ayayaaq River: I Name of river from its mouth neak Ayiyak Mesa along the Kuukpiq River to its headwaters to the west of current Little Chandler Lake.

Atigun River: I North Flowing River. Upper Dį'hąįį Estate. The Dį'hąįį abandoned the estate in 1855. Their name for the river has been lost. Denaakk'e word for this river was Tlaakk'oł Neekk'e. It was one of their last trade routes into the region.

Beyada' Tene: General area of Cantwell, Alaska.

Ch'ataanjik, Tseet'o Huno': Dzk, Lt Currently Ray River.

Ch'oonjik: "Porcupine Quill River", on maps as Porcupine River.

Chuu Choo Vee: Dzk Arctic coastline.

Dietrich River: River feeding into the upper Koyitł'ots'ina. Di'hąįį Estate

Dizeènjik: Colleen River.

Draydlaya Chaget: On maps as Chatanika.

Easter Creek: Upper Killiq River region.

Eł tseeyh no': Dn "Windy River" and "Ochre Colored Spruce River" (also K'iitł'uu Dzk, Kiiñaqvak I).

Fish Creek: Enters the Neek'ekelno' from the south.

Han Gwachoo, Nagwichoonjik: Eastern dialect river. Presently the Mackenzie River.

Hadwinjik, also Haweenzik: A possible typo in the latter, interjected a Z where there should have been a J. On maps as Hadweenzic. Jette with C. Tema'anyułta original spelling, Hadwinjik. Enters the Yukon from the north. Also Oozhriinjik, Oozhriigwits'ik in Dzk. Enters the Yukon River between Teedriinjik and K'iidotin Gwitsik from the north.

Heegwinjik: A small northern tributary of the Hadwinjik. Possibly a trade route to the Di'hąį Estate. Located on the southside or a ridge that connects to the area of the Teedriinjik/K'aiiehchu'njik.

Hudochaaget: Dn Presently on maps as Dall River.

Hugaadzaat No': River that enters the Koyitł'ots'ina from the North.

Hula-Hula River: See Teets'iinjik.

Hulghaatne: Dn. Former name for the upper Kobuk River.

Imailim Kuuŋa: I The Imelyik River middle Noatak River area.

Innugararuck's Village: Camping site at Inyorurak Pass.

Innoko River: River flowing into the Lower Yukon from the south.

Inyorurak Pass: I Pass to the east of Itivluk Pass.

Ipnavik: I. River at the headwaters of the Kuukpik/Colville.

Itilyiurgiak Creek: Enters the Aalaasurauq from the west.

Itivliim Kuuŋa: I On maps as Etivluk River

Itivluk Lake: Narvaŋuluk former settlement on Etivluk Lake on maps.

Itivluk: I River flowing north into the upper Kuukpik. Itivliim Kuuŋa. Itivluk, Etivluk as spelled on maps.

Itivluk Lake: I Also Narvaŋuluk and Etivluk.

Ivasak: Tributary going north.

K'aii'eehchu'njik: Dzk "Willow Water River." On maps as East Fork Chandalar.

Kaŋiq River: I Currently the Buckland River, in south Kotzebue Sound. See also Kk'otsoh No'.

Kaŋigqat: River flowing north to Tagiaq. On maps as Kongakut.

Kiruqtagiak Creek: Enters the upper Maqpik River.

Kodeel No': On maps as the Kateel River.

Kk'oonootne: River entering the Koyitł'otsina from the south. Below entry of the Aalaashuk. On maps as the Kanuti River.

Kk'otsoh No': Denaakk'e name for Kaŋiq River. A headwaters tributary is Tleek'edetlnaa'. On maps as Buckland River.

Kobuk Kovak: Formerly **Hulghaatne** in its' upper reaches.

Koyuk River: I River entering Norton Sound from the northeast.

Kuskokwim drainage: Major River flowing into Bristol Bay.

Kuugruaq: I: On maps as Canning River. Formerly **Vyàh K'it**, Dzk.

Kuukpiq/Kuukpik: I On maps as Colville River. Flows to Tagiaq.

Łihteeraadal Łeeridiidal/Qaaktuġvik, and Nanjyuughat/Qikiqpagruk: Barter Island.

Łeeridiidal, Łihteeraadal, and Qaaktuġvik: Barter Island in Dzk. and Nanjyuughat/Qikiqpagruk. On maps as Barter Island.

Maqpik River: Intersects with the Ayiyak/Ayayaaq River from the south.

Meloghezeet no': Dn Enters the Yukon from the northside.

Nagwichoonjik: Dzk Eastern Gwich'in Nation dialect. Han Gwachoo Western Dialect. Currently on maps as the Mackenzie River.

Nanjuughat/Qikiqpagruk: Dzk "An island close to the mainland." Hershel Island.

Neek'eklehno': Dn On maps as South Fork Koyukuk River.

Njuunjik: Dzk: Also on maps as Juunjik.

Noataaq: I Noatak River.

Noonekuh No': Dn Presently on maps as Jim Creek, Central Brooks Range.

Nuataam kuuŋa: I Also Nunataaq, Noataaq, Noatak.

Ooghe Kuh No': Dn Kkaayeh dialect. Kk'uyetl'otsene, Kk'oyetl'otsine, and Koyitł'ots'ina: Presently the Koyukuk River.

Okpikruak: I River along middle Kuukpiq/Kuukpik flowing from the south.

Okokmilaga River: I River flowing from the east into the Killiq.

Oozhriinjik, Ureenjik: Dzk. Called Moon River because of its crescent shape. Very rare. Also Hadwinjik in Jette, earliest illicitation.

Oozhriinjik Gwits'ik: Mouth of Oozhriinjik.

Qaaktuġvik: I On maps as Barter Island. Also Łeeridiidal, Łihteeraadal in Dzk.
Qalugruaq, Qalugruak: Salmon River. In Burch as Qalugruam Kuuŋa
Qaŋmaliq: I On maps as Anaaqtuuvak River.
Qikiqpagruk/Nanjyuughat: Hershel Island
Saġvagniqtuuq: I Currently on maps as Sagavanirktok River.
Teedriinjik: Enters the Yukon River from the north in the Yukon Flats.
Teets'iinjik: "The river with many caches." Or/also "The river with many small driftwood pieces." On maps as the Hula-Hula: River going north.
Tlaa Chux No': "Big Rock Creek" Stream coming in from the North at the foot of the Yukon River Rapids.
Tleek'edetlnaa': a tributary of the Kk'otsoh No' (Buckland River) that leads to the Koyuk River and other passed to the southeast.
Trail Creek: Enters the Teedriinjik from the south.
Tozitna: Dn A north tributary to the Yukon below Tanana River entry.
Tryahtsi'nik: Neets'ąįį Estate, "Otter Tail Creek."
Tseet'o Huno', Ch'ataanjik: On maps as the Ray River.
Ts'eet'o Hutl'ot: Dn "Headwaters of Ts'eet'o' Huno'."
Ts'eeteetna: On maps as the Pah River.
Unakserok River: Eastern drainage into Aalaashuk River.
Uree Gwits'ik: Mouth of Ureenjik Dzk also Hadwinjik Gwits'ik.
Ureenjik: Dzk, Oozhriinjik. Dzk. Called Moon River because of its crescent shape. Very rare. See Hadwinjik.
Wulik River: I Kivalliñaq Estate River flowing from the east into the sea.
Yukon: Yukon River.

Lakes, Passes, Features, Mountains

Alatna Hills: To the east of Aalaashuk and north of the Koyitł'ots'ina.
Amiloyak Lake: I To the north of Agiak Lake and south of Chandler Lake.
Anaqtuuvak Pass: I Formerly Naqsraq Pass.
Cape Krusenstern: Northwest Arctic.
Delong Mountains: Mountain range to the west of the Ipnavik.
Anaqtuuvak River: I Formerly the Qaŋmaliq.
Atigun Pass: A mountain pass on the former Di'hąįį Estate.
Atłiq: I Former settlement on the middle of the Smith Lakes between the Ipnavik and Etivluk rivers. Along the southern headwaters of the Kuukpiq.
Chandler Lakes: A group of lakes at the headwaters of the Maqpik River.
Draydlaya: Chatanika River.
Endicott Mountains: Range to the north of Alatna Hills.
Gwazhał Cordillera: Brooks Range.
Igliqliqsiuġvik: An area along the middle Kobuk River.
Inyorururak Pass: Pass to the east of Itivluk Pass.
Itivluk: I Itivluk Pass On maps as Howard Pass.
Ivasaaqtignillik: I Presently Portage Creek, upper Noatak River.
Kalukruatchiak Point: I Bluff near the confluence of the Killiq and Kuukpik.
Kaŋmalik, also Qaŋmaliq: On maps as Anaktuvuk River.
Kiiñaqvak: Also Eł tseeyh no' Dn, K'iitł'uu Dzk, presently the John River.
Killiq: I Presently on maps as Killik River
K'iitł'it: Dzk 1. Headwaters of the "Birch Bark Shavings" River. Headwaters of the K'iitł'uu (also Eł tseeyh no' Dn, Kiiñaqvak I).

PLACENAMES **133**

K'iitł'it Pass: Dzk 1. "Headwaters of the Birch Bark Shavings" River. 2. Also Naqsraq in Nunamiut Iñupiaq. 3. On maps as Anaktuvuk Pass.

K'iitł'uu: Dzk 1. "Birch Bark Shavings River" Dzk, also Eł tseeyh no' Dn, Kiiñaqvak I., 2. The settlement below the mouth of the Koyitł'ots'ina and the Eł tseeyh no'. Settlement and river with the same name.

Kikitaliorak Lake: I Settlement site about 20 miles to the east of Itivlik Pass and to the southwest of Narvaŋuluk.

Kinyiksukvik Lake: I Former Nendaaghe settlement.

Kinyiksukvik Lake: Site of settlement.

Kipmuk Lake: I Site of Qupyuq settlement upper Noatak region.

Kiruqtagiak Creek: Creek that ends to the west of Little Chandler Lake. Formerly the Ayiyak/Ayayaaq River.

Kotzebue Sound: Northwestern Alaska arm of the Chukchi Sea.

Kuugruaq: Drains north into the Tagiaq. Also Vyùh K'it in Dzk. On maps as the Canning River.

Laki: An Icelandic volcano which erupted in 1783.

Łel'one: Mountain southeast of Ts'eet'o' Huno' upper regions.

Maniilaq: Upper Kobuk. Maunluk River on maps.

Maqpik River drainage: I River draining which enters the Ayiyak/Ayayaak River from the south near Tuktu Bluff. Currently Chandler River on maps.

Naqsraq: I "1. a ridge that divides watersheds of rivers; **a pass**, a valley or passage in the mountains; 2. low point of a hill; (i) to travel via the lowest point; 3. (t) to travel via its lowest point." In Sivuniŋit Dictionary. On maps as Anaqtuuvak Pass. Also Dzk K'iitł'it.

Naqsraġlugiaq: I A mountain in the middle of Naqsraq Pass. Represents the middle of the pass from whence the rivers flow in opposite directions.

Narvaŋuluk: I Former settlement site along the Aalaasuraq. Formerly the name of Etivluk Lake on maps.

Nendaaghe: Former Denaa name for the upper Noataaq.

Noochu Loghoyet: Menhti xwt'ana Lt Estate: Trading site.

Noolaaghe Doh: Kayaah: Settlement on an island. Trading site.

Norton Sound: Northwestern Alaska inlet of the Bering Sea.

Mount Papiġuq: Mountain at the headwaters of the Noatak River.

Natmaqtuġiaq, Natmaktuġiaq and Nakmaktuak: I On maps as Ambler Pass.

Nunataaq: I Upper Kobuk River peoples' name for the former Nendaaghe Estate area and the river, Noataaq, Nuataam kuuŋa.

Okokmilaga River: I River flowing from the east into the Killiq/Killik.

Old and New Rampart: HBC outposts along the Ch'oonjik.

Oolah Pass: Between the headwaters of the Ikillik River and the Koyuktuvak Creek.

Okpikruak: I River along middle Kuukpiq/Kuukpik flowing from the south.

Pupik Hills: I Hills to the west of Anigaak River.

Qaaktuġvik: Barter Island.

Qikiqpagruk: Hershel Island.

Quunġunaq: I On maps as Gull Pass in the Noatak headwaters.

St. Lawrence Island: Island in the Bering Straits.

Schwatka Mountains: Range between the upper Noatak and Kobuk rivers.

Shaktoolik: Community on coastal Norton Sound.

Shoo: Place name in the Yukon Flats, approximately 25 miles northwest of Gwichyaa Zhee.

Smith Lakes: 3 small lakes between the Ipnavik and Itivluk rivers. Middle Lake former site of Atłiq settlement.

Taah K'ehoolaanh, Taah K'ehoolaanh Dehn: Dn Presently Walker Lake in the upper Kobuk River.

Tambora: A volcano in Indonesia which erupted 1815 to 1816.

Tagaiq: I On maps as the Arctic Ocean.

Teelaii Tthal: Dzk A caribou corral on the southern shore Van K'eedii. Last owner Juuzii Tr'ootsyaa John Drit.

Teetł'it Zhee: "Drainage House," on western Canadian maps as Mcpherson.

Tigara Peninsula: I Currently on maps as Lisburne Peninsula.

Tohot'anhde: Dn On maps as Morelock Creek.

Tooloouk: I Camp or settlement below confluence of Itivluk and Kuukpik. Reshaped Denaakk'e word Too Loghe, headwaters. However, since this is at the confluence of two rivers, Too Loghyet.

Troth Yeddha': Troth Yeddha' was renamed College Hill at the University of Alaska Fairbanks. Then in 2013 College Hill was renamed Troth Yeddha', its original Lower Tanana place name. Also Tsoł Dlela'.

Troth Yeddha' Bena': Settlement at foothill of Troth Yeddha'.

Tsee Choo Ddhah: Dzk "Big Beaver Mountains." On maps as the White Mountians.

Tsee Kon' Ddhah: Name of the Tsee Choo Ddhah as they lose elevation and move further to the west. "Beaver House Mountains."

Tseet'o Dlela': Mountains to southeast of Tseet'o Huno' ending in this ridge. Continuation of Tsee Choo and Tsee Kon' Ddhah across the Yukon River. In Taghachwx Lower Tanana dialect.

Tseet'o Huno': Area of the middle and upper Tseet'o Huno', literally, "Inside the beaver house or beaver sitting in a ball" river.

Tukuto Lake: Lake between the upper Ipnavik and upper Itivluk river.

Tulugag Lake: I A lake about 5 miles north of the present community of Anaktuvuk Pass.

Uluskuk Bluff: I Bluff at the confluence of the Qaŋmaliq and Kuukpik rivers.

Van K'eedii (K'ehdii): One lake on top of another. On maps as Old John Lake.

Glossary IV
Family and Personal Names

Denaa

Aldzak: Aldzak Kkohkkee. Nendaaghe Kkohkkee, husband of Tł'eevih and Deedzii, father of Dik Sarah, Shiizin. Nachats'an Jessie Aldzak, and Mary Aldzak Khyahtthoo. Aldzak may mean to "fasten with nail or peg." In J. Jette, "proper to extreme upper dialect." Also "One who grabs ahold and sees things through to the end, persistent pursuit of his/her goal."

Anaraaq, Anaraak: Personal name of the Upper Kobuk region and Anaraaq Anaraak Fred Ozhriikaii of the Khyahtthoo extended family. A very old name with no known translation in Iñupiaq. Orzhriikaii, "a name that was left as a gift from those passed on."

Ch'idził Koxki: Eastern Taghachwx Lower Tanana leader who lived between K'iidootin and Teedriinjik along the Yukon River at the mouth of the Hadwinjik.

Chief Henry: Denaa elder.

Ch'ooghwałzhii: In McDonald Choowhulhzi 1867 (RMc) Too Tleekk'e elder who came into Neets'ąįį county to trade. May have been a Koxki.

Chukasi, George: Brother of Doyuk Alexander and Thomas Teegoogeetsii.

Doyuk K'eeldzeettl Alexander: Brother of George Chukasi and Thomas Teegoogeetsii.

Eliza Jones: Denaakk'e linguist, researcher, ethnogeographer, ethnohistorian, Denaa elder.

Ella or Aalaa: Men's name. Ella Frank Drit, Ella Joseph Kellum Khyahtthoo. This is a name that originates in the Northern Denaa estates of Nendaaghe and Saaqił Estates, as in Aalaasurauq, Aalaashuk, and Aalaasuk.

Gookąąhtii Koxki: Western Taghachwx Lower Tanana koxki. Raised on the Di'hąįį Estate by his father Drit II.

Hester John Evan: Oral historian and story teller from Nenena, Alaska.

Hirshi: Captured Too Loghe woman at Naqsraq.

Juuzii: Men's name Juuzii John Tr'ootsyaa Drit. Not translated. Man's name of Dį'hąįį or Nendaaghe origin.

K'etłts'en' : "Sideways or to the side." Hannah K'etłts'en' Seenaaneeyo. In the Rosenberg photograph collection, UAF Archives.

Sahtaii: (Sa'taii or Shaht'aii) A Too Tleekk'e youth in McDonald visit to Neets'ąįį in 1867. If spoken in Dzk his name could mean, Sa'taii, "star trail," or Shahtaii, "Strong as me."

Senito: Of the Ts'eeteetna' group of former Saaqił Estate who moved to an area along the Yukon River later called Kokrines. Father-in-law of Alfred Mayo, trader. Witness to the death of Father Seghar, 1886.

Shiizin Aldzak: Nendaaghe. Only son of Aldzak, husband of Susan Drit, father of Ch'ataiigwatrat Myra John Aldzak Tizyaa Kakavihchik. A Denaakk'e personal name. If pronounced in Dzk would mean. "My breath, my soul."

Shiizin Gehikti': Nendaaghe. Only son of Gehikti' and Gehik Vihn.

Senaaneeyo William: which means, "he followed me," and possibly "he followed me (across)." In Jette, possibly Tsenani'o, might be "he brought something out." Too Loghe. Husband of Hannah K'etłts'en' Senaaneeyo Senaaneeyo. Parents of Lilly Senaaneeyo Pitka, Divaadido Joseph William Senaaneeyo, and Ellen Bets'e tl'ee Doh Daa Dleno (advice giver) ej/sp Senaaneeyo Moses Naqasudne Dech'oyeełno. Senaaneeyo, "He followed me."

Tajutsik, Tullik, and Qawatik: Three Too Loghe involved in battle at Naqsraq. As per Panniaq.

Tema'anyułta: Charlie "Kali" Tema'anyułta aka Isaac **Yerontoradił'o**. Translator and placename expert hired by Jules Jette in 1904. Named all the hydronyms on the Taghachwx Estate.

Viłiiyił'yo': Too Loghe. William, Beaver Creek William, Husband of Khagooheenjik Nich'it gwileii Agnes Hashinlai', father of Kenneth, Edmond, Agnes, William, Belle and Ellen. Viłiiyił'yo' means something like, "Ho! What is that?'

Yerontoradił'o: Isaac Yerontoradił'o aka Charlie **Tema'anyułta**. His stepdaughter was Jennie Isaac. Also known as Old Isaac. May be important in other stories about "Old Isaac." His stepdaughter may have married up the Koyitł'ots'ina and he was known to have traded at Tanana.

Yeyelthudodolno Eva Jack: Adopted Little Beatus and Kathleen, Nedo'edaadle', maternal grandmother of Yerełno Sam Joseph.

Group Too Loghe names: Qawatik, Tajutsik, Tullik, Doyuk, K'eeldzeettl, Shaht'aii, Ch'ooghwałzhii, Senaaneeyo', and Viłiiyiłyo'.

Dinjii Zhuh

Adaa vitsii Ahaa Anna Joseph Vahan Ko'nii'ak Drit: Di'hajj daughter of Nitch'it Trooni and Ko'nii'ak, married to Dritzhuu Edoor Edward Drit. Mother of Joseph, George, Herbert/Albert, Rachel, Mary, Lucy, and Myra.

Anaraaq, Anaraak: Personal name of the Upper Kobuk region and Anaraaq Anaraak Fred Ozhriikaii of the Khyahtthoo extended family. A very old name with no known translation in Iñupiaq. Orzhriikaii, "A name that was left as a gift from those passed on."

Ch'adzahti': Gok'eech'ahtthaii Gook'ahtthak Kookathak John Ch'adzahti' Tanacross refugee, Gook'eech'ahtthaii, "He went after them with an adze, knife or spear with the intention to mortally wound." Gook'ahtthak, "He clubbed them soundly." Kookathak, HBC spelling.

Ch'idii: Mary Ch'idii Khyahtthoo Dzeegwaajyaa Ko'nii'ak. The last known child and daughter of Khyahtthoo John. Wife of Jospeh Dzeegwaajyaa, and then wife of Vindeegwiizhii John Ko'nii'ak. Ch'idii means, "Something left over." As the last child and a girl, she ate the left-overs.

Ch'eeghwałti': Thomas Khehkwaii Vuntut. Raised by Dahjalti'.

Ch'idził Koxki: Baptized Archibald Garrett by McDonald. Also Archie, Argee, White Eye, Ch'indee K'aa. Taghachwx xwt'ana Koxki. Ch'idził, meaning "an ice crystal".

An ice crystal hit his eye during a snow storm and his iris became white. Ch'indee K'aa, "gray white eye."

Ch'igiioonta': Nendaaghe Denaa, first husband of Dik Sarah Aldzak, father of Deeghozhraii Vatr'oogwiltsii John Ch'igiioonta'. Chiigii oonta', "he/she holds a child," also "he/she holds an unborn calf (for the elders to eat)." The underlying meaning of the name means that he was such an exceptional provider that he brought this food meat for the elders, because having less or no teeth they were able to eat this meat easily. This name is two words that have been contracted.

Ch'igoozhrii, Moses: An original Neetsąįį resident who imparted Dinjii Zhuh K'yaa place names of the upper Sheenjik/Khiinjik. Later Vuntut Estate resident. First wife Elizabeth Shaaveezhraa mother of Enoch, William, Peris, Peter, Myra, and Hannah. 2nd wife Caroline Joseph Saityen.

Ch'igwihch'in Lucy Geh'ikti' Drit: Daughter of Geh'ik Vihn and Geh'ikti', wife of Drizhuu Frank Fraum Drit.

Ch'ijinjaa John Di'ch'i' Zhyaa Shit'iigwiłtthat: Son of Neeshih, nephew of Shit'iigwiłtthat Simon.

Ch'iji'oonta' William: Dzk Brother of Drit II, paternal uncle of Ditsiigiitł'uu Drit Khehkwaii. Ch'iji'oonta', 'he/she is holding (an animal's) antlers."

Ch'ik'i'tsoo vahan Ch'igiioonta': 1st wife of Deeghoozhraii John Vatrogwiltsii Chi'giioonta'. Died in an epidemic that took her and her small daughter, Ch'ik'i'tsoo. Ch'ik'i'tsoo "fair hair" (hair with light brown highlights.) She was the sister to Doyuk Old Alexander, George Chukasi and Thomas Teegoogiitsii.

Ch'ik'i'tthankal Khyahtthoo, Adam: Ch'ik'i'tthankal, bald head. Older Khyahtthoo family member. In McDonald as Tshitshikul.

Ch'indeeghoo Vatroogwilts'ii John Ch'igiioonta': Ch'indeeghoo, "Round eyes." Vatroogwiltsi'ii, "He has a large nape of the neck."

Ch'itłee Khai' William Sasa Saityen Shuman: Son of Andrew Saityen and Emma Peter Gwats'oo. Married to Salina, Maggie, and Fannie. Ch'itłee Khai' is the skin and fur around the knee cap of the caribou, a very tough hide.

Ch'iyikgwatthah Mary Ch'iji'oonta'Vitsiik'iitł'aa Ch'igiioonta': Ch'iyikgwatthah: a very vocal person, garrulous, talkative, literally, "a hot mouth."

Vitsiik'iitł'aa: 'her grandfather is from K'iitł'aa.' This word is the way an HBC employee heard the word and wrote it down. Probably K'iitł'uu, unless that is in Di'haįį dialect.

Daanitysaa: Oldest daughter of Dahjalti', possibly adopted. Uncertain, may be Maria Ch'iji'oonta', the wife of William Ch'iji'oonta'.

Dahjal: The first-born son of Dahjalti'.

Dahjalti': Dahjalti' Khehkwaii of Dagoo and Neets'ąįį Estates. Also Shininduu K'eezhiizhal. Shininduu "Ashes on my face." K'eezhiizhal "He walks and breathes expanded awareness and presence into every step." The father of Dahjal, Deenaatsyaa f., Treenahtsyaa Ellen Dahjalti' Shit'iigwiłtthat, and Shohtsal John Dahjalti'. Possibly an uncle of Eliza Dahjalti' Ch'iji'oonta', but was raised in his household.

Deedzii: Second co-wife of Aldzak, mother of Nachats'an Jessie Aldzak and Mary Aldzak. Also Deedzii Alice Khyahtthoo. Two different people. Di'haįį dialect, possibly "One who fleshes skin." Deedzii Aldzak was older of the two. Possible translations of original Denaakk'e names.

Deeghoozhraii Ch'indeeghoo John Vatr'ogwiltsii Ch'igiioonta': The only surviving child of Ch'igiioonta' and Dik Sarah Aldzak. Di'haii. Deeghoozhraa, "Dark round eyes," Vatr'ogwiltsii, "Big nape of the neck." Some men were known as bear hunters. Deeghoozhraii was one of them. Later perhaps due to injury he became a fisherman, always had fish.

Deets'i' Khagooheenjik: Nendaaghe hut'aane. Younger brother of Khagooheenjikti', husband of Ditsiigiitł'uu Drit's younger sister. Father of his only child, Leviti' John Khagoohenjikti'. Deets'i', no one had a direct translation for his name. May be a cryptic reference to the tail of *Yahdii*, the celestial shamanic guide for all Dinjii Zhuh. Vits'i', the tail of Yahdii, the Big Dipper.

Dhindeegwaazhii Thomas Khyahtthoo: Nendaaghe, Draanjik, died 1913 ECR. The brother of Vits'ii'ik, Vi'iitr'ik Wilson. Known to McDonald as Thomas Black. The third husband of Ilikaq Lucy Shigyaa Tr'oonii Saityen and raised Lucy's granddaughter, Soozun Dahjalti'. 2nd wife Eliza.

Dik: "On the edge," also "Along the border." Dik Sarah Aldzak Ch'igiioonta' Drit also Sarah Shaaghan Dik. A renowned oral historian and transmitter of legends. In dialect variant, Ndik.

Dinjiitil David Di'chi' Choo Dzeegwaajyaa: Nendaaghe, oldest of 3 orphaned brothers taken in by Dahjalti', married to unknown woman, father of Nideech'i' Solomon and Dinjiitil Simon Dzeegwaajyaa.

Dinjiitil Simon Alvee Zee Khii Choo Salmon Dzeegwaajyaa: The brother of Nideech'i' Solomon Dzeegwaajyaa. Father of William Salmon Dzeegwaajyaa and Eliza Dzeegwaajyaa Drit Khyahtthoo.

Dinjii Ts'ik Shajol Peter John Ch'igiioonta': The father of Stephen Peter Ch'igiioonata'. Husband of Soozun John Dahjalti'. Dinjii Ts'ik, "thin man", Shajol, "my staff." Named after a powerful dinjii dazhan named Dinjii Ts'ik who lived on the Saakił Estate of the upper Kobuk River.

Ditsiigiitł'uu Drit: Di'haii. Son of Drit II, nephew of Ch'iji'oonta' William, second husband of Ilikuq Lucy Saityen, Nachats'an Jessie Aldzak Saityen, Dik Sarah Aldzak, Shiiłiiteerahdyaa Gehik, and Neeshih. First husband of Njaandii. Ditsiigiitł'uu, "Named after his grandfather or father. Drit, "fast adroit."

Drit II: Di'haii. Brother of Ch'iji'oonta' William, father or stepfather of Gookąąhtii Koxki and father of Ditsiigiitł'uu Drit Khehkwaii.

Drits'ik Mary Drit: Di'haii. The daughter of Nachats'an NahtthaiiJessie Aldzak and Ditsiigiitł'uu. Drits'ik, akin to "Her father's (Drit) rib," or "A sliver of her father's heart."

Dritzhuu Edoor Edward Drit: Di'haii, Neets'aii. The son of Sarah Shaaghan Dik and Ditsiigiitł'uu Drit Khehkwaii. Husband of Adaa vitsii ahaa Anna Ko'nii'ak Drit. Father of Joseph, George, Herbert/Albert, Rachel, Mary, Lucy, Myra. Dritzhuu, "Child of Drit."

Drizhuu Frank Fraum Drit: Younger brother of Dritzhuu Edoor Drit. Same mother, same father.

Dzeegwaajyaati': Nendaaghe hut'aane: Father of Dzeegwaajyaa, Ko'ehdan, a younger brother, Dinjiitil David, Ndik, and Dinjiinindal Joseph Dzeegwaajyaati'.

Elizabeth Shaaveezhraa Moses Ch'igoozhrii: Draanjik, sister of Thomas Shaaveezhraa, 1st wife of Moses Ch'igoozhrii, mother of Enoch, William, Peris, Peter, Myra, and Hannah.

Emma Peter Gwatsoo Etchit: Draanjik. The daughter of Peter Gwats'oo, mother of Ch'itłee Khai' William Sasa' Joseph Shuman Saityen, with Andrew Gaashiik'yuu Saityen.

Gaashiik'yuu Andrew Saityen: Nendaaghe, Neets'ąįį. The son of Ilikuq Lucy and Saityen. Father of William Sasa' Shuman with Emma Gwats'oo Etchit, and Phoebe Andrew Saityen Stevens, and Sarah Ghoo Andrew Peter Saityen Drit with his first wife (name unknown). Gashiik'yuu means "He snowshoed in spite of adversity." Raised his maternal two youngest siblings, Joseph Vahan Drit and Silas Drit, the children of Ditsiigiitł'uu Drit.

Geh'ik, Geh'ik Vihn, Geh'ikti: Nendaaghe family who became refugees. Geh'ik, "Rabbit coat." Geh'ik Vihn, "The mother of rabbit coat." Geh'ikti', "The father of rabbit coat."

Goghwaii and brother: The adopted sons of Dahjalti'. Warriors.

Gookąąhtii Drit Koxki: Taghachwx xwt'ana koxki near Tseet'o Huno', a brother or half/brother of Ditsiigiitł'uu Drit Khehkwaii. Gookąąhtii, "The uncle who watches over them."

Gok'eech'ahtthaii Gook'ahtthak Kookathak John Ch'adzahtì': Tanacross refugee, Gook'eech'ahtthaii, "He went after them with an adze, knife or spear with the intention to mortally wound." Gook'ahtthak, "He clubbed them soundly," or "He beat them soundly in a wrestling move." Kookathak, Rmd and HBC spelling.

Gozhizhi Joseph Tsal Dzeegwaajyaa: Neets'ąįį, Vuntut, son of Ndik and Joseph Vahan Dzeegwaajyaa.

Gwah'aii John Drit: Di'hąįį. The son of Nachats'an Aldzak and Ditsiigiitł'uu. Husband of Nitch'it Lal Mary. Gwah'aii means "Near," and "On the side."

Gwahtłaati': Extended Khyahtthoo family, the son or grandson of Ch'aa Alexander Khyahtthoo. Gwahtł'aa means "Something ill fitting." May also have other meanings. Unknown.

Gwii'ee'chit Dray Chiito' Draichiiatat John Hardisty Shahnyaati': Tanacross refugee. Gwii'ee'chit, "He was thrown towards us." Deenduu khaihkwaii. Draychiito', "Man who made treaty at Draydlaya Chaget," among the Menhti Lower Tanana. Shahnyaati', 'The father of Shahnyaa ,'' a first born son. See also Shahnyaati'. Shahnyaa means "He says to me," or "He told me."

Gwitee'aa Henry Khyahtthoo: son of Gwizhoo Frizzy James William Hardisty Khyahtthoo. First wife, Jane Roderick Khyahtthoo, and later Maria Henry Gwats'oo. He had two children (Paul and Sarah) with Jane Roderick Khyahtthoo, and none with Maria Henry Gwats'oo. Maria had all her children with first husband Thomas, and then one with her second husband also named Henry.

Gwizhoo Frizzy James William Hardisty Khyahtthoo: Nendaaghe, Too Loghe, Neets'ąįį. The son of Khyahtthoo John's brother, mother unknown. Husband of Jane, family unknown and Ann, family unknown. Father of Beatrice and Zeh Gwitee'aa Henry Khyahtthoo, who was adopted by his Uncle Deek'an.

Hareedzee Joseph "Joe #6" Khagooheenjikti': Informant for Robert McKennan and Frederick Hadleigh-West. Nephew of Deets'i' Khagooheenjikti'. The son of Khagooheenjik Vihn and Khagooheenjikti'. The brother of Khagooheenjik Nich'it Gwilęįį Agnes Hashinłąį' Viłiiyiłyo' and 1st cousin of John Leviti' Khagooheenjikti' who was raised in the same household.

Herbert: Nendaaghe hut'aane, Extended Khyahtthoo group. HBC porter, student of Reverand Robert McDonald, Lived at Teetł'it Zhee, later in Dawson, Yukon Territory of Canada, then returned with his family to the Draanjik Estate.

Herbert Halvir Ginkhii Albert Tritt Drit: Neets'ąįį. The son of Ann Ko'nii'ak and Dritzhuu Edward Edoor Drit. First wife Laura John Vindeegwinzhii and 2 children, who died in an epidemic. Second wife Sarah Ghoo Saityen. Father of Isaac, Martha, Paul, Abel, and George. "Halvir," an attempt to say Herbert, Ginkhii, "Preacher."

Ilikuk, Ilikuq: Ilikuq Lucy Saityen Shijuu tr'oonii Drit Shigyaa tr'oonii Khyahtthoo. A co-wife of Saityen, a co-wife of Ditsiigiitł'uu Drit, and wife of Thomas "Blind Thomas," Khyahtthoo. Mother of Neeshooch'it John Saityen, Shovat t'oo Tsinehvee Gamen Robert Drit, Juuzii John Tr'ootsyaa Drit, and Shaanaavee vahan Drit Dahjalti'. Shijuu tr'oonii, "We regard her as our little sister." Or "I have no younger sisters." Shigyaa tr'oonii, "I ran out of snares (to catch a man)."

Isaac Tritt Drit: Great grandson of Ditsiigiitł'uu Drit Khehkwaii. Neets'ąįį gwich'in.

Its'oo Roderick Khyahtthoo: See Vihts'oo Roderick Khyahtthoo.

Joseph Dzeegwaajyaa: Nendaaghe. Youngest of 3 brothers adopted by Dahjalti', first husband of Mary Ch'idii Khyahtthoo. Father of Laura, Albert and Charlie.

Johnny Frank Drit: Neets'ąįį. Son of Ch'igwihch'in Lucy Gehikti' and Drizhuu Fraum Frank Drit, husband of Sarah John Ko'nii'ak. A renowned storyteller and oral historian.

Juuzii John Tr'ootsyaa Drit Khehkwaii: Di'hąįį and Neets'ąįį. The son of Ilikuq Lucy Saityen Shijuu Tr'oonii Drit and Ditsiigiitł'uu Drit Khehkwaii. Raised on the Di'hąįį Estate. Moved to the Neets'ąįį Estate circa 1856. His mother married Vindeegwaazhii Thomas Khyahtthoo and the family relocated to Neets'ąįį Estate. Operated Teeląįį Tthal on shores of Van K'ehdii. Juuzii, untranslated Dn name, Tr'ootsyaa unknown translation. Last owner of Tee Ląįį Tthal. Husband of Mary. Father of Joseph Juuzhar, Susan Aldzak, Harriet Stewart, John, Peter, and David Itrik.

K'aiiheenjik Khehkai': Famous Eastern Gwich'in Nations community leader. The man who raised Dahjalti' Khehkwaii.

Katherine Joseph Senaaneeyo Peter Ch'igiioonta': Linguist, translator, author, and historian. Daughter of Annie Viłiiyiłyo' and Davaadido' Joseph William Senaaneeyo.

Khagooheenjik: Khagooheenjik Nitch'it gwileii Hashinlaii' Agnes William Viłiiyil'yo'. Daughter of Khagooheenjikti' and Khagooheenjik Vihn, mother of Kenneth, Edmund, Ann, Belle, William, and Ellen. Khagooheenjik means "The child was delivered breech." Nich'it gwileii means "She lost her mother as a young girl," and Hashinlai' means "I flowed down the river with them." In Denaakk'e as Hishinlai'.

Khagooheenjikti': Father of Khagooheenjik and Joseph Marcel Joe #6. Uncle and stepfather of nephew John Leviti'. Nendaaghe Denaa, Neets'ąįį.

Khaiidhiiluu: An Umialik near the Nendaaghe region. In the Tł'eevihti' story.

Khii Choo: Iqaluġruaqpak I Dzk translation of Iñupiat personal name meaning "big fall silver and/or chum salmon." Upper Noatak River.

Khii Choo Simon John Dinjiitil Nilthaati' Adzee Alvee Salmon Dzeegwaajyaa: Khii Choo, fall silver or chum salmon, Nilthaati', father of Nilthaa his oldest child, of the Dzeegwaajyaa family line. In the early days people were often baptized twice, either by different preachers and/or their understanding of the ceremony was not clear. The family surname became Salmon. This man was a HBC porter along with his older brother Solomon Nideech'i' Dzeegwaajyaa. Possibly circa 1865.

Khyahtthoo Kkohkkee: John Teetsii Tsik. Nendaaghe hut'aane Denaa, head of Khyahtthoo extended family who ended up in the Shiinjik River valley by 1848 as the main meat and caribou skin providers for the Hudson's Bay Company in Gwichyaa Zhee. Khyahtthoo, "Bear trap."

Kǫ'ehdan Dzeegwaajyaa: Nendaaghe hut'aane Denaa with a Dzk personal name. In the Kǫ'ehdan Story, Chapter 3. Son of Dzeegwaajyaa, older brother or half brother of Dinjiitil David Di'chi' Choo Dzeegwaajyaa.

Kwatlatyi, Netro, Josie (an attempt at Juuzii), Kakavihchik, Kendi: Eastern Gwich'in Nation surnames.

Łihteerąhdyaa Gehik Dzeegwaajyaa Shiłihteerąhdyaa Drit: "One whom we take back and forth," a Nendaaghe hut'aane Denaa woman who was first wife of Kǫ'ehdan; abducted and recaptured and then co-wife of Ditsiigitł'uu Drit Khehkwaii. Drit renamed her Shiłihteerąhdyaa which means "My one whom we take back and forth." Daughter of Gehikvihn and Gehikti'.

Lucy Viłiiyił'o' Ch'igiioonta' Ch'adzah: Too Loghe, Di'haii, and Draanjik daughter of Maria Viłiiyił'o' and unknown first husband. Co-wife of Deeghoozhraii Vatro'gwilts'ii Chigiioonta. Only surviving child, Alice Ch'igiioonta' Ch'ijihnah'in.

Maggie William Ch'iji'oonta' Ch'igiioonta' Gilbert: Neets'aii oral historian. Wife of Titus Peter Ch'igiioonta' and then James Gilbert.

Nach'aatsan: Nach'aatsan Natthaii Jessie Saityen Drit, a daughter of Aldzak and Deedzii Nach'aatsan Vahan. First wife of Saityen, co-wife of Drit Distiigitł'uu. Mother of Gaashiik'yuu Andreww Saityen, John Gwahaii Drit, Bella Ditr'ik Drit Chadzahti', Mary Drit, Joseph Vahan Drit and Silas Drit.

Ndik Tinjiitil Dinjiinindal Dzeegwaajyaa: Nendaaghe. One of 3 brothers adopted by Dahjalti'. Husband of Joseph Vahan Drit, father of Joseph Tsal Dzeegwaajyaa

Neeshih: The sister or cousin of Shitiigwiłtthat Simon and mother of Ch'ijinjyaa John Di'chi' Zhyaa. Neeshih, "She walks."

Neeshooch'it John Saityen: Written in Albert Tritt Journal as Neetthoochit, (something akin to having your ass beaten), by Stephen Tsee Gho' as Neeshooch'it (in wrestling to be thrown to the ground) literally "he threw me to the ground." This is in the Di'haii dialect, modern spelling would be Neeshook'it. Said by Trimble Gilbert 2022 as Neeshoogit, literally "he stabbed me." Because the two older versions of the name are consistent, I am staying with that spelling and interpretation.

Nideech'i' Solomon Dzeegwaajyaa: Neets'aii, son of Dinjiitil David Dzeegwaajyaa. Husband to Belle and Ch'itchyaazhuu Elizabeth, co-wives. Father of Ginnis, Peter, Sophie, Myra, Paul, and Maggie.

Nitch'it Tr'oonii Ko'nii'ak: Nendaaghe, Di'haii Wife of Ko'nii'ak. Nich'it Tr'oonii, "Last girl in the family." Mother of Vats'acharahthan Thomas, Vitsiideeyuunyaa (a son), Vindeegwiizhii John, Ann Vitsii Ahaa, and Louise.

Nitsih ghaih gaii Louise Ko'nii'ak: Di'haii, Neets'aii daughter of Nitch'it Tr'oonii and Ko'nii'ak. Wife of Oozhriikaii, Fred Anaaraq, Nendaaghe, Too Loghe, Neets'aii. Mother of Deetreech'yaa Simon, Deetreezhuu Robert, Daniel/Donald, (Vuntut) Enoch, Ellen, Mary Dzan, Lucy Esau Crow, Jimmy, Zhoh Gwats'an John.

Olti': Father of Ool, regional headman who was killed by his nephews.

Ooluu and Olim: Dzk Attempt to say William.

Oozhriikaii Fred Anaaraq Khyahtthoo: Nendaaghe, Too Loghe, Neets'aii Khyahtthoo extended family. Husband of Nitsih ghaih gaii Louise Ko'nii'ak. Father of Deetreech'yaa Simon, Deetreezhuu Robert, Daniel/Donald,(Vuntut) Enoch, Ellen, Mary Dzan, Lucy Esau Crow, Jimmy, Zhoh

Gwats'an John. "The last of those from the Moon River."

Peter Kaii: Maybe William as surname. Kaii; "The last of his family left to us."

Phoebe Bebe Andrew Saityen Steven: Daughter of Gaashiik'yuu Andrew Saityen and wife of Little Steven from Eagle, Alaska. Mother of Sarah Stevens Malcolm.

Robert John Ch'igiioonta': Younger brother of Dinjii Ts'ik Shajol Peter John Ch'igiioonta'. Photographs in Frank Schrader USG report.

Saityen, Saityet, Sannik, Satnik, Sayyen: No translation. Well known Nendaaghe Hut'aane Denaa Kkohkee and warrior. Well known from Iñupiaq story tellers throughout the Northwest Arctic. Possibly "blade," "sai'ye," or "knife," or "tsaaye." In Denaa, possibly "rock meat cache" in upper Kobuk Iñupiaq dialect. Circa 1820–1838/42. Husband Nachaats'an Jessie Naathaii Aldzak Drit and father of Andrew Gaashiik'yuu Saityen. Husband of Ilikuq Lucy Saityen and father of Neeshooch'it John Saityen.

Sarah Etchit Shaaveezhraa: Dzk Draanjik gwich'in. Daughter of Chutugti' Khaihkwaii and un-named unknown mother. Sister of Black River Charlie Chutug and John Shuman Etchit. Second wife of Joseph Shaaveezhraa. Mother of Ellen, and stepmother of Ch'itł'ee Khaii William Sasa' Shuman Saityen, the first born son of Emma Gwats'oo Etchit, the first wife of John Shuman Etchit.

Sarah Ghoo Saityen Tritt Drit: Dzk Daughter of Gaashiik'yuu Andrew Saityen and unknown/not named mother. Wife of Herbert Albert Tritt Drit. Mother of Isaac, Martha, Paul, Abel, and George. Raised Olim William Tritt.

Shaaghan Dik, Sarah Aldzak: Dzk. Dik Sarah Aldzak Nendaaghe. Daughter of Aldzak and Tł'eevih. Oral historian and genealogist. Wife of Ch'igiioonta' and Drit. Mother of Deeghoozhraii Vatroogwiltsii John Ch'igiioonta', Edoor Edward Dritzhuu Drit, and Fromm Frank Drizhuu Drit. Circa 1820 to circa 1900. Possibly adopted Mary.

Shaanaavee Alice Dahjalti' Peter: "Things are hazy for me." She was extremely near sighted. Daughter of Shaanaavee vahan and Shohtsal John Dahjalti'. Wife of Peter. Mother of Lucy, Sarah, and Eva.

Shaanaavee vahan Drit Dahjalti': Only daughter of Ilikuq Lucy Saityen and Drit Khehkwaii, wife of Shohtsal John Dahjalti', mother of Alice, Soozun, and Jilzhit Julius John Dahjalti'.

Shahnyaati', Gwi'eech'it: Baptized as John Hardisty. Tanacross refugee, Deenduu khaihkwaii. Also Dray Chiito' and Draichiiatat, "The man who made treaty at Draydlaya Chaget" among the Menhti Lower Tanana.

Shajol:l See Dinjii Ts'ik .

Saveah Khaihkwaii: Also Shreeveeyaa. An older cousin of Shahnyaati' who became Khaihkwaii in the area of Shoo, about 25 miles Northwest of Gwichyaa Zhee.

Shaaveezhraa Thomas: In Mcdonald as Suvera, Chivera, and Siverzya. Brother of Elizabeth Shaaveezhraa Moses Ch'igoozhrii and half-sister Ellen. Known as Blind Thomas in Episcopal Church Records, died 1913. Married to Sarah Ellen Saityen.

Shininduu: Childhood name of K'eezhiizhal Dahjalti' Khehkwaii

Shiizin Joseph Aldzak: The son of Tł'eevih and Aldzak, only brother of Sarah Aldzak with the same mother. Husband of Susan Tr'ootsyaa Drit and father of Ch'ataiigwatrat Myra Aldzak John Tizya Kakyvihchik, an only child.

Shit'iigwiłtthat Simon Deets'at L'original Laryil Ralyil: Nendaaghe, Neets'ąįį: Shit'iigwiłtthat, 'Someone hit me in the back,' Deets'at: hunched over, L'original a name given him by (probably) Antoine Hoole of the HBC. Ralyil: an attempt by Dzk speaker to say L'original. Also Laryil.

Shoh Tsal John Dahjalti': Only surviving biological son of Dahjalti' Khehwaii, husband of Shaanaavee Vahan Drit, father of Shaanaavee Alice Dahjalti' Peter, Soozun Dahjalti' Ch'igiioonta', and Julius Jilzhit John Dahjalti'.

Silas Drit: Di'hąįį. The son of Nachats'an Aldzak and Ditsiigiitł'uu. Husband of Eliza Dzeegwaajyaa Drit.

Simple: Semple family: Extended Khyahtthoo family.

Soozun John Dahjalti' Peter Ch'igiioonta': Neets'ąįį genealogist, oral historian, and prayer healer. Circa 1877–1949

Shovat t'oo Tsinehvee Gamen Robert Drit: First child of Ilikuq Lucy Saityen and Distriigiitł'uu Drit Khehkwaii. Husband of Annie Dazhyaa, Tanacross. Father of Jonas, Ned, Julia, James, Andrew, and Zakius. Shovat t'oo, was curled up in a black bear skin, Tsinehvee, he escaped a terrible occurrence (epidemic), Gamen, unknown translation.

Stephen Tsee Gho' Tsyaa Tsal Peter Ch'igiioonta': Dzk Neets'ąįį genealogist, oral historian, and prayer healer. 1906–1997

T'ąąval Henry William Saityen: The grandson of Andrew Saityen, husband of Jennie Thomas Shaaveezhraa William Saityen, father of Albert, Thomas, Charlotte, John, and, Ellen.

Tatlik: Kkaayah hut'aane guide for Zagoskin.

Teech'i'tsoo Vich'i'nintaii Gwalul Stronghead Joseph Khyahtthoo: Nephew of Teetsii Tsik John Khyahtthoo. Name of father and mother unknown. Husband of co-wives Christina, Mary Ch'iji'oonta', Ann widow of older brother, Katherine John Ch'adzah, and Laura Shit'eegwiłtthat Ch'iji'oonta. Father of Galuke Calib Calif Joseph Kellum (one person), Andrew Joseph Khyahtthoo, Saa Emma Joseph McDonald Felix, and Myra Joseph David Kaii Adams

Teegoogeetsii Thomas: Brother of Doyuk Alexander and George Chukasi. Teegoogeetsii, "they are housed here and there."

Teetsii Tsik John Khyahtthoo: (Dzk) Also Khyahtthoo Kkohkee (Dn): Teetsii Tsik is a personal name which means, "A skinny Tl'eeyegge hut'aane person," or "a skinny twig in the pile of river driftwood." He lived up the Dizeènjik.

Tsiiteelyaa Isaac: Nendaaghe Extended Khyahtthoo family. Tsiiteelyaa was a porter. He portaged for the HBC very early on. Tsiiteelyaa, literally, "he/she takes things from one storage place to another."

Tł'eevih: A small alpine stream fish that clings to rocks. The name is given for the tenacity of the individual. The only known daughter of Tł'eevih vihn and Tł'eevihti', first co-wife of Aldzak. Mother of Dik Sarah Aldzak and Shiizin Joseph Aldzak, and perhaps unknown others.

Tł'eevihti': Dzk Father of Tł'eevih, Nendaaghe female warrior.

Tł'eevih vihn: Dzk The mother of Tł'eevih, Nendaaghe hut'aane female warrior.

Toh Val'i' Gehik: Nendaaghe, Di'hąįį: daughter of Gehik vahan and Gehikti', wife of Vindeegwizhii Ko'nii'ak. Mother of Phillip, Laura and Lucy.

Treenahtsyaa Ellen Dahjalti' Shiteegwiłtthat: Daughter of Dahjalti' Khehkwaii.

Tsee Gho': Beaver Teeth. Tsee Gho' Tsyaa Tsal Stephen Peter Ch'igiioonta'.

Tsyaa Tsal: Young boy. Tsee Gho' Tsyaa Tsal Stephen Peter Ch'igiioonta'.

Vats'ach'arahthan Vats'at Ch'araathan Vit'ishitr'ijahthan Thomas Ko'nii'ak: Nendaaghe, Di'hąįį, Teetł'it. A porter for the HBC. Settled in Teetł'it Zhee adopted the surname Thompson and Thomas. Father of Peter Thomas and others.

Vats'ahch'arahthan: "We leave things to his good judgment."

Vihts'ooik Teeki'oonjik Roderick Khyahtthoo: in census as Itsoo. Because the snow owl is viewed as a powerful messenger and strongly associated with shamanic arts his name was changed to Itsoo, a cryptic reference to the snow owl. Vihts'ooik, "Snow owl robe." Teeki'oonjik, "The one among them who got an arrow."

Vindeegwiizhii John Ko'nii'ak: Nendaaghe, Di'hąįį Younger brother of Vats'ahch'arahthan and Vitsii Deeyuunyaa. Vindeegwiizhii, 'he has intelligent eyes, or his eyes are moving.' Husband of Toh Val'i' Gehik and later Mary Ch'idii Khyahtthoo. Father of Phillip, Laura, Lucy, James, Sarah, Peter, and Christian.

Virginia Jean Barber Flett Ch'igiioonta': Widow of first husband Robert Flett, mother of Jacob Dzeegwat Flitt. Second husband, Robert John Ch'igiioonta', none of their children survived into adulthood.

Vitsii Deeyuunyaa Ko'nii'ak: Younger brother of Vats'ahch'arahthan.

Vitsii Deeyuunyaa, "Follows his grandfather's example and advice."

Vitsii'ik, Vi'iitr'ik Wilson: Nendaaghe, Neets'ąįį Extended Khyahtthoo family. Brother of Thomas Dhindeegwaazhii Married to Deedzii Alice. Father of Natthal William Vi'iitr'ik, Jinjyah, Christina and possibly Andrew who married into the Vitrekwa family.

William Sasa' Ch'itłee Khai'Saityen Shuman: son of Andrew Saityen and Emma Gwats'oo. Raised by Thomas Shaaveezhraa and Sarah Etchit. His adopted uncle was John Shuman Etchit. He took his surname. Also Ch'itłee Khai'. Surname William.

Iñupiat

Aakałukpak: Akuniġmiut warrior from the middle Kobuk region. Saityen story.

Aguaqutsit, Amoquiq, Aanaŋuluk, Angukak, Aqsiataujaq, Ilawaguluk, Kaunulak, Kiatsaun, Makkalik, Pamiulak, Suvlu, Tatpana, Ula, and Ularjuaq: a group of Nunamiut men involved in the final expulsion from Naqsraq. Recounted by Panniaq.

Anaraaq, Anaraak: Personal name of the Upper Kobuk region. A very old name with no known translation.

Asatchaq Jimmy Kiḷigvak: The last Iñupiat shamanic practices informant of Tigara, an oral historian, relayed the story of pre-contact practices of whaling rites among the Tikiġaġmiut, cultural guardian. 1891–1980

Ilikuk: A relative of Panniaq.

Ilikuk, Ilikuq: Ilikuq Lucy Saityen Shijuu tr'oonii, Drit, Shigyaa tr'oonii Khyahtthoo. A co-wife of Saityen Kkohkkee, a co-wife of Ditsiigiitł'uu Drit Khehkwaii, and wife of Thomas "Blind Thomas,' Khyahtthoo. An original Saaqił hut'aane. Mother of Neeshoochit John Saityen. Oral historian.

Immałurauq Joe Sun: Immalurauq Joe Sun of Shungnak. Upper Kobuk oral historian.

Isisan Justus Mekiana: Nunamiut oral historian.

Iqaluġruaqpak: I Personal name of man, meaning "Big fall silver and/or chum salmon." Upper Noatak River.

Kakinya: Elijah Kakinya, Nunamiut oral historian.

Kataksiñaq: The hunting partner of Qatiya'aana, the adopted brother of Saityen. In Chapter 3.

Khaiidhiiluu: Dzk An Umialik near the Nendaaghe region. Tł'eevihti' story. Several possible Dzk translations "I dragged myself through the winter," or "I dragged winter throughout the season," or "I dragged a whole bunch of skins," or "I dragged (something) slowly." That something could be anything, such as an oomiak.

Maŋuyuk: I Sister of Qayiayaqtualuk, Kiviliġmiut.

Maptiåaq Billy Morry: Of the Nunamiut community.

Masruana Jenny Jackson: Upper Kobuk oral historian.

Mekiana, Isisan Justus: Nunamiut oral historian.

Naiyuq Rachel Craig: Nunamiut translator and oral historian.

Navaġiaq: Iñupiaq man who fought off Indians at Auksaakiaq.

Nutaaq Doreen Simonds: Iñupiaq elder, oral historian, linguist, translator, stage and screen artist, life stages doula, and earth keeper.

Omigaloon: Umialik in Nuvuk in Maquire 1852–54.

Oquilluk, William A.: Iñupiaq author of "People of Kauwarek."

Panniaq: Panniaq Simon Paneak, Nunamiut oral historian.

Passak: A 10 year old Denaa boy raised by Omialik Omigaloon.

Qalhaq Barbara Atoruk: Kuuvaum Kaniaġmiut genealogist, translator.

Qatïya'aana: The adopted brother of Saityen.

Qayiayaqtualuk: Kiviliġmiut man and his sister Maŋuyuk

Qïvlïuraq: The nephew of Saityen.

Quqquq, Ilikuk, and Uqriññunalġaa: Relatives of Panniaq.

Saityen: Nendaaghe: Sayyen, Saiyyen, Sai'ya, Saityet, Satnik, and Sannik. Perhaps other spellings or associated names.

Sivviq Chester Sevek: I 3rd great grandson of Qayiayaqtualuk and Kiviliġmiut culture bearer.

Suvlu (Sowlu): Grandfather of Panniaq Simon Paneak.

Tatqviñ Ruthie Ramoth-Sampson: Iñupiat linguist, translator, educator, and scholar.

Uqriññunalġaa: A relative of Panniaq.

Uularaġuaraq: A young Akuniġmiut warrior in the Saityen story.

Lower Tanana

Ch'idził Koxki: Eastern Taghchwx Estate leader.

Gookąąhtii Koxki: Western Taghchwx Estate leader.

Xodalttheyh Kwska: A young Toghotili Tu Tl'ot Lower Tanana Estate refugee who fled to Toklat Estate and became a Kwska, community leader among the Toklat Estate people.

Tanacross

Gok'eech'ahtthaii Gookahtthak John Ch'adzahti': Gok'eech'ahttaii, "To stab or club others as in the final blow," Gookahtthak: "He killed or knocked out with his ch'anghwarh," (a club with sharp edges or protruding basalt or sharpened bones). Ch'adzah; "Dancer," perhaps a song and dance leader. Husband of Ditsii Ahndii Drits'ik Belle Ch'adzahvahan Drit Ch'adzah. Brother of Alice, and maternal great aunt (maternal grandmother's sister) of Hester John Evan.

Gwi'eech'it Dray Chiito' Draichiiatat Shahnyaati': Fled Tanacross as a young refugee, was raised by Dahjalti' Khehkwaii on the Neets'ąįį Estate and became the Deenduu Khaihkwaii.

Shreeveeyaa Saveah Gwiyaati' Khaihkwaii: Fled Tanacross as a young boy. Became a Gwichyaa leader around Shoo.

Please note all the personal names in the charts have not been included.

Glossary V
Indigenous Word Definitions

Anaullaun: I A club made often with a stone or bone attached to a haft or handle. The same as ch'ankhwarh in Dzk

Apsalliq: Tigara word for maintaining silence after the death of loved ones. Also Natchksut (natchiksaq). Upper Kobuk to fast for a period of 3 to 5 days in seclusion for deceased.

Ch'ankhwarh: Dzk A club made often with a stone attached to a haft or handle.

Ch'eekwaii: Dzk word for Iñupiat or Yupiit people. Also **Needaavał**, in Nunamiut as Nutaaviłiich, possibly many Needaavał.

Ch'itsyaa: One of three marriage groups among the Dinjii Zhuh.

Ch'ivihtr'ii: Tied sharp stone barbs attached to the bottom of snowshoes to kill or wound anyone hiding under the snow.

Daa, daak: Dn "Verb theme meaning in Group 5, "the following themes express the movements of a mass of objects or of amorphous substances." In Koyukon Athabascan Dictionary, Jetté and Jones, ANLC, 2000.

Daaghe: Dn 1. Dead people. 2. Spirits. 3. Souls. 4. Ghosts of the dead.

Denaa: Dn 1. Mankind. 2. A man. 3. Real human being. Self-ethnonym of Tl'eeyegga hut'aane.

Denaakk'e: Dn Language of the Denaa and Tl'eeyegge hut'aane.

Deyene: Dn Dialect variant of Deyenenh, medicine man or shaman.

Deyenh: Dn A very strong shaman or medicine man.

Deyenenh: Dn Shaman or medicine man as he/she uses and casts senh. According to Miranda Wright, "An inspirational functionary equivalent in the colloquial usage to the term shaman." Variant Deyene.

Dik: Dzk "On the edge," or "on the edge of." Also, Ndik a dialect variant.

Dinjii dazhan: Dzk 1. Person who manipulates or appears to manipulate the energy of shan. 2. A person who works with spiritual energy with intention.

Dinjii Zhuh: Dzk 1. Children of man. 2. Mankind. Self-ethnonym for people labelled as Gwich'in.

Dinjii Zhuh K'yaa: Language of the Dinjii Zhuh.

Divee ch'illig: Dzk "Sheep song," a victory dance.

Gwazhał: Dzk "A swelling." As Gwazhał Cordillera.

gwich'in: Dzk 1. "Looks like, similar in aspect", 2. "gwich'in roh," "looks like it, must be," 3. Dweller of a certain region.

Hun/han: Dzk A large river.

hut'aane: Dn Resident of.

Hutlaane: Dn   Rules of behavior and relation to the greater spirit of the universe.

Iñuksuk: I   A rock cairn.

Iyaġak: I   A "rock" in the Upper Kobuk Iñupiaq dialect. Also Uyaġak in the Northern Iñupiaq dialect. See Uyaġak.

Iyaġaqtat: I   A meat storage pit lined with grass or willows and covered with willows and rocks in the upper Kobuk dialect.

Kaii: Left over, a gift from the deceased, and in this case the last member of his family left (to us) alive.

Khaiits'a/khaints'a': Dzk   The last born child of a man or woman or family.

Khaihkwaiii, Khehkwaii, Khehkai': Dzk A community leader. In order: Gwichyaa gwich'in dialect, Neetsaii gwich'in dialect, Eastern Gwich'in Nations dialect.

Kanyuumavik: I   A meeting place of Nunamiut and Too Loghe people which later became a place name.

Kayyaavak: I   An area between Hunt Fork and Qaŋmaliq. Hunt Fork a stream flowing from the west into the K'itł'uu.

Ke'eenee': Dn   Bad, malicious medicine, sorcery.

Kkohkkee: Dn   Denaa community leader.

Koxki: Taghachwx community leader.

Kuuŋa: I   A river.

Kwska: Lower Tanana community leader.

Manaqtuq: I   A floating seal retrieval hook.

Natchksut (natchiksaq): Spelling unclear. Upper Kobuk region. "To fast for 3 to 4 days in seclusion after the passing of a person/s." Also, *Apsalliq* "maintaining silence for 4 to 5 days" in Tigara.

Naats'aii: Dzk   A marriage group. Also Noltseene in Dn.

Ndik: Dik: Dialect variations of the same word meaning "On the edge," and "at the edge of."

Needaavał: Dzk "Swinging back and forth in a walking gate." Dinjii Zhuh word for Iñupiat or Yupiit people. Isisan Justus Mekiana understood the word as Nutaaviłiich.

Nen: Dn   Noun theme meaning 1. Spinal. 2. Ridge. 3. Backbone. 4. Sloping.

Nendaaghe: Former Denaa name for the upper Noataaq River.

Nihteeindrat: Dzk Literally "Where the streams are clawed in either direction in the mountain pass." Meaning a mountain pass.

Niuviq: I   Nunamiut dialect trading partners.

Njuu: Dzk 1. An island. 2. A group of mountains without passes. 3. To crawl.

No'/na': Dn River, creek, stream.

Noltseene: Dn   Denaa marriage group. Also Naats'aii in Dzk.

Nunataaq: I   Area of the former Nendaaghe Estate.

Nunataq, Nunachi-, nunataaqiġvik: I North Slope dialect sod, semi-subterranean meat cache.

Nutaaviłiich: Isasan Justus Mekiana interpretation of Needaavał, Dzk word for Iñupiat and Yupiit people.

Omialik: Iñupiat leader, whaling captain, wealthy man.

Oonjit, Vanodlit: Contractions of *vanangoodlit*, for Euro-Americans.

Qilya (Qiḷa): I   Shaman's power; shaman's spirit; conjuring spirit. May possibly be akin to the energy of senh and shan.

Sookk'eł: Dn   Sunny side or sunny river banks. Also Saaqił, as pronounced by Masruana Jenny Jackson and also Saaqił.

Saiyat, saiyatat, siġluaq, siġluuraq: I   Northwest Arctic dialect. A Semi-subterranean meat cache.

Sai'ye: Dn   A blade.

Senh: Dn "The word senh refers to manifestations of the dynamic aspect of nature as centered, focused, and transmitted through the potency of nature, which might be characterized in western terms as an impersonal force in all things... Senh is not merely power or energy, but procreative power derived from an ultimate source not personified but conceptualized as existing, diffused, transmitted, and manifested throughout the universe." Miranda Wright in "The Last Great Indian War," 1995.

Shan: Dzk 1. Spiritual energy. 2. Cosmic energy flow. 3. Creative energy flow that permeates everything in the universe. Akin to prana. According to Johnny Frank Drit, shan "is just like electricity."

Sighok'elaayh: Dn Trading Partner

Sookeł: Dn Possibly sunny banks

Teenjaarahtsyaa: One of three marriage group of the Dinjii Zhuh.

Teetsii: Dzk 1. A pile of driftwood along a river bank. 2. Teetsii gwich'in: generic term for Denaa people.

Tł'eevih: Dzk A small fish that clings to rocks in alpine regions.

Tl'eeyegga: Dn "To go down into the (house)."

Tl'eeyegga hut'aane: Dn 1. Inhabitants of the area. 2. An ethnonym of Denaa people. 3. Tl'eeyegga, "to go down into the (house)" plus hut'aane "residents of." "Residents of those who go down into the house (home)."

Tsaał: Dn Darkness

Tsaaye: Dn A knife, *also* sai'ye as a blade.

Ugruk: Bearded seal.

Umiak: I A sea worthy boat covered with ugruak, bearded seal skins.

Umialik: I An Iñupiat community leader and/or a whaling captain.

Uyaġak: I 1. Rock in Northern Iñupiaq dialect. Also, Iyaġak

Vahan: Dzk The mother of firstborn male child. A formal address when prefaced with a person's name in Teknonymy system. Also, the mother of her children.

Vanchil dazhoo: Medicinal plant used in Tł'eevihti' story. Also, vank'il dazhoo.

Vanangoodlit: Dzk "For him/her there became more land than they were previously aware of." Word for Euro-Americans.

Vihn: Dzk The mother of firstborn female child. In a formal address when prefaced with a personal name. A part of the Teknonymy system of naming.

Glossary VI
Chronology

1760: Tł'eevihti' born (Nendaaghe hut'aane Denaa)
1780: Estimated formation of historic Kivalina residential group began
1783: Icelandic volcano Laki erupts. Subsequent Tree growth rings nearly non-existent from Kobuk Region Alaska for this year, illustrating growth disruption caused by Laki eruption.
1789: Arrival of Scottish explorer Sir Alexander Mackenzie along the Nagwachoonjik (currently the Mackenzie River)
1800: Drit (II) born. Dį'haii. Tłeevih (daughter of Tł'eevihti') born. Nendaaghe.
1816: Russian Naval Officer Otto Von Kotzebue's first trip to Kotzebue Sound.
1815–1816: First attack on Atliq. Iñupiat begin the eviction of the Nendaaaghe hut'aane.
1815–1816: Aldzak married Tł'eevih after 1815/1816.
1816: Ch'iji'oonta born. Ditsiigiitł'uu Drit Khehkwaii born.
1816: Coastal Iñupiat communities began to feel the shortage of women, and to see the trade route bottleneck that was created by Nendaaghe hut'aane occupation of the upper Nendaaghe.
1817: Kotzebue's second expedition to Kotzebue Sound thwarted by solid sea-ice off the coast of St. Lawrence Island.
1816–1818: Presumed date range for devastating famine/winter described by William A. Oquilluk, Soozun Dahjalti' John Ch'igiioonta', Treenahtsyaa Ellen Dahjalti' Shit'eegwiłtthat, and Ernest Burch.
1819: All Iñupiat communities began to feel the shortage of women, and to see the trade route bottleneck that was created by Nendaaghe hut'aane occupation of the upper Nendaaghe. Coastal Iñupiat communities attack the western Nendaaghe settlement of Ko'ehdan's family.
1819: Imperial Russian Naval Officers Mikhail Vasiliev and Gleb Shishmarev enter Kotzebue Sound.
1820: Retaliation party of Ko̧'ehdan razed Nuvuġaluaq settlement.
1821: A party of fifteen Nendaaghe hut'aane men killed in revenge of *Navaġiaq*.
1819–1822: A group of Nendaaghe hut'aane travel east and join the Neets'aii.

Dahjalti' Khehkwaii takes Ko'ehdan's younger brothers Di'chi' Choo David Dzeegwaajyaa, Ndik Dzeegwaajyaa, and Joseph Dzeegwaajyaa as small boys.

1820s–30s: Internecine conflicts within the Gwich'in Estates and within the Tanacross Estates.

When the Tanacross group was involved in internal conflicts revolving around who would control trade routes through their country, Gwi'eech'it as a young boy escaped with his life with a group of other refugees. He is taken in by Dahjalti' Khehkwaii and raised on the Neets'aii Estate.

1822: Kuukpiġmiut attack on Atłiq. Nendaaghe abandon Atłiq and Tukuto. Nendaaghe retreat to Itivluk Pass, the Aalaasuraq, Aalasuk, and Killik river valleys.

1822: Saityen and/or his parents displaced from the Nendaaghe Estate. Move onto the Saaqił Estate along the upper Kobuk.

1822: Khyahtthoo family abandoned Nendaaghe, move to Too Loghe Estate.

1826: Frederick W. Beechey in search of the Sir John Franklin Expedition in Alaska reported on Nuvuġaluaq.

1837–1841: Saityen Kk'ohkee dies of his injuries at Sannikmik along the Upper Aalaashuk. Nachats'an Jessie, Andrew Gaashiik'yuu Saityen and Ilikuq Lucy and Neeshooch'it John Saityen, his two young wives and their sons join Dits'iigiitł'uu on the Di'haii Estate.

1837/38: Major interncine conflict between Nendaaghe and resident Saaqił hut'aane Denaa of the upper Kobuk. The Nendaaghe flee the upper Hulghaatne and move onto the Too Loghe Estate.

Nendaaghe hut'aane displaced from the Saaqił estate by the Saaqił people and the Akuniġmiut Iñupiat. Too Loghe host Nendaaghe hut'aane and related Saaqił hut'aane refugees. Second group of Nendaaghe refugees move to Neets'aii Estate including the Shit'iigwiłtthat and Khagooheenjikti' families.

1837/38: The Saaqił faced ultimatum to become Iñupiat or leave the Saaqił Estate as Denaa. Those who flee the Saaqił Estate leave in three groups; from west to east, the 1. Selawik group go down the Kk'otsoh No' to the headwaters of rivers going towards Norton Sound and the Kodeel No', the 2. Ts'eeteetno' group leave down the Ts'eeteetno to the headwaters and mouth of the Hugaadzaat No', and along the Yukon River from the mouth of the Koyitł'ots'ina to the Meloghezeet No', 3. Aalaashuk group portage to the Aalaashuk and down it to the Koyitł'ots'ina, Kk'onootne and along the north bank of Yukon River.

Post 1838: Period of increased antagonism between Too Loghe and the Kaniaġmiut, Killiġmiut, and Qaŋmaliġmiut (later collectively known as the Nunamiut). Kobuk River not the Kobuk for its full length.

After 1838: Khagooheenjikti' came into the household of Dahjalti' with his younger brother Deets'i'.

1838: Alexander Kashaverov came into the Kaŋiġmiut region (Buckland

River) and met a group of Kk'otseh hut'aane Denaa people.

1838–1839: Smallpox epidemic spread from Lower Yukon region and up to Norton Sound and up the Yukon River.

1842: Exceptionally cold winter.

1842–1843: Russian Lt. Lavrentiy Zagoskin exploration along the Yukon and lower Koyitł'ots'ina.

1843: Heavy rains to the Yukon attributed to Agung volcanic eruption in Indonesia.

1848–1854: HMS Plover voyage to western arctic.

1847: Alexander Hunter Murray and the Hudson's Bay Company arrive in Gwichyaa Zhee.

1847: The introduction of guns in the Yukon Flats.

1847: Final displacement of the Too Loghe and Nendaaghe hut'aane from K'iitł'it/Naqsraq Pass.

1847: Two communities of people living in close proximity in the upper Koyitł'ots'ina, the former Too Loghe Denaa and the Di'haii gwich'in.

1847: Shininduu K'eezhiizhal Dahjalti' Khehkwaii passed. He arranged for the Khyahtthoo family to move onto the Neets'aii Estate. By 1848/9 the Khyahtthoo family become the major suppliers of caribou skins, and caribou skin products to the Hudsons' Bay Company employees.

1847/1848: Too Tleekk'e, Di'haii, Taghachwx Lower Tanana, and Kk'oonootne hut'aane take control of the settlements of Too Loghe, Sełyee Menkk'et, and Dobendaatltonh Denh on the Kk'onootne Estate.

1850: The 20 warriors of the Taghachwx Lower Tanana are now reduced down to 8 warriors

1850: Shahnyaati' allows several warriors to raid Sełyee Menkk'et and Too Loghe.

1850: The Di'haii, Taghachwx xwt'ana, and Deenduu gwich'in mercenaries destroy the settlements of Sełyee Menkk'et and Too Loghe in the upper Kk'oonootne.

1850s: Dzeegwaajyaa, Khagooheenjik, Gehikti', Saityen, and Ko'nii'ak families all considered Neets'aii and Di'haii gwich'in.

1847–1855: Ditsiigiitł'uu Drit Khehkwaii's five younger children were born between 1847 and 1855.

1850: Too Tleekk'e are displaced from the upper Kk'oonootne.

1851: Only 6 people remaining in the community of the Taghachwx xut'aana Denaa people.

1852: Traders from Yukon/Tanana confluence come up to Gwichyaa Zhee for the first time.

1853: The Too Tleekk'e (formerly Too Loghe hut'aane) , now fully resident along the Neekk'eklehno' and upper Koyitł'ots'ina, come to Fort Yukon for the first time to trade.

1855: Ditsiigiitł'uu Drit Khehkwaii (age 35-38), dies.

1855: The Di'haii abandoned the upper Koyitł'ots'ina.

Acknowledgments

The author wishes to acknowledge the Gates of the Arctic National Park and Preserve and Jeffrey T. Rasic for the designing and publication of the "Map of Athabascan and Iñupiat Estates of Northern Alaska, c. 1800, Citation: Raboff, Adeline Peter (2020). Cultural Resource Report NPS/GAAR/CRR-2020/002, National Park Service, Fairbanks, Alaska," and for the update on this map in 2024 for this publication.

A note about the map. Saakił is written on the map as Saakił, however after consultations with an Iñupiat speaker, and a linguist, it appears that the Denaakk'e word Sookk'eł meaning "sunny side" has been reshaped.

Iñupiat speakers do not follow the consonant S with an O, only with an A or AA. Throughout the text I will refer to the Saakił as the Saaqił Estate in keeping with Iñupiat spelling. The next iteration of this map will reflect this change.

And to Haley McCaig for providing the Timeline, Settlements of the Nendaaghe, and the Trade Routes of the Di'hąįį. Thank you kindly. To Adam K. Freeburg for his touch-up and topographic reliefs of those maps.

Thanks to: Smith, Gerad, and James Kari. 2023. The Web Atlas of Alaska Native Traditional Place Names. ArcGIS Storymap, published online November 15, 2023

Any errors or oversights are totally the responsibility of this author.

Special thanks to Carole Anderson for her editing. Much appreciated.

And for a small grant from Native Movement.

www.ingramcontent.com/pod-product-compliance
Lightning Source LLC
Chambersburg PA
CBHW041510220426
43661CB00047B/1523